1 and 2 Thessalonians

D0615674

New International Biblical Commentary

1 and 2 Thessalonians

David John Williams

New Testament Editor,
W. Ward Gasque

PEABODY, MASSACHUSETTS 01961-3473

Copyright © 1992 by Hendrickson Publishers, Inc.
P.O. Box 3473
Peabody, Massachusetts 01961–3473
All rights reserved.
Printed in the United States of America

ISBN 0–943575–86–9

Library of Congress Cataloging-in-Publication Data

Williams, David John.
    1 and 2 Thessalonians / David John Williams.
        p.   cm. — (New International biblical commentary; 12)
    Includes bibliographical references and indexes.
    ISBN 0–943575–86–9 (pbk.)
        1. Bible. N.T. Thessalonians—Commentaries. I. Bible.
    N.T. Thessalonians. English. New International. 1992.
    II. Title.   III. Title: One and two Thessalonians   IV. Series.
    BS2725.3.W55   1992
    227'.81077—dc20   92-5252
                                                                    CIP

Table of Contents

Foreword vii

Abbreviations xi

Introduction 1

1 Thessalonians

§1 Address and Greeting (1 Thess. 1:1) 21
§2 Thanksgiving for the Thessalonians' Faith
    (1 Thess. 1:2–10). 25
§3 Paul's Ministry in Thessalonica (1 Thess. 2:1–16) 36
§4 Paul's Longing to See the Thessalonians
    (1 Thess. 2:17–3:5) 53
§5 Timothy's Encouraging Report (1 Thess. 3:6–13) 61
§6 Living to Please God (1 Thess. 4:1–12) 69
§7 The Coming of the Lord (1 Thess. 4:13–5:11) 80
§8 Final Instructions (1 Thess. 5:12–28) 94

2 Thessalonians

§1 Address and Greeting (2 Thess. 1:1–2) 109
§2 Thanksgiving and Prayer (2 Thess. 1:3–12) 110
§3 The Man of Lawlessness (2 Thess. 2:1–12) 121
§4 Stand Firm (2 Thess. 2:13–17) 133
§5 Request for Prayer (2 Thess. 3:1–5) 139
§6 Warning Against Idleness (2 Thess. 3:6–15) 144
§7 Final Greetings (2 Thess. 3:16–18) 151

For Further Reading 153

Subject Index 159

Scripture Index 163

Foreword
New International Biblical Commentary

Although it does not appear on the standard best-seller lists, the Bible continues to outsell all other books. And in spite of growing secularism in the West, there are no signs that interest in its message is abating. Quite to the contrary, more and more men and women are turning to its pages for insight and guidance in the midst of the ever-increasing complexity of modern life.

This renewed interest in Scripture is found both outside and inside the church. It is found among people in Asia and Africa as well as in Europe and North America; indeed, as one moves outside of the traditionally Christian countries, interest in the Bible seems to quicken. Believers associated with the traditional Catholic and Protestant churches manifest the same eagerness for the Word that is found in the newer evangelical churches and fellowships.

We wish to encourage and, indeed, strengthen this world-wide movement of lay Bible study by offering this new commentary series. Although we hope that pastors and teachers will find these volumes helpful in both understanding and communicating the Word of God, we do not write primarily for them. Our aim is to provide for the benefit of every Bible reader reliable guides to the books of the Bible—representing the best of contemporary scholarship presented in a form that does not require formal theological education to understand.

The conviction of editor and authors alike is that the Bible belongs to the people and not merely to the academy. The message of the Bible is too important to be locked up in erudite and esoteric essays and monographs written only for the eyes of theological specialists. Although exact scholarship has its place in the service of Christ, those who share in the teaching office of the church have a responsibility to make the results of their research accessible to the Christian community at large. Thus, the Bible scholars who join in the presentation of this series write with these broader concerns in view.

A wide range of modern translations is available to the contemporary Bible student. Most of them are very good and much to be preferred—for understanding, if not always for beauty—to the older King James Version (the so-called Authorized Version of the Bible). The Revised Standard Version has become the standard English translation in many seminaries and colleges and represents the best of modern Protestant scholarship. It is also available in a slightly altered "common Bible" edition with the Catholic imprimatur, and the New Revised Standard Version appeared in 1989. In addition, the New American Bible is a fresh translation that represents the best of post–Vatican II Roman Catholic biblical scholarship and is in a more contemporary idiom than that of the RSV.

The New Jerusalem Bible, based on the work of French Catholic scholars but vividly rendered into English by a team of British translators, is perhaps the most literary of the recent translations, while the New English Bible is a monument to modern British Protestant research. The Good News Bible is probably the most accessible translation for the person who has little exposure to the Christian tradition or who speaks and reads English as a second language. Each of these is, in its own way, excellent and will be consulted with profit by the serious student of Scripture. Perhaps most will wish to have several versions to read, both for variety and for clarity of understanding—though it should be pointed out that no one of them is by any means flawless or to be received as the last word on any given point. Otherwise, there would be no need for a commentary series like this one!

We have chosen to use the New International Version as the basis for this series, not because it is necessarily the best translation available but because it is becoming increasingly used by lay Bible students and pastors. It is the product of an international team of "evangelical" Bible scholars who have sought to translate the Hebrew and Greek documents of the original into "clear and natural English . . . idiomatic [and] . . . contemporary but not dated," suitable for "young and old, highly educated and less well educated, ministers and laymen [*sic*]." As the translators themselves confess in their preface, this version is not perfect. However, it is as good as any of the others mentioned above and more popular than most of them.

Each volume will contain an introductory chapter detailing the background of the book and its author, important themes, and other helpful information. Then, each section of the book will be expounded as a whole, accompanied by a series of notes on items in the text that need further clarification or more detailed explanation. Appended to the end of each volume will be a bibliographical guide for further study.

Our new series is offered with the prayer that it may be an instrument of authentic renewal and advancement in the worldwide Christian community and a means of commending the faith of the people who lived in biblical times and of those who seek to live by the Bible today.

W. WARD GASQUE
Provost
Eastern College
St. Davids, Pennsylvania

Abbreviations

Abbott-Smith	G. Abbott-Smith, *A Manual Greek Lexicon of the New Testament*. Edinburgh: T. & T. Clark, 1937.
ASV	American Standard Version
AV	Authorized or King James Version of 1611
BDF	F. Blass, A. Debrunner, and R. W. Funk, *A Greek Grammar of the New Testament and Other Early Christian Literature*. Chicago: University of Chicago Press, 1961.
Best	E. Best, *The First and Second Epistles to the Thessalonians*. HNTC. New York: Harper & Row, 1972.
Bruce	F. F. Bruce, *1 & 2 Thessalonians*. WBC 45. Waco, Texas: Word, 1982.
CBQ	*Catholic Biblical Quarterly*
cf.	compare
ExpT	*Expository Times*
f.(ff.)	and following verse(s) or page(s)
Findlay	G. G. Findlay, *The Epistles to the Thessalonians*. Cambridge: Cambridge University Press, 1925.
Gk.	Greek
Heb.	Hebrew
JB	The Jerusalem Bible
JBL	*Journal of Biblical Literature*
Lightfoot	J. B. Lightfoot, *Notes on the Epistles of St. Paul*. London: Macmillan, 1904.
LXX	Septuagint (pre-Christian Greek version of the Old Testament)
marg.	margin
Milligan	G. Milligan, *St. Paul's Epistles to the Thessalonians*. London: Macmillan, 1908.

Morris	L. Morris, *The Epistles of Paul to the Thessalonians*. Leicester: Inter-Varsity Press, 1984.
Morris, *Themes*	L. Morris, *Word Biblical Themes: 1, 2 Thessalonians*. Dallas: Word, 1989.
Moulton-Milligan	J. H. Moulton and G. Milligan, *Vocabulary of the Greek Testament*. London: Hodder & Stoughton, 1930.
MS(MSS)	manuscript(s)
NBD	J. D. Douglas, ed. *The New Bible Dictionary*. London: Inter-Varsity Fellowship, 1962.
NEB	New English Bible
NIDNTT	C. Brown, ed. *The New International Dictionary of New Testament Theology*. 3 vols. Exeter: Paternoster Press, 1975–78.
NIV	New International Version
NovT	*Novum Testamentum*
NTS	*New Testament Studies*
Phillips	J. B. Phillips, *The New Testament in Modern English*. London: Geoffrey Bles Ltd., 1958.
1QH	Thanksgiving Hymns, Qumram Cave 1
RSV	Revised Standard Version
RV	Revised Version of 1881
Saunders	E. W. Saunders, *1 Thessalonians, 2 Thessalonians, Philippians, Philemon*. Atlanta: John Knox Press, 1981.
SBL	Society of Biblical Literature
Schmithals	W. Schmithals, *Paul and the Gnostics*. New York: Abingdon, 1972.
v.(vv.)	verse(s)
Williams, *Acts*	D. J. Williams, *Acts*. NIBC 5. Peabody, Mass.: Hendrickson Publishers, 1990.
Williams, *Promise*	D. J. Williams, *The Promise of His Coming*. Homebush West, Australia: Anzea Publishers, 1990.
ZNW	*Zeitschrift für neutestamentliche Wissenschaft*

Introduction

Man is but a breath of wind,
His days are like a shadow that passes away.
Part the heavens, O Lord, and come down,
Touch the mountains and they shall smoke . . .

Happy that people who have the Lord for their God.

"Struck down but not destroyed" by what happened in Philippi (cf. 1 Thess. 2:2), the missionaries Paul, Silas, and Timothy (Luke, who probably accompanied them earlier, may have stayed behind) made their way along the *Via Egnatia*, through the Amphipolis and Appolonia, to Thessalonica. The city stood on or near the site of an earlier settlement, Therma, which took its name from the nearby hot springs. The two may once have existed side by side, for Pliny the Elder speaks of both Thessalonica and Therma; but in time Therma disappeared or was absorbed into the other.

Thessalonica was founded by Cassander and named after his wife, the daughter of Philip II of Macedon and the half-sister of Alexander the Great. When the last of the Macedonian kings fell to the Romans, Thessalonica became the capital of one of the four republics into which the country was then divided (167 B.C.). Twenty years later (148 B.C.), when the republics were then amalgamated into one Roman province, it became the provincial capital.

Although made the seat of the Roman government of the province, because it sided with the eventual victors of the battle of Philippi (42 B.C.), Thessalonica was granted the status of a "free city," governing itself on Greek rather than on Roman lines by its own magistrates, the politarchs as Luke correctly names them in Acts, and assembly, the *dēmos* of Acts 17:5.

The city prospered. Its fine harbor, fertile hinterland, and position astride vital trade routes ensured its prosperity. As Melitus observed long ago: "So long as nature does not change, Thessalonica will remain wealthy and fortunate."[1] To this day it is a flourishing center, and in Paul's day it was one of the great seaports of southeastern Europe, with an estimated population of about 200,000. Its Jewish population appears to have been correspondingly large, as one would expect. There was much that would draw a trading people to this city. Thus, when the early Christian missionaries arrived, they found a synagogue.

The Founding of the Church

Paul and his colleagues followed their usual practice of visiting first the synagogue (Acts 17:2), and they met with good success: "Some of the Jews were persuaded and joined Paul and Silas, as did a large number of God-fearing Greeks and not a few prominent women" (Acts 17:4). The fact that the best results came from the Gentiles associated with the synagogue rather than from the Jews themselves, as seems to have been commonly the case, demands some explanation. Who were these "God-fearing Greeks"?

"Wherever the Jews went in the Gentile world, their presence gave rise to two conflicting tendencies. On the one hand, the Jew possessed the knowledge of the one true God; and amidst the universal corruption, idolatry, and superstition of the ancient world, this saving knowledge exercised a powerful attraction."[2] On the other hand, this knowledge was enshrined in a law that in many respects proved much less attractive. Consequently, among those who were drawn to Judaism there were varying degrees of commitment. Some went the whole way, submitting to instruction, circumcision and baptism, leading on to sacrifice in the temple, although in practice this latter requirement may have been waived where travel to Jerusalem was not easy. These were the "proselytes," the "converts to Judaism" of Acts 2:10 and 6:5, among whom women outnumbered men because of the requirement of circumcision. Others, while not prepared to go so far, nevertheless worshipped and studied in the synagogues. These were the "God-fearers" or "worshipers of God" as they were also called (*phoboumenoi*, Acts 10:2, 22; 13:16, 26; *sebomenoi*, Acts 13:43; 16:14; 17:4, 17; 18:7).

Two distinct groups could be found in the synagogues of the Diaspora (and sometimes in practice three, for the proselytes were not always accepted by those who were Jewish by descent). Of these two groups the Christian mission discovered the God-fearers to be the more responsive. They were, indeed, the key to the rapid and successful planting of the church throughout the Mediterranean world. Described on one occasion as a "providentially prepared bridgehead into the Gentile world," they were an informed audience, familiar with the Scriptures and the messianic hope of the Jews. But at the same time they were profoundly aware that they themselves were excluded from that hope as long as they remained as simply God-fearers. These God-fearers

> always remained second-class citizens. Proselytes were buried in the Jewish cemeteries in Jerusalem and Rome and elsewhere, . . . but not "god-fearers." From an official point of view, despite their visits to synagogue worship and their partial observance of the law, the "god-fearers" continued to be regarded as Gentiles, unless they went over to Judaism completely through circumcision and . . . baptism.[3]

It is hardly surprising, then, that when they were told that "the messianic hope had come alive in Jesus, that in him the old distinction between Jew and Gentile had been abolished, that the fullest blessings of God's saving grace were as readily available to Gentiles as to Jews," many of the God-fearers embraced the Good News.[4] They seemingly formed the nucleus of many of the early Christian congregations (along with a scattering of Jews and proselytes), and through them the gospel reached the Gentile world beyond the walls of the synagogue.

But if the Diaspora synagogues provided the Christian missionaries with a prepared and responsive audience, they often became the source of their most bitter opposition. The synagogue in Thessalonica was no exception. "On three Sabbath days, [Paul] reasoned with them from the Scriptures, explaining and proving that the Christ had to suffer and rise from the dead" (Acts 17:2f.; see disc. on 1 Thess. 5:10). But that was all the time they would give him. We assume that Paul and the others then withdrew and established a separate congregation, but Luke tells us nothing of this in Acts. By telling us only the story of the missionaries' relationship with the synagogue, he gives the impression that they were in Thessalonica for only those three Sabbath days. Paul's letters, however, show that they were there for a much longer period—long enough for a church to be established with its own leaders (1 Thess. 5:12) and for outlying areas to be reached with the gospel (1 Thess. 1:7); long enough for the "traditions" to be passed on (2 Thess. 2:15; 3:6), evidently with systematic and sometimes repeated teaching (see disc. on 2 Thess. 2:5); long enough for the church in Philippi to send Paul gifts more than once (Phil. 4:16; for the expression "again and again," see disc. on 1 Thess. 2:18); and long enough to warrant the missionaries' working "night and day" rather than being a burden on their converts and, at the same time, setting their converts a good example (1 Thess. 2:9; 2 Thess. 3:8).

A. J. Malherbe suggests that they worked from Jason's house. He draws attention to the *insula*, a type of apartment house commonly found in first-century cities that "would contain a row of shops on the ground floor, facing the street, and provide living accommodations for the owners and their families over the shop or in the rear." They would also have "living quarters for visitors, employees, and servants or slaves."[5] Jason, who "welcomed" Paul and his companions (Acts 17:7), was apparently well-to-do and perhaps the proprietor of such an *insula*. If so, it would have provided lodgings for the missionaries, a place where they could work, and a base for their preaching and teaching.

In time, however (and we assume that it was a matter more of months than of weeks),[6] the mission, as far as Paul and his colleagues were concerned, came to an end—not of their own volition, but as the result of Jewish opposition. The Jews, resenting perhaps the loss of influential God-fearers such as Jason and the "prominent women," determined to rid the city of the Christian missionaries and to destroy the Christian church. They formulated a plan to bring the missionaries before the assembly on a charge of sedition. To give some grounds for this charge, they "rounded up some bad characters from the marketplace" and organized them into staging a riot (Acts 17:5; cf. 14:4f., 19; 17:13; 1 Thess. 2:14–16). No charge was better calculated than this to achieve their end, for it put the city at risk of losing its status as a free city. With the stage thus set for the successful prosecution of the missionaries, the rioters "rushed to Jason's house in search of Paul and Silas in order to bring them out to the *dēmos*" (Acts 17:5, not "crowd" as in NIV). But their plan went awry, for the two could not be found, and without them they could lay no charge (Timothy does not seem to have rated attention).

Frustrated, the rioters resorted to dragging "Jason and some of the other brothers before the politarchs," accusing them of offering hospitality to the seditionists. Because of the noise of the melee, the charge had to be shouted. Paul and Silas were accused of having "caused trouble all over the world, . . . defying Caesar's decrees." Unless Paul's preaching was misconstrued as a prediction of a change of ruler, it is difficult to find any justification for the charge. Imperial decrees expressly forbid forecasts like "saying that there is another king" (Acts 17:7). The same charge is leveled against Jesus (cf. Luke 23:2; John 19:12, 15) and is as ill-founded now as it was in his case. But to the Jews, "Christ" meant "king," and since this was the title by which the emperor was called in the lands to the east of Rome, they could maliciously accuse the Christians of proclaiming a rival to Claudius. That Christians so often called Jesus "Lord" further colored their accusation, for the emperors were also called by that title (see note on 1 Thess. 1:1).

These charges disturbed both "the crowd and the city officials." Serious charges like these had to be treated as such. But after investigating the charges, the politarchs did not find the evidence as compelling as the accusers hoped (cf. Acts 17:9, they "let them go"), although they did penalize the Christians. "They made Jason and the others post bond" to ensure, as we suppose, that they kept the peace. This meant that the missionaries could no longer preach in public, and this explains their sudden departure. In 1 Thessalonians 2:15, 18 Paul reflects on this turn of events, which he unhesitatingly attributes to Satan himself. Paul might not have taken his dismissal so tamely had Jason and the others not been involved. As it was, he and Silas could only accept what happened.

The departure of the missionaries did not end the harassment of the Christians. The Thessalonian church was subjected to persecution that seemed to Paul as severe as that endured earlier by the Jewish Christians at his own hands (1 Thess. 2:14; 3:1–5; 2 Thess. 1:6). Nor did his departure lessen the calumnies of the Jews against him in particular, so that we find him defending himself against numerous charges in his first letter to the church (see below on The Writing of 1 Thessalonians).

Under cover of darkness, perhaps fearing further violence should they be seen, the missionaries were sent by "the brothers" to Berea, some forty-five miles southwest of Thessalonica (see disc. on 1 Thess. 1:4 for "brothers"). After a promising start to the work there, Paul was forced by the arrival of Jews from Thessalonica to move on, leaving Silas and Timothy behind to continue the work (Acts 17:10–14). Paul was accompanied by some Berean "brothers" to the coast (perhaps to Dion) and thence, either by road or by sea to Athens (Acts 17:15). Here, as we learn from 1 Thessalonians 3:1f., he was rejoined by Timothy whom he then sent back to "strengthen and encourage" the Thessalonians. Silas did not catch up with Paul, as far as we know, until he and Timothy, the latter returning a second time from Thessalonica, rejoined him in Corinth.

The Writing of 1 Thessalonians

The news that Timothy brought concerning the Thessalonians was, on the whole, good, and 1 Thessalonians was written in response to that news. There is no mistaking the note of relief that sounds throughout the letter (see disc. on 1 Thess. 1:2–10). Several times Paul had wanted to return himself, but he had been unable (1 Thess. 2:17f.); now he was overjoyed to hear that they were prospering, despite what had happened to him when he was there, and despite what the Thessalonians themselves had endured. We may be able to piece together Timothy's report to Paul: (1) The Thessalonian Christians' example inspired faith. Their witness to Christ had become "a model to all the believers in Macedonia and Achaia (Greece)" (1 Thess. 1:6–10). (2) Some in Thessalonica, probably Jews, were misrepresenting Paul, accusing him, as it would seem from his defense, of cowardice and of being interested only in making money out of his converts. This was an easy accusation to make, since at that time itinerant preachers who lived off their gullible hearers were commonplace.[7] But Paul insists his motives are pure and reminds his readers how he and his colleagues conducted themselves. The very strength of his defense, however, may suggest that some of the Thessalonian Christians were in danger of believing what his accusers were saying (1 Thess. 2:1–12, 17f.).

Timothy perhaps reported another danger, (3) that of the Thessalonians' slipping back into heathen ways. That would explain Paul's stress in this letter on maintaining the Christian standard of holiness (1 Thess. 4:1–8; 5:22–24). (4) Clearly there was some anxiety within the church about members who had died. Would they share in the blessings of Christ's return, or had death robbed them of their reward? Paul sets the survivors' minds at rest. He assures them that, whether dead or alive at Christ's return, no believer in Christ is disadvantaged (1 Thess. 4:13–5:11). (5) Perhaps related to their expectation of Christ's return, but perhaps keyed to social factors that had nothing to do with it, some in the church were not simply out of work but were unwilling to work and had become a burden on others for their support. Paul gently rebukes them (the rebuke is much stronger in the second epistle) and asks the church to "warn those who are idle" (1 Thess. 5:14; cf. 4:11). (6) There seems also to have been some lack of respect for the church leaders, brought about perhaps by the leaders' lack of diplomacy in dealing with the ones not willing to work (1 Thess. 5:12f.). And (7) there may have been a tendency on the part of some members to treat the gift of prophecy, or perhaps all spiritual gifts, with contempt (1 Thess. 5:19–22).

We have adopted what is the simplest and, we think, the most likely scenario of the circumstances behind Paul's writing this letter. However, another scenario has been proposed that sees most of the matters set out above as symptoms of an incipient Gnosticism. W. Lütgert, for example, claims that an early Jewish Christian Gnosticism was evident, not only in Thessalonica, but in the churches in Philippi, Corinth, and those represented in the Pastoral Epistles.[8] These gnostics, he says, believed that the eschatological kingdom of God had fully come—they espoused what might be called a "realized eschatology" (see disc. and note on 1 Thess. 2:12), in which the gift of the Spirit and their own ecstatic experiences evidenced that the Parousia (the return of Christ) had already occurred (see disc. on 1 Thess. 2:19). Far from being regarded as an objective event, the resurrection was viewed as spiritual, taking place only in the lives of believers. Religious enthusiasm took precedence with these gnostics, he says, over the need to earn a living.

Walter Schmithals draws on Lütgert's thesis and contends that gnostic missionaries opposed Paul both here in Thessalonica and elsewhere; moreover, they charged Paul (1) with speaking without the power of the Spirit (cf. 1 Thess. 1:2–2:2) and (2) with deception and error (cf. 1 Thess. 2:3). Paul's exhortations to the Thessalonians to shun immorality and to respect their leaders must be seen against the background of gnostic permissiveness and their challenge to authority. Robert Jewett also owes something to Lütgert,[9] but he rejects the idea that the group in Thessa-

lonica was of the same kind as those who troubled Paul elsewhere.
They lacked, he claims, certain features of Gnosticism (e.g., the
identification of knowledge with the Spirit and a docetic Christ)
and should be placed only on the fringe of that movement. He
agrees, however, with Lütgert, Schmithals, and others in supposing that this Thessalonian "fringe" had turned eschatology into a
present spiritual experience and had abandoned the Christian
ethics of work and sex.

Central to such theories is the proposition that the Thessalonians believed that the kingdom had come. But when we
examine what Paul himself says, especially in 2 Thessalonians
2:1–12, while there is no disputing that the idea of realized
eschatology was in the air (e.g., v. 2), it is equally evident that it
was not the viewpoint of Paul's readers. The problem for them
was what to make of such a notion in the light of their own firmly
held belief that something was still to come (a "future eschatology" assumed, for example, in the teaching of 1 Thess. 4:13–18;
see further the disc. on 2 Thess. 2:1–12). As for "those who are
idle," to see in them evidence of a gnostic incursion into the
church is to overlook the fact the missionaries had already en-
countered the problem when they were in Thessalonica and had
warned against it (see disc. on 2 Thess. 3:6, 10). Similarly, the
exhortations to sexual morality and the plea that the Thessalonians should hold their leaders "in the highest regard" are best
seen not as evidence of Gnosticism but as evidence of the imma-
turity of the Thessalonian church.

The Authenticity of 1 Thessalonians

Few people would question that Paul wrote this letter. The
external evidence is solid. It was accepted as Scripture by Marcion (ca. A.D. 140) and by the Muratorian Fragment, which dates
a little later than Marcion in the second half of the second century. The letter is not quoted until Irenaeus (ca. A.D. 180), but the
similarity of language between it and some earlier writings suggest that it was in circulation by the first half of that century.[10]

The address names Paul as sender (together with Silas and
Timothy, but see disc. on 1 Thess. 1:1 and 3:1). But more significantly, its language and ideas are those of the apostle (see,
e.g., disc. on 3:10; 4:1–12, 13, 16; 5:12, 15, 24). His association with
the others agrees with the evidence of Acts that they were his

colleagues at this time, assuming that the letter was written from Corinth during the so-called second missionary journey. Some see contradictions in the details of Acts and 1 Thessalonians as touching the movements of the people concerned, and on that basis, they question the letter's authenticity. But it must always be understood that, while Acts is a remarkably accurate account of what it chooses to tell us, it does not choose to tell us everything. It should not surprise us, then, to find evidence in the letter of movements not recorded in Acts. We have already suggested a satisfactory reconstruction of events which shows Acts and 1 Thessalonians to be complementary, not contradictory. Any grounds in these details for doubting that Paul wrote the letter are imaginary.

The contents point to an early date. Evidence of a developed church structure is absent. "Those who work hard among you" are mentioned (1 Thess. 5:12), but these leaders have no titles and there is no evidence of a hierarchy within their number (cf., e.g., Phil. 1:1). Moral and practical dilemmas faced the church rather than theoretical difficulty, which might have been the case in a later day. Further, the major doctrinal concern of the letter— what would be the fate of believers who had died before the return of Christ—could have been a problem only in the earliest days of the church. The question raised by the Thessalonians would soon have been answered (as it is in this letter) and the problem laid to rest.

The letter has every appearance then of belonging to the time when Paul himself was still active. That being the case, it is hard to imagine how anyone other than Paul could have written it. Surely no one could have passed off a forgery while he was there to disown it. He shows in 2 Thessalonians 2:2 how intolerant he is of such an attempt; in addition he is careful to ensure his own letters are unmistakably his (see disc. on 2 Thess. 3:17).

The Date of 1 and 2 Thessalonians

Luke's account of Paul's time in Corinth (Acts 18:1–17) gives us a rare peg on which to hang Pauline chronology. He mentions that the apostle's presence there coincided with Gallio's appointment as the proconsul of Achaia. Proconsular governors normally took office on 1 July and held office for only one year. The year in which Gallio governed Achaia can be determined by an inscription at Delphi, which records the emperor's reply to an inquiry from Gallio. This is dated after the twenty-sixth acclamation of Claudius as *Imperator*. These acclamations occurred at frequent but irregular intervals and by themselves do not establish a precise date. But other inscriptions found elsewhere enable scholars to set fairly narrow parameters for the date of the Delphi inscription. Two of these inscriptions (*Corpus Inscriptionum Latinarum* 3.476, 1977) show that the twenty-second and the twenty-fourth acclamations belong to the eleventh year of Claudius' reign (25 January A.D. 51 to 24 January 52). A third, found on a monumental arch of an aqueduct in Rome, dedicated on 1 August A.D. 52, shows that by this time Claudius had received his twenty-seventh acclamation. On this basis, Gallio's term of office most likely extended from July A.D. 51 to June 52. That same year, therefore, also saw Paul in Corinth.

Of course, Paul stayed in Corinth for more than one year (Acts 18:11), and we do not know whether Gallio's term of office was early or late in relation to Paul's time in the city. Neither can we determine when, during the year that Gallio visited, Paul was brought before him. The circumstances suggest, however, that Paul had been in Corinth long enough to have made the impact that prompted the Jewish action against him. This might put Paul's arrival in the city as A.D. 50 or early in A.D. 51. The impression given by Acts is that, soon after Paul's arrival, Silas and Timothy rejoined him; further, it appears that shortly after that—"Timothy has just now come to us from you"—he wrote 1 Thessalonians, say A.D. 51 (see disc. on 1 Thess. 3:6).

Before long, Paul received further news of the church in Thessalonica. It was still encouraging news. They were still holding firm despite renewed persecution, and, as far as his own standing was concerned, he no longer needed to defend himself to them; at least, no such defense is offered in the second epistle. But they still needed help concerning some matters. This prompted Paul to write 2 Thessalonians, probably only a matter of weeks or at the most a few months after the first letter, and near enough to the same year, A.D. 51.

The Writing of 2 Thessalonians

Specifically, there are two matters that Paul deals with in the second epistle. The first is doctrinal. Evidently a report was circulating in the church that "the day of the Lord had already come." Paul responds to this in 2:1–12 by explaining that certain events must precede the Parousia, two in particular: "the rebellion" and the appearance of "the man of lawlessness." Since neither of these had taken place, any report to the contrary was plainly false. The second matter is of a more practical nature and something addressed in the earlier letter: namely, the problem of "those who are idle." Apparently the gentle reproof of 1 Thessalonians produced no effect. A much harder line was required, so Paul lays down the principle that "if a man will not work, he shall not eat" (2 Thess. 3:6–15).

The Authenticity of 2 Thessalonians

Although Paul is named as the author, just as he is in 1 Thessalonians, and in association as before with Silas and Timothy, scholars are less likely to agree that 2 Thessalonians came from Paul's hand.[11]

Those doubting that Paul wrote it claim that the eschatology of 2 Thessalonians differs from that of 1 Thessalonians to the point of contradiction. In the first letter, Paul regards Jesus' coming as imminent; in the second that sense of imminence is absent, and instead the emphasis is on what will precede the Parousia. This is a fair observation. But it is a difference of emphasis only, not evidence of a contradictory eschatology. Each letter addresses a particular issue, and until the question was raised of when the coming would be—the question addressed in 2 Thessalonians—there was no call for Paul to discuss it in the earlier letter, where the quite different issue was being addressed of what the fate of the dead would be.

Furthermore, it is asserted that the language of the first letter implies that its readers were Gentiles: "You turned to God from idols . . . " (1:9; see above on The Founding of the Church), whereas 2 Thessalonians, with its numerous allusions to the OT, implies that they were Jews (see esp. 2 Thess. 1:5–10; 2:1–12).[12] But the fact that 2 Thessalonians draws so much on the OT may say more about its author than the readers, while the fact that the OT is more in evidence here than in the first letter is because of its subject matter. Its theme is the day of the Lord, concerning which the OT says much (see disc. on 2 Thess. 1:3–12 for the author's possible use of an earlier source for many of the OT allusions).

Moreover, the two letters are said to be different in tone, the first warm and friendly, the second formal and cold. But this is too sweeping a generalization. Much of the warmth of the first is generated by Paul's self-defense, which he no longer needed to make, as it seems, in the second. Take these passages out and the difference in tone between the two letters would be imperceptible.[13] Conversely, the alleged coldness of the second letter rests on only a few passages in which a more formal tone is adopted, as in 1:3, "We *ought* always to thank God . . . " (cf. 1 Thess. 1:2, "We always thank God . . . ") and in which the author asserts his authority. "We command . . . " (3:4, 6, 10, 12; but cf. 1 Thess. 4:11). But alongside these expressions are others, such as his calling his readers "brothers" (1:3; 2:1, 13, 15; 3:1, 6, 13, 15; see disc. on 1 Thess. 1:4) and his enthusiastic references to their progress (e.g., "your faith is growing more and more," 1:3); these reflect a warmth of affection no less than that in 1 Thessalonians (see disc. on 2 Thess. 1:3–12 for the possible influence of liturgical language on the alleged formality of the epistle).

This mixture of affection and authority is typically Pauline. Moreover, the likeness of 2 Thessalonians to Paul's other letters does not end here; it is also reflected in its ideas and language. Pauline words, phrases, and constructions abound (see, e.g., disc. on 2 Thess. 1:2; 2:1, 17; 3:5). In this matter of language and thought, the likeness of 2 Thessalonians to 1 Thessalonians is especially noticeable. This similarity, however, is something of a two-edged sword. It has been enlisted as an argument against the authenticity of 2 Thessalonians on the grounds that a man of Paul's ability, in writing to the same church within a short space of time, would not have repeated himself to the extent that he does but would have found other forms of expression. But the similarity argues even more forcibly for a common authorship of the two letters than it does against Paul's authorship of the second. Surely no forger would have imitated Paul so successfully. As Leon Morris observes, "the imitator (if there was one) must have thought with the very mind of Paul."[14] In defense of the traditional authorship, William Neil accounts for the similarity between the two letters by suggesting that Paul had read through "the customary draft copy of his first letter before writing the second" and that its language and ideas were, therefore, still fresh in his mind.[15] This is not an unlikely scenario, since it may have been a misunderstanding of what he had written in

1 Thessalonians that he was correcting in 2 Thessalonians. (On the other hand, the problem addressed in the second letter may have been due to another letter which was not his; see below and the disc. on 2 Thess. 2:2).

Besides all this, the external evidence for Paul's authorship of the second letter is strong. Polycarp, Ignatius, Justin, and the Didache, all in the first half of the second century, appear to have known it. Both the Marcionite canon and the Muratorian Fragment include 1 Thessalonians, and it is quoted by Irenaeus and later writers as Pauline (e.g., Ireneaus, *Against Heresies* 26.4).

The Sequence of the Letters

The idea is sometimes canvassed that 2 Thessalonians was written before 1 Thessalonians. According to this view, the shorter letter is filled out and enriched by the other. Advocates of this theory find support for their view in the recurring phrase, "now about" in 1 Thessalonians 4:9, 13; 5:1. The same phrase recurs in 1 Corinthians, marking Paul's answers to the Corinthians' questions. From this, the inference is drawn that Paul wrote 2 Thessalonians first; it precipitated a number of questions to which Paul responded with 1 Thessalonians. But the comparison with 1 Corinthians will not stand, for the context confirms that Paul is not answering the Thessalonians' questions but is using this formula to introduce a discussion of what they already knew.

That 2 Thessalonians is the earlier letter is argued also on other grounds. Paul's statement in 1 Thessalonians 5:1 that he had no need to write to them "about times and dates" makes the best sense, it is argued, if he had already written 2 Thessalonians 2:1–12. Again, at the end of 2 Thessalonians, Paul draws attention to his signature. That he should do so seems more appropriate in his first than his second letter. Also in the letter that is called the first, he refers to the leadership of the church, to a persecution that the church had already suffered (cf. 2 Thess. 1:4 where the church is still suffering), and to the death of some of its members. All of this, it is said, demands a longer span of time between the founding of the church and the writing of 1 Thessalonians than the traditional date and order of the letters allow. Finally, there is a problem within the church that Paul refers to in 2 Thessalonians 3:11 as though learning of it for the first time ("We hear that some among you are idle . . . "). In 1 Thessalonians 5:14, however, he speaks of the same problem as a matter of common knowledge and as something that the church must take in hand.

Taking these arguments in order, (1) there is no need to postulate 2 Thessalonians 2:1–12 as the background to the "times and dates" of the other letter. On any showing, Paul's ministry in Thessalonica included preaching about the Parousia; this sufficiently accounts for the reference of 1 Thessalonians 5:1. (2) The reference to his signature in 2 Thessalonians 3:17 may be better explained by the possibility that in 2:2 he is responding to a spurious letter that was circulating in his name (see above on The Writing of 2 Thessalonians and the disc. on 2 Thess. 2:2). For their future reference, should the question of authenticity ever come up again, they should know that his letters could be clearly identified. This is "the distinguishing mark in all my letters," he explains. "This is how I write." (3) Our reconstruction of the events of Paul's ministry in Thessalonica, and of what followed until the missionaries were reunited in Corinth, allows ample time for the situation reflected in 1 Thessalonians to have developed (see above on The Founding of the Church). (4) As for the references to persecution, "despite the aorist *epathēte* in 1 Thessalonians 2:14, it is not clear," says Bruce, "that the afflictions of 1 Thessalonians belong to the (recent) past in contrast to the present afflictions of 2 Thessalonians."[16] Perhaps the most that can be said about these references in both the epistles is that they point to what was an ongoing fact of life for this church. (5) Finally, with regard to the problem of idleness, when Paul says in 2 Thessalonians 3:11 that he and his colleagues had heard of the matter, this does not necessarily mean that they had heard of it only then or only once. The reference may be to a later report which confirmed what Timothy had already told them (such a report may also have mentioned the Thessalonians' mistaken ideas about the Parousia; see disc. on 2 Thess. 2:1–12).

In short, none of the arguments for reversing the traditional order of the two letters is convincing, while there are solid reasons for retaining that order. Paul's explanation in 1 Thessalonians 2:17–3:5 of his state of mind—his "intense longing" to see the Thessalonians—and of the measures that he had taken because of it presupposes that this was his first letter. The same holds true for the note of relief now that he has an encouraging report of the church. If indeed 2 Thessalonians is more formal in tone than the other (see above on The Authenticity of 2 Thessalonians), this might reflect a more settled state of mind now that he knew how matters stood. It might also reflect that he was having to deal with a recalcitrant group who had disregarded his earlier warnings. The problem with the idle is, in fact, only one of several areas in which a progression can be seen from 1 Thessalonians to 2 Thessalonians. Another is in the references to persecution. The church had already suffered, as we have seen, in 1 Thessalonians, but there is reason to think that part of Paul's purpose in writing was to encourage the church in the face of what inevitably lay ahead: "You know quite well," he wrote, "that we were destined for (trials)" (1 Thess. 3:3). And by the time he wrote 2 Thessalonians, the inevitable had happened, and the church was suffering persecution again. A third area in which a progression can be traced is in the teaching about the Parousia. In 1 Thessalonians 4:17, Paul gives what seems to be a new piece of instruction (as far as this church is concerned) about believers being "caught up . . . to meet the Lord in the air." But this teaching appears to be presupposed in 2 Thessalonians 2:1 in the reference to "our being gathered to him," thus Paul is building in the second letter on the instruction given in the first. We conclude, then, that Paul wrote the two letters and that he wrote them in their canonical order.

The Letters Today

When the dust of these questions settles, what really matters is what these letters say to Christians today. Some of the issues in the letters may not be those we face, but even so, we can learn from how they are discussed. Paul had no doubt about his authority. He believed himself to be a man "approved by God," appointed by Christ (1 Thess. 2:4, 6) and called "to proclaim . . . the whole will of God" (Acts 20:27). On that basis he said "anything that would be helpful" (Acts 20:20), whether what he said was a "comfortable" or an "uncomfortable" word in the ear of his hearers. His only criteria were the helpfulness of the word and the wholeness of the ministry of the word; they certainly did not include the comfort of his hearers. He would put a "flea in their ear" if need be (see disc. on 1 Thess. 2:4). But his proclamation of "the whole will of God" was tempered always with love. He was like a "mother caring for her little children" or a father "encouraging, comforting, and urging" them on (1 Thess. 2:7, 11f.). In

discussing often difficult issues, Paul was both gentle and authoritative, faithful to God's word, but "fatherly" (in the best
sense) in applying it (see, e.g., disc. on 2 Thess. 3:15).

These letters still speak to us today. Some of the issues may
not be those that we face, but, for the most part, their teaching is
timeless and often timely for today's church. These letters were
addressed to a small church in a large and overwhelmingly
pagan society, a church under constant pressure to conform to
the norms of that society. Many today can identify with the
Thessalonians in this situation and can learn from Paul's sustained call to holiness that overcoming the pressure to conform
demands consecration, not complacency.

But, then it might be asked, Why be holy? The answer to
that question and, at the same time, the best incentive to live
consecrated lives, is the truth that Jesus will return. Nowhere is
that truth more vividly declared than in the Thessalonian letters.
"With this in mind," says Paul speaking of that return, "we pray
. . . that . . . Jesus may be glorified in you, and you in him,
according to the grace of our God and the Lord Jesus Christ"
(2 Thess. 1:11f.). In this, he sums up what the letters say to
Christians today: Be ready, be holy; to which we can only add
our own Amen.

Notes

---

1. Cited by J. B. Lightfoot, *Biblical Essays* (London: Macmillan,
1893), p. 255.

2. R. B. Rackham, *The Acts of the Apostles* (London: Methuen, 1901),
p. 240. See also J. Murphy-O'Connor, *St. Paul's Corinth* (Wilmington, Del.:
Michael Glazier, 1983), p. 80.

3. M. Hengel, *Acts and the History of Earliest Christianity* (London:
SCM Press, 1979), p. 89.

4. F. F. Bruce, *New Testament History* (New York: Doubleday, 1971),
pp. 276f.

5. A. J. Malherbe, *Paul and the Thessalonians* (Philadelphia: Fortress
Press, 1987), p. 17.

6. W. Ramsay, *St. Paul the Traveller and the Roman Citizen* (London:
Hodder & Stoughton, 1930), p. 233 estimates a stay of six months.

7. See M. Dibelius, *Studies in the Acts of the Apostles* (London: SCM Press, 1956), p. 156: "Paul's mission might easily have been confused by the public with the activities of wandering speakers, mendicant philosophers, pseudo-prophets, and sorcerers. Therefore the missionary's first concern had to be to dissociate himself from them by emphasizing that his aims were not self-seeking."

8. W. Lütgert, *Die Vollkommenen im Philipperbrief und die Enthusiasten in Thessalonich* (Gütersloh: C. Bertelsman, 1909), pp. 547–654.

9. R. Jewett, "Enthusiastic Radicalism and the Thessalonian Correspondence," *SBL Seminar Papers* 1 (1972), pp. 181–232.

10. G. Milligan, *St. Paul's Epistles to the Thessalonians* (London: Macmillan, 1908), p. lxxii, thinks that "two passages in Ignatius and one in the *Shepherd of Hermas* may perhaps be taken as showing acquaintance with its contents."

11. For a recent representative of those who doubt the Pauline authorship of 2 Thessalonians, see G. S. Holland, *The Tradition That You Received from Us: 2 Thessalonians in the Pauline Tradition* (Tübingen: Mohr-Siebeck, 1988), pp. 59–127.

12. A long time ago, the great German scholar Adolf von Harnack made the suggestion, which was later taken up by others, that the church in Thessalonica was divided into two congregations, one Gentile, the other Jewish, and that the two letters were addressed to each respectively. Cf., e.g., K. Lake, *The Earliest Epistles of St. Paul* (London: Rivingtons, 1914), pp. 83ff. However, there is little to commend this theory. Had Paul been writing to two such congregations, he would surely have made this clearer in the letters. We have no evidence that the church was divided. A better suggestion is that of E. E. Ellis, "Paul and his Co-Workers," *NTS* 17 (1970–71), pp. 437–52, that the second letter was addressed to the church leaders. But even this comes up against the fact that the two letters seem to be sent to the same people, namely, "the church of the Thessalonians."

13. See J. E. Frame, *The Epistles of St. Paul to the Thessalonians* (Edinburgh: T. &T. Clark, 1912), p. 35.

14. L. Morris, *Word Biblical Themes: 1 & 2 Thessalonians* (Dallas: Word, 1989), p. 6. See also D. F. Watson's review of Holland, *Tradition You Received* (*JBL* 108 [4, 1989]), pp. 748–50: "If 1 and 2 Thessalonians share a similar, very standard rhetorical outline and a few verbal and thematic similarities, then Paul just as well as a pseudonymous author could quite reasonably be its author. Differences in content could easily be attributed to the same author's varying approach to meet a different rhetorical exigence."

15. W. Neil, *The Epistles of Paul to the Thessalonians* (London: Hodder & Stoughton, 1950), p. xxiii.

16. F. F. Bruce, *1 & 2 Thessalonians*, WBC 45 (Waco, Tex.: Word, 1982), p. 146.

1 Thessalonians

1:1 / **Paul** frequently associates himself with others in the prescripts of his letters (cf. 1 Cor. 1:1; 2 Cor. 1:1; Gal. 1:1f.; Phil. 1:1; Col. 1:1; 2 Thess. 1:1; Philem. 1). In most cases it must be doubted that the others made any material contribution to the letters, being named simply out of courtesy, and so in this case. The letter bears all the hallmarks of a Pauline epistle (see Introduction on The Authenticity of 1 Thessalonians and disc. on 3:1), such that it is difficult to believe that **Silas and Timothy** had any hand in what was written apart from giving Paul an up-to-date report on the situation in Thessalonica and some counsel as to what should be said **to the church of the Thessalonians**. **Silas and Timothy** had, of course, shared with Paul in the establishment of that church, and Timothy had only recently returned (as we suppose) from revisiting the scene of their former labors. It is understandable, therefore, that they should be named in the address.

The address follows the normal pattern of letters of that time, naming the writer(s) first, then the recipient(s), and finally giving a word of greeting. Sometimes this structure became for Paul the vehicle of an extended theological statement, as in Romans 1:1–7. Here it remains relatively simple. Because the letter is written to the church (no matter that it was addressed in the first instance to a particular group of Christians at a particular time), we may read it as Paul's letter (and God's word) to us (see Introduction on The Letters Today).

The greeting of **peace** was, and still is, the usual greeting among Jews. Properly, it signified far more than peace does with us. Our concept of peace is largely negative: the absence of war; theirs signified well-being in the widest sense, and here, in the spiritual sense in particular (cf. 5:23; 2 Thess. 1:2; 3:16). The usual Greek greeting was "Rejoice" and the similarity of that word (*chairō*) with **grace** (*charis*) has led some to think that Paul was making a play on the two words. But this could equally as well be a variant of the greeting, "Mercy and peace," that was current in some Jewish circles (cf. 2 Bar. 78:2). At all events, we are carried by the greeting to the heart of the Christian gospel, for we have been saved by the grace of God ("the extravagant goodness" of God, cf. 1 Thess. 5:28; 2 Thess. 1:2, 12; 2:16; 3:18) that we might have peace with God. One wonders (although this is the first evidence of it) whether the greeting, **Grace and peace**, had become a liturgical formula (see disc. on 5:28 for the association of grace with the Lord Jesus Christ, and cf. 2 Thess. 1:2).

Elsewhere Paul adds to this greeting the phrase, "from God the Father and the Lord Jesus Christ" (cf. Rom. 1:7; 1 Cor. 1:3; 2 Cor. 1:2; Gal. 1:3; Eph. 1:2; Phil. 1:2; 2 Thess. 1:2; 1 Tim. 1:2; 2 Tim. 1:2; Titus 1:4; Philem. 3) or simply, "from God our Father" (Col. 1:2). Thus we might ask whether we should add the phrase **in God the Father and the Lord Jesus Christ** to the greeting. The Greek would allow it, and it would thereby indicate the *place* (*en*, "in") in which grace and peace are to be found rather than the *source* (*apo*, as in the formulae above) from which they come. But NIV adopts the consensus view that the phrase belongs rather with **the church of the Thessalonians**, expressing the idea that the church was at rest in God. In the world it had no rest. It was a persecuted church. However, the promise was that no one could snatch followers of Christ out of the Father's hand, and they rested secure in that (cf. John 10:29 and see disc. and note on 2 Thess. 1:4 for the church as God's possession). But notice, to be **in God** is also to be **in . . . the Lord Jesus Christ**. The one preposition (in the Greek) governs both persons, thus drawing the Father and Jesus together whom, by implication, we know either together or not at all (cf. 3:11; John 10:28–30). The fact that the Father and the Son are thus linked in this the earliest of Paul's letters implies that it was already the practice (stemming from the first disciples' experience of Jesus) to afford the Son divine status (see further disc. on 3:11). As Morris observes, "It is not easy to see how any created being, anyone less than God, could be linked with God the Father in such a way. How can the Thessalonian church be 'in' the Lord Jesus Christ if he is no more than a first century Jew?" (Morris, *Themes*, p. 31).

The description of God as **Father** adds the dimension of love to the thought of God's care for the church, while the title **Lord** bears further witness to Paul's estimate of Jesus. The use of this title comes out of the early church's belief in the resurrection of Jesus, which, more than anything else, convinced them that God had made him both Lord and Christ (Acts 2:36).

Additional Notes   §1

1:1 / In God . . . and the Lord Jesus Christ: Not only is this phrase with the preposition **in** (*en*) unusual in a greeting, as noted above, but insofar as it speaks of the church as being "in God," it is unusual in any Pauline context. He might speak of boasting "in God" (Rom. 2:17; 5:11) or even of being hidden "in God" (Eph. 3:9; Col. 3:3), but he never speaks of the church or an individual being "in God" as he speaks of their being "in Christ." Acts 17:28 is no exception. That text refers to the life we have in him by virtue of creation, not of redemption; and in any case, the line is not Paul's but probably from Epimenides of Crete. Best takes the preposition as instrumental, "the Christian community brought into being by God."

There are a number of references in the OT to **God** as **Father** (e.g., Exod. 4:22; Deut. 32:6; Hos. 1:10; 11:1), but in most cases these describe the relationship between God and his people as a whole, or between God and the king. Evidence that individuals thought of God as their Father is sparse. The same can be said of intertestamental Judaism, and in the whole of the Qumran literature there is just one passage where the epithet, Father, is applied to God (1QH 9.35f.). Judaism of the first century A.D. and later did call God by this name but not often, and generally with stress on the idea of obedience to the Father. Few thought of God as the Father of the individual. "There is no instance," for example, "of the use of *Abba* (Father) as an address to God in all the extensive prayer literature of Judaism, whether in liturgical or in private prayers" (J. Jeremias, *New Testament Theology* [New York: Scribners, 1971], p. 65). If anything, first-century Judaism tended increasingly to think of God as remote from the individual, to which the teaching of Jesus provides a unique and radical corrective. The scribes put God in the seventh heaven; Jesus taught that he is near and cares for each of us. This teaching is reflected, for example, in the prayers of these two letters (1 Thess. 3:11–13; 2 Thess. 2:16f.; 3:5), where God is portrayed as "not remote and uncaring. He is deeply concerned about his people. He is active in bringing about their growth in Christian qualities, and his concern and his activity will persist to the end" (Morris, *Themes*, p. 13).

The Lord Jesus Christ (cf. 1:3; 2:15, 19; 3:11, 13; 4:1, 2; 5:9, 23, 28; 2 Thess. 1:1, 2, 7, 8, 12; 2:1, 8, 14, 16; 3:6, 12, 18). Lord (*kyrios*) is not a name but a title. It is used in a variety of ways but, with reference to ordinary people, most commonly as a polite form of address, much like our "sir" (e.g., John 12:21). More importantly, however, it forms part of the religious vocabulary of the day. Pagan gods receive the title "lord," and sometimes, in that connection, it is applied to the Roman emperors to express their divinity. Paul would have been aware of this and mindful that in using the title of Jesus he was putting Jesus in the highest place in pagan terms. But, without question, the immediate background to his use (in common with that of the church generally) is the LXX, where "Lord" frequently renders the Hebrew *Yahweh*, the name of God. The application of the title to Jesus stems from his resurrection whereby he "was declared . . . to be Son of God" (Rom. 1:4). Paul employs this title ambiguously at times; whether he means God the Father or God the Son is not clear. In most cases, however, the reference appears to be to the Son. "There is but one God, the Father . . . and there is but one Lord, Jesus Christ" (1 Cor. 8:6; for Father, see disc. on 1:8; 2 Thess. 3:1, 3, 4, 5; for Son see disc. on 1 Thess. 1:10; 3:8, 12; 4:6; 4:15–17; 5:2, 12, 27; 2 Thess. 1:9; 2:2, 13; 3:16).

Similarly **Christ** is a title, but, due in large measure to Paul, it soon came to used as a proper name. "Christ" comes directly from the Greek word *Christos*, which translates the Hebrew *mešiaḥ* (messiah), meaning "anointed one." In the OT, various people are anointed with oil and thereby set apart for a particular office in the service of God, such as priests (Lev. 4:3; 6:22) and kings and perhaps prophets (1 Kings 19:16). The kings especially are called "the Lord's anointed" (e.g., 1 Sam. 24:10; 2 Sam. 19:21; 23:1; Ps. 2:2; Lam. 4:20). In some instances a person or persons might be called *mešiaḥ* who had not been literally anointed but who, nevertheless, served God's purpose in some way (the patriarchs, Ps. 105:15; Cyrus the Persian, Isa. 45:1; the nation Israel, Hab. 3:13). Thus there were many "anointed ones," but over the years the expectation grew that in due course God would send not just *an* anointed one, but *the* anointed one who would inaugurate God's kingdom in the final and fullest sense (see note on 2:12). This expectation can be traced in the OT, although the title Messiah is hardly, if at all, applied there to the coming one. In that connection, the title belongs to a later period, including the period of the NT. At this time, according to A. Edersheim, *The Life and Times of Jesus the Messiah* (London: Longmans, Green & Co., 1890), vol. 2, pp. 710–41, the rabbis understood 456 OT passages to refer to the Messiah. Thus, when Paul called Jesus by this title, he was using a term that would arouse significant associations in the minds of all those in touch with rabbinic teaching. He uses the title ten times in each of the Thessalonian letters (1 Thess. 1:1, 3; 2:6, 14; 3:2; 4:16; 5:9, 18, 23, 28; 2 Thess. 1:1, 2, 12; 2:1, 14, 16; 3:5, 6, 12, 18).

§2 Thanksgiving for the Thessalonians' Faith (1 Thess. 1:2–10)

Paul's letters typically follow the address and greeting with Paul's thanksgiving for his readers. It is the celebration of their new life in the context of which he can deal with their mistakes and misunderstandings. This letter follows that pattern (the only exception is Galatians). Indeed, here the note of thanksgiving sounds well beyond this section, being heard again in 2:13–16, 3:9–10, and in 3:11–13, where its sound mingles with that of prayer (Paul Schubert, *Form and Function of the Pauline Thanksgiving* [Berlin: Töpelmann, 1939], pp. 17–27, suggests, indeed, that the thanksgiving begun in 1:2 extends for the next forty-three verses!). In the passage before us, it is also mingled with prayer, or at least a report of prayer for the Thessalonians (vv. 2b–3). The grounds of the thanksgiving in vv. 4–10 provide an interesting supplement to the story of the church's foundation in Acts 17.

1:2–3 / We . . . thank God. The plural **We** reflects the association of Silas and Timothy with Paul in the address and suggests that they have some part in what is written, if only in providing Paul with more recent news about the Thessalonians. This should be compared, for example, with 1 Corinthians and Philippians, where Paul links other names to his own in the address but follows with the singular, "I thank God." The addition of the words **always** (*adialeiptōs*, cf. 2:13; 5:17) and **for all of you** (despite the fact that there were some problem people in the church) is some measure of Paul's love for the Thessalonians. Out of this love his thanksgiving flows. The phrase **for all of you** could be read with either **we . . . thank God**, as NIV, or **mentioning . . . in our prayers**.

In the Greek, three participial phrases follow, qualifying Paul's opening statement. Thus we learn that the thanksgiving is made in the *context* of prayer, literally, by "making a remembrance of you (but in the sense of **mentioning**, cf. Rom. 1:9; Eph. 1:16; Philem. 4) "in the time of our prayers" (*epi tōn proseuchōn hēmōn*). That is, whenever they pray they include thanksgiving for the Thessalonian church.

The second participial phrase expresses the *grounds* of the thanksgiving in their remembering three things in particular about the Thessalonians. These three things correspond with the familiar triad of graces occurring elsewhere in Paul and other NT writers (cf. 5:8; Rom. 5:1–5; 1 Cor. 13:13; Gal. 5:5; Col. 1:4f.; Heb. 10:22–24; 1 Pet. 1:21f.).

1. Their **work produced by faith** (the three nouns, **work, labor, endurance,** *ergon, kopos, hypomonēs,* of this passage recur in Rev. 2:2). This short phrase sums up what must be our response to the gospel. We are saved by grace through faith—all that is necessary has been done for us by grace (the work of God in Christ), and we take hold of it through faith (our trust in Christ as the Savior; for "faith," see further disc. on 3:2, and for "salvation," see disc. on 5:8). Thus we are not saved *by* works—our works—but we are saved *for* works, specifically the "good works, which God prepared in advance for us to do" (Eph. 2:8–10). These are expressed in his commands and summed up in the two great commands to love God and neighbor (Mark 12:29–31; Rom. 13:8–10). Paul could not conceive of a merely intellectual religion. Faith must be demonstrated in practice; evidently, this was happening in the Thessalonian church.

2. Their **labor prompted by love**. This phrase makes the same point as the other: namely, that the Thessalonians are making their Christian profession visible. The practice of their belief is evident for all to see. But, whereas the **work produced by faith** focuses on the word **faith**, i.e., on the means of entering into relationship with God, this phrase draws attention to the nature of that relationship with God. It is one of love. "We love because he first loved us." But "he has given us this command: Whoever loves God must also love his brother" (1 John 4:19–21)—another form of the two great commands, obedience to which is the **labor prompted by love. Labor** (*kopos,* cf. 2:9; 3:5; 2 Thess. 3:8 and 1 Thess. 5:12 for the corresponding verb) is a stronger word than *ergon,* **work,** but no difference is intended here. Obedience is always hard work!

3. The missionaries' third recollection of the Thessalonian church concerns their **endurance inspired by hope in our Lord Jesus Christ**. Endurance (*hypomonē*, cf. 2 Thess. 1:4; 3:5) characterizes those who are unswerving in purpose. It is not a passive virtue but an active one, as its association with labor and work suggests. The Thessalonians' endurance was rooted in both the past and present. It sprang from their consciousness of the grace of God in Christ and of the love of God which now enfolded them (see disc. on 1:4). But further, it is sustained by what still lay ahead. The NT understands **hope** not merely to mean wishful thinking but to possess a certainty about the future based on the promises of God (cf. 2:19; 4:13; 5:8; 2 Thess. 2:16). Specifically the hope is **in our Lord Jesus Christ**. The Greek reads literally, "the hope of," but the genitive is objective. Jesus—and more precisely his return—is the content of their hope. In line with this, Paul speaks of "the hope of salvation" in 5:8, and in 5:9 of the Thessalonians as waiting still "to receive salvation through our Lord Jesus Christ" (cf. Rom. 5:2; Col. 1:27). There is no question that they are saved, but Paul generally reserves that term for the future, though he sometimes uses it of the present state of believers (cf. Rom. 8:24; 1 Cor. 1:18; 15:2; 2 Cor. 2:15; Eph. 2:5, 8; 2 Tim. 1:9; Titus 3:5). But some of the benefits of salvation such as "the redemption of (their) bodies" (Rom. 8:23) will come only with the return of Jesus. Thus we are introduced to what will become the single most important theme of these letters (for **Lord** and **Christ**, see note on 1:1).

NIV links the phrase, **before our God and Father** with Paul's "remembering," but in the Greek text the phrase comes at the end of the verse and may be better linked with what is remembered of the Thessalonian church. This especially concerns their **endurance inspired by hope in our Lord Jesus Christ**, since it follows immediately on that phrase. In support of this view, we note that the same phrase, **before our God and Father** (identical in the Gk. though not in NIV) is closely associated in 3:13, as it would be here, with the thought of Christ's return. It suggests that all that they did and endured was done with an awareness of God and that he was in control.

1:4 / Where NIV begins a new paragraph, the Greek continues with the sentence begun in verse 2. We have now the third participial phrase qualifying the statement, "we . . . thank God," and expressing further the *grounds* of the thanksgiving. The importance that Paul gives to thanksgiving (cf. Rom. 1:8, "First, I thank . . . God") lies in his recognition that, whatever part he or others might play, in the final analysis it is God who opens hearts (cf. Acts 16:14)—the new life of the Thessalonian Christians is due to God. And this is the point that Paul makes in this verse. **We know . . . that he has chosen you** (lit. "knowing your choice, election"; *eklogē*, in the NT always of the divine choice, cf. Rom. 9:11; 11:5, 7, 28; also *klēsis*, "calling," 2 Thess. 1:11). Election in the OT concerns the nation (cf. Deut. 4:37; 1 Kings 3:8; Isa. 41:8f.; 43:10; 44:1f.; 45:4; 49:7), although it begins with an individual, Abraham (Neh. 9:7). In the NT it concerns the individual, and, in a sense, *the* individual, Christ, so that election becomes ours only when we are "in Christ" (cf., e.g., Eph. 1:3–14). Thus the element of human choice enters into the process. If we choose to be in Christ, we have been chosen by God. There is nothing arbitrary, therefore, about election. Our choice makes us his elect. At the same time it makes us "somebodies" who in the eyes of the world may be "nobodies." Election gives us a value that otherwise we would not have, for God chose us, not because of what we were, but despite our being sinners and simply because he is the kind of God he is (cf. 1 John 4:8, 16; also Rom. 5:8 and 1 John 4:10). Our election is entirely an expression of God's love. Notice then, how Paul links these two ideas in this passage by calling the chosen those **loved by God** (cf. Deut. 33:12; Neh. 13:26; Sir. 45:1; Bar. 3:36; m. 'Abot 6.1). The perfect tense of the participle expresses the thought that the love, once shown to us in Christ, continues to enfold us. (See 2 Thess. 2:13 and probably Jude 1 for a similar use of *ēgapēmenoi*.) The adjective *agapētos* more often expresses this idea, but the participle may put greater emphasis on God's continuing love. **Brothers** is one of the earliest names used by Christians of themselves and certainly the most frequent in the NT. The roots of the Christian use lay in the Jewish practice of calling one another "brother" (cf. Acts 2:37; 7:2; 13:15; 28:17), but for Christians it came to have a deeper meaning (cf. Matt. 23:8; Mark 3:34). They were those whose new birth had made them members of the one heavenly family and children of the one heavenly Father. The name is a reminder that, despite our differences, we are one, and that there is "one God and Father of all" (Eph. 4:6; cf. 1 Thess. 1:1). The many occurrences of the name in these letters (twenty-one times), more than might have been expected even from its frequent use elsewhere, may be taken as a measure of Paul's affection for the Thessalonians. Needless to say, **brothers** includes both men and women.

1:5 / The conjunction introducing this verse in the Greek, *hoti*, is ambiguous. It could be taken as "that," making verse 5 an amplification of verse 4, as in RV: "knowing your election, how that our gospel came to you." On this understanding, the emphasis appears to be on their hearing the gospel as evidence of their election. Or it could mean **because,** as in NIV. We know that he has chosen you, says Paul, **because our gospel came to you**. On this view (which we accept as the more likely), it is the preaching, not the hearing, that is the evidence and, more particularly, the circumstances in which the gospel was preached. For it came, **not simply with words, but also with power**. No preaching can be effective without the infusion of divine power (touching all concerned—the preacher and the hearer alike), while effective preaching—and this is Paul's point—demonstrates that God has chosen the hearers. (It is proof, too, that the preachers themselves have been chosen.) The gospel is described as **our gospel** in the sense that this is what they were to preach (cf. 2 Thess. 2:14; 2 Cor. 4:3; also "my gospel," Rom. 2:16; 16:25; 2 Tim. 2:8), but it is "the gospel of God" in the sense that it is peculiarly God's or that it originates from God (2:2, 4, 8, 9; Rom. 1:1; see further disc. on 1:8). In terms of its content, though, it is described as "the gospel of his Son" (3:2; 2 Thess. 1:8; Rom. 1:9; 15:19; 1 Cor. 9:12; 2 Cor. 2:12; 9:13; 10:14; Gal. 1:7; Phil. 1:27; cf. also Rom. 1:1–3, "the gospel of God . . . regarding his Son").

The association of **power** (*dynamis*) with the gospel is a familiar Pauline theme (see Rom. 1:16; 1 Cor. 1:18, 24). This reference may be to "signs, wonders, and various miracles" that accompanied the preaching (Heb. 2:4)—what Paul refers to elsewhere as "the things that mark an apostle" (2 Cor. 12:12); or Paul may be referring to the changed lives of the Thessalonians. Either way, "the power of the Spirit" was at work (Rom. 15:19). Hence Paul's reference to **the Holy Spirit** (written in the Gk. without the definite article, emphasizing, perhaps, his activity; cf. 1:6; Rom. 5:5; 9:1; 15:13, 16, 19; 1 Cor. 12:3; 2 Cor. 6:6; note that the Third Person of the Trinity has now been introduced; see disc. on 1:1 and cf. 1:3f.). The Spirit is the source of power; he is also the source of **deep conviction**, or so the juxtaposition of the three

phrases, **with power, with Holy Spirit, . . . with . . . conviction,**
would seem to imply. **Conviction** (*plērophoria*) carries the sense
of being convinced about a matter. Paul probably still has the
preachers in mind, their conviction about the gospel being a
factor in the Thessalonians' response. But it is possible (as Bruce
and others) to take the word as applying to the hearers and to the
Spirit's role in convincing them of the truth of what they heard
and, beyond that perhaps, in giving them a general confidence
in God. As Morris notes, this concerns "the God who has a
purpose for them and who will surely bring that purpose to pass"
(Morris, *Themes*, p. 90). At all events, the verse ends with the
preachers in mind. What they preach, they live. There is a consistency in their ministry such that their lives exemplify their message. The final clause in the Greek is connected to the rest of the
verse by the conjunction *kathōs*, which marks a close correspondence between what precedes and what follows: as our gospel
came to you with power, said Paul, so **you know how we lived
among you for your sake**. That final phrase, **for your sake** (*di'
hymas*, "because of you"), suggests that lifestyle is a matter of deliberate choice on the part of the preachers (cf. 2:9; 2 Thess. 3:7).

1:6–7 / This consistency of practice with belief was evident, no less, in the Thessalonian Christians. These verses are
introduced (in the Gk.) by "and" (*kai*) and furnish the second (as
we read the Gk.; see disc. on 1:5) of the two reasons for the
statement in verse 4. The writers knew that God had chosen the
Thessalonians because, first, he had sent them effective preachers
and, second, the preachers had met with a ready response: **You
became imitators of us and of the Lord** (see note on 1:1). Lifestyle
is the only evidence that others have of our standing with God.
Paul is thus sure that the Thessalonians are in good standing. Paul
appears to claim in this verse that he and his colleagues are to be
imitated equally with the Lord. Such a claim would be too pre-
sumptuous by far. Rather, what he means is that the preachers so
mirror Christ in all that they do, that they themselves are models
of Christ to others: "You became imitators of us and *therefore* of the
Lord." Could we say that? We should remember that, to begin with,
the Thessalonians had no Christian examples to follow other than
Paul and his colleagues (see further disc. on 2 Thess. 3:7). In time,
they found other models and became imitators of the churches in
Judea (cf. 2:14).

The second half of verse 6 sets out how the Thessalonians became imitators of the missionaries. Like Paul, Silas, and Timothy (and indeed like others before them, cf. Acts 5:41; 16:22–25; Rom. 5:3, 5; 2 Cor. 6:10; Col. 1:24, including Christ himself, cf. Heb. 12:2), **in spite of severe suffering**, they had **welcomed the message with the joy given by the Holy Spirit** (for *dechomai*, "to receive gladly," "to welcome," see disc. on 2:13). The NT takes it for granted that Christians will suffer. Indeed, Paul later states that we are destined (by God) for suffering (see disc. on 3:3). Why this should be, we do not know. But we do know that suffering builds character (cf. Rom. 5:3–5; James 1:12; 1 Pet. 1:6f.) and there may be a hint of this in the juxtaposition of suffering and joy. Joy is a distinguishing mark of the Christian, for it has its basis in our relationship with God (and therefore derives from his grace) and is a gift of his Spirit who is at work in us (see further disc. on 5:16). The precise nature of the "severe suffering" of the Thessalonians is not explained—why should it be? Both the writer and the readers knew what was meant. The word *thlipsis* implies pressure from without, and clearly in this instance, its cause was the pressure of persecution (cf. 3:3, 7; 2 Thess. 1:4, 6; for the verb, *thlibomai*, 3:4), almost certainly instigated by the Jews who had earlier succeeded in having the missionaries driven from the city (cf. 2:14–16; Acts 17:5–10). But for all that, the Thessalonian Christians were themselves **a model** of Christ **to all the believers in Macedonia**, their own province, **and Achaia**, the neighboring province to the south (modern central and southern Greece).

1:8 / By way of further explanation (note the conjunction *gar*, "because") Paul remarks that the Thessalonians' imitation of the missionaries included preaching as well as practice. **The Lord's message rang out from you.** This is literally, "the word of the Lord," a phrase common in the OT and later in Acts, but appearing only here and in 2 Thessalonians 3:1 in the Pauline writings. But Paul enlists other, similar phrases like "the word," "the word of God," "the gospel of God." The word is the gospel, and it is the gospel of which "the Lord" is the author (see disc. on 1:5). As elsewhere in the NT, it is unclear who is meant by the Lord, for the Son (Jesus) no less than the Father is called by this name. In this instance we should probably understand the reference to be to the Father (see note on 1:1). The verb "to ring out" (*exēcheō*), found only here in the NT, suggests the call of a trumpet and brings to mind Paul's metaphor of 1 Corinthians 14:8: "If the trumpet does not sound a clear call, who will get ready for battle?" The clarion call of the gospel had sounded from Thessalonica **not only in Macedonia and Achaia,** but **everywhere**.

This, at least, is the sense of what Paul says. But in midstream he changes the structure of the sentence. "The Lord's message" is replaced as the subject by **your faith in God** (for **faith**, see disc. on 3:2), and strictly, the latter had become known. "Everywhere" refers only to Jewish-Christian communities, and even then it may be hyperbole (cf. Rom. 1:8; 2 Cor. 2:14; Col. 1:6). It is commonly suggested, however, that Priscilla and Aquila may have heard of the faith of the Thessalonians in Rome before coming to Corinth (Acts 18:2), as Paul would have learned, and "what was known at Rome could be presumed to be known everywhere" (Morris). Certainly at Corinth, Paul and the others had no **need to say anything about it**. News of their faith (and equally, no doubt, of their "work produced by faith," etc., 1:3) had gone before them. However, before long, he boasted to the Corinthians about their faith (2 Thess. 1:4) and their work, along with that of all of the Macedonian churches (2 Cor. 8:1–5).

1:9–10 / As verse 8 explains verse 7, so verses 9–10 explain verse 8 (notice again the conjunction *gar*). The subject **they** is indefinite—anyone at all might have reported what was happening in Thessalonica. This is how the missionaries heard of their own part in the story—**what kind of reception you gave us**—from the lips of others. The unusual expression literally means, "What kind of entrance we had." It implies a warm reception and, again, suggests the familiar Pauline metaphor of the open door (cf. Acts 14:27; 1 Cor. 16:9; 2 Cor. 2:12; Col. 4:3). The best part of the story, however, was how they **turned to God from idols**. There is a striking correspondence between this report and that of Paul's preaching in Acts 14:15. Together with Acts 17:22–31, these verses give some indication of Paul's approach to pagans in which the denunciation of idolatry played an important part. We should thus read his description of God as **the living and true God** against this background. The Greek lacks the definite article; the phrase is literally, "a living and true God" (cf. Acts 14:15; Rom. 9:26; 2 Cor. 3:3; 6:16; 1 Tim. 3:15; 4:10; Heb. 3:12; 9:14; 10:31; 12:22; 1 Pet. 1:23), but there is no danger of misunderstanding.

Only one God fits this description. He alone lives, and therefore, he alone is "real," the sense of *alēthinos*, **true.**

In greater detail, what it meant to turn to God receives a twofold definition. First, it means **to serve** him, with the infinitive expressing the goal of salvation and the tense (present) making the point that our goal in being saved is to serve him always. The word means "to serve as a slave" (*douleuō*, see also Rom. 12:11; 14:18; 16:18; Eph. 6:7; Phil. 2:22; Col. 3:24; for Paul's use of the noun of himself, see Rom. 1:1; Gal. 1:10; Phil. 1:1; Titus 1:1), which highlights that our service is to be absolute—there is no time and there are no circumstances in which God is not Lord and we are not his slaves. Second, it is **to wait for his Son from heaven**. The juxtaposition of these ideas of serving and waiting complement one another. There is no other way in which to wait for God than to serve God here and now (cf. Acts 1:6–8). Again, the present tense of the infinitive expresses the thought of being always on the lookout for Christ's return. The Thessalonians needed no urging in this; sadly that is less true of Christians today who have largely lost sight of his return and, therefore, lack that incentive for mission and for a more Christlike way of life. The phrase **from heaven** (*ek tōn ouranōn*), signifies the Son's divinity (cf. 4:16 and see disc. on 1:1).

Verse 10 introduces the distinctly Christian element into this report. Others, such as Jews, might have called upon the Thessalonians to turn from idols, but for Christians, the other side of that coin was that they should turn to God through his Son **whom he raised from the dead—Jesus, who rescues us from the coming wrath**. We notice again a striking correspondence to an account in Acts, this time with Paul's speech to the Athenians in Acts 17:22–31, which is largely an appeal to them to turn from idols. Also the speech associates the thought of judgment with the risen Jesus. The resurrection attests Jesus to be "the man (whom God) has appointed" for this purpose (Acts 17:31). In Acts, the thought of Jesus' coming is expressed as a threat; here it is held out as the hope of our salvation. Notice the use of his human name both here and in Acts: thus Paul identifies God's appointed savior and judge with the man of Nazareth. The present tense **who rescues** should not be overemphasized. As a title it must be understood as timeless and meaning something like "the Deliverer." But that *rhyomai* (cf. 2 Thess. 3:2) was chosen, and not some other word, draws attention to the danger in which sinners stand. They need to be "saved" in the sense of "rescued," and that is precisely what Jesus does. He rescues us from the coming wrath of the eschatological judgment. The preposition, *ek*, **from**, underlines the thoroughness of his achievement. The reality of the wrath "revealed from heaven (i.e., God) against all the godlessness and wickedness of men" (Rom. 1:18; cf. 1 Thess. 2:16; 5:9) is insisted upon in Scripture, and we must not shut our eyes to its grim certainty. As righteous and holy, God responds to human sin, but this should not be thought of as merely "an inevitable process of cause and effect in a moral universe" (C. H. Dodd, *The Epistle to the Romans* [London: Hodder & Stoughton, 1932], p. 20). It is inevitable, but it is something personal. God will actively drive the sinner from his presence (no matter that his love longs to bring the sinner home) until the sinner turns for rescue to the Savior, on whom God's wrath has been redirected (cf. Mark 15:34), and in whom God's love is revealed. Thus, through Christ the Savior and the sinner's taking hold of what he has done, God's purpose is fulfilled, for he "did not appoint us to suffer wrath but to receive salvation" (5:9; see also disc. on 2 Thess. 2:11). See further Leon Morris, *The Apostolic Preaching of the Cross* (Grand Rapids: Eerdmans, 1956); R.V. G. Tasker, "Wrath," *NBD*, p. 1341, and H. C. Hahn, "Anger, Wrath," *NIDNTT*, vol. 1, pp. 105–13.

Additional Notes §2

1:5 / **Our gospel** (*euangelion*): In classical literature this word designated the reward given for good news. Its later transference to the good news itself belongs to the NT and early Christian literature. Even in the LXX its only definite occurrence (2 Sam. 4:10) carries the classical meaning. And yet, the NT usage probably stems from the LXX, not from the noun, but from the verb *euangelizomai*, and in particular from the use of the verb in Isa. 40:9; 52:7; 60:6; 61:1 concerning the announcement of restoration after the Babylonian exile. The whole context (Isa. 40–66) of these occurrences is reinterpreted in the NT with reference to salvation through Jesus Christ (cf. Luke 4:18 with Isa. 61:1 and Rom. 10:15 with Isa. 52:7).

1:9 / **You turned to God from idols**: It would appear that from the outset, the majority of the Thessalonian Christians were of Gentile origin. The first converts came into the church by way of the synagogue as God-fearers (Acts 17:4; see Introduction on The Founding of the Church). These words serve, then, as an adequate description of their background and may have sprung to Paul's lips as the language commonly used in preaching to pagans. We have noted above the parallel with Acts 14:15. But is it Pauline language? Bruce points out that this summary of the Thessalonians' conversion experience lacks some of the distinctives of Paul's preaching, such as God's grace and the cross of Christ (cf., e.g., Rom. 3:25; 1 Cor. 2:2; Gal. 3:1; 6:14). This, together with the rhythmical structure of the passage, may indicate a pre-Pauline formula which has left its mark also on Acts (Bruce). This is not to say, of course, that Paul could not or did not make the language his own. There is ample evidence of his readiness to take up a form of words from the tradition and to incorporate it into his own writing or preaching (e.g., 1 Cor. 11:23–26; 15:3–8).

§3 Paul's Ministry in Thessalonica (1 Thess. 2:1–16)

In the thanksgiving, Paul incidentally touched on their ministry in Thessalonica, but he now speaks of that ministry more directly, defending his own and his colleagues' conduct against Jewish slanders. The matters touched on include: (1) the circumstances of their coming to Thessalonica and their motives in being there (2:1–6); (2) their conduct towards the Thessalonians (2:7–12); and (3) the response of the Thessalonians to their message and the ensuing hardship caused by that response (2:13–16). Because of their hostility toward the Jews and based on the assumption that they reflect the fall of Jerusalem in A.D. 70 (for the latter, cf. 2:16c especially) the last four verses have been regarded as an interpolation by some interpreters. The argument for a post-70 date for these verses is supported, some argue, by their similarity of theme and language to passages in the Synoptic Gospels, especially Matthew 23:29–36. But this similarity can be as easily accounted for by supposing that Paul and the synoptics drew on a common tradition. Nothing in verse 16 compels us to see behind it the disaster of A.D. 70, although it does speak of the eschatological wrath of God of which that event became a sign and symbol. But given the circumstances in which Paul was writing, it is no more surprising that he should write in this way (remember, Paul was human!) than that, in other circumstances, he should take a gentler line.

2:1 / It is not apparent in the NIV, but this verse is linked to the previous section and, specifically, to verse 9. It offers a further explanation of what was said there (notice again the conjunction *gar*, "because"). That link is reinforced by the repetition of the unusual word *eisodos*, translated in verse 9 as "reception" and here as **visit**. What others had reported of the Thessalonians' reception of the missionaries, the Thessalonians themselves knew to be true: their **visit to** them **was not a failure**. The Greek word is *kenos* (fem. *kenē*), "empty," and, while the reference is to their mission in general, it should be understood to include their preaching in particular, which was not empty in terms either of conviction—they had preached "not simply with words, but also with power . . . with . . . conviction" (1:5)—or of content—they preached the gospel (v. 2)—or, indeed, of conversions. With regard to the latter especially we should notice the perfect tense of the verb *gegonen*. What was true at the time of their visit remains true. The Thessalonian converts' changed lives prove the genuineness of their conversion.

2:2 / Still on the theme of their preaching, Paul adds that they had **dared to tell** the Thessalonians **his** (God's) **gospel** (see disc. on 1:5 for the gospel of God). This statement is introduced in the Greek by the strong adversative, "but" (*alla*): far from being a failure, their mission saw the very positive achievement of their "speaking (the gospel) freely" (*parrēsiazomai*, cf. Acts 9:27, 29; 13:46; 14:3; 18:26; 19:8; 26:26; Eph. 6:20; in the NT it includes the sense of speaking boldly, hence NIV "we dared to tell"). Boldness of speech characterized preachers of the early church and bore witness that God was with them. So Paul says that they had spoken **with the help of** their **God**. Considering their previous situation at Philippi, where they had **suffered and been insulted** (cf. Acts 16:16–40 and see Williams, *Acts*, ad loc.), and given the situation at Thessalonica, where they had met with **strong opposition**, their boldness of speech testified to human courage no less than to God's help. On the information that we have, it seems that the opposition stemmed from the Jews (cf. 2:14–16; Acts 17:5–19). In referring to it, Paul uses the Greek word *agōn* which described the contests of the Greek games. This term may imply that he is not prepared to take their opposition lying down but would be an active contender in the contest for the hearts of the Thessalonians (there is a fine line between turning the other cheek and standing up for what is right; cf. Luke 6:29; Acts 23:3).

2:3 / The "strong opposition," a calling into question Paul's motives, had been directed chiefly at Paul and had continued even in his absence, after the Jews forced him to leave Thessalonica. Hence his need to defend his motives. The missionaries' **appeal** (using the noun, *paraklēsis*, in the same sense as the verb *parakaleō* in 2 Cor. 5:20; see disc. on 1 Thess. 3:2) did **not spring from error** (*planē*, which can mean either "deceit," leading others astray, or "error," being led astray oneself). NIV is probably right to understand it as self-deception, "error," though Bruce thinks that Paul may have intended the double meaning: "They were neither deceivers nor deceived" (cf. 2 Tim. 3:13). There is no Greek verb corresponding to the "does not spring" of NIV, but some such verb is clearly understood. It would be better put in the past tense, "did not spring," with reference primarily to their mission.

Nor did their appeal spring from "impurity" (*akatharsia*, NIV **impure motives**, cf. 4:7). This word generally carries a moral sense, and here, it may suggest sexual immorality. There was nothing of that kind in the missionaries' desire to make converts. Nor were they **trying to trick** the Thessalonians. *Dolos* meant originally "a bait," and from that "a trap," and from that, "any means of tricking another." With this word, the preposition changes from the *ek* governing the previous two nouns and denoting origin (NIV . . . does not spring "from") to *en* with the dative, meaning in this instance, "in the context of." With their preaching still his theme, Paul denied—and we assume that this denial reflects the accusation of the Jews—that it took place in a context in which their entire ministry was given over to deception.

2:4 / Again Paul employs the strong adversative *alla*, "but" (see disc. on 2:2). Far from having such motives, the missionaries were, in fact, **men approved by God to be entrusted with the gospel**. This description complements the reference in verse 2 to "his gospel"—the gospel is God's in terms of its origin and his to entrust to its preachers (see disc. on 1:5). As for the preachers, the verb *dokimazō* applied to them was used of testing metals, and from that, of any test, and then of the approval of what had passed the test (cf. 5:21). Its perfect tense here suggests that they had long since passed the test. They were approved by God and that approval remained. Such approval made it unthinkable that their appeal to the Thessalonians stemmed from error or impure motives (2:3). Their motives and their message alike centered on God. **We speak**, says Paul using the present tense to express what was always their practice, **not trying to please men but God** (cf. 2:15; 4:1). Here again, Paul may be refuting his opponents' accusation that his preaching was designed to please people—that he was, in this sense, ever ready to "become all things to all men."

He was, of course, always ready to be so, only not in that sense, not in the sense of compromising his preaching. Rather, he sought to accept and be accepted by all, "that by all possible means (he) might save some" (1 Cor. 9:22). In his preaching, he set himself "to proclaim . . . the whole will of God" (Acts 20:27), whether it pleased his hearers or not (cf. Gal. 5:11). The verse ends with the verb that Paul used earlier (*dokimazō*, but now as a participle describing God). God who approved them, **tests our hearts**, he declares. This is, in effect, an invocation to God to witness to the purity of their motives (cf. 2 Cor. 4:2). The "heart" (*kardia*, cf. 2:17; 3:13; 2 Thess. 2:17; 3:5) is a comprehensive term for the inner self, "the seat of the rational as well as the emotional and volitional elements in human life" (Abbott-Smith). God is commonly described in Scripture as the searcher and tester of hearts (1 Chron. 28:9; 29:17; Ps. 7:9; 139:23; Prov. 17:3; Jer. 11:20; 12:3; 17:10; Acts 1:24; 15:8; Rev. 2:23).

2:5–6a / Continuing to refute the charges that he sought to please men (v. 4), Paul denies he resorted to tricks of the trade such as **flattery**. The Greek is literally "neither did we come (*ginomai*, 'become') in a word of flattery," where "word" refers to their preaching. This denies that flattery played any part in their preaching style. Flattery (*kolakeia*) implies manipulation—it is flattery designed to achieve the flatterer's ends, a common enough feature of public speaking in both Paul's day and our own.

The second charge that Paul disavows is that they **put on a mask to cover up greed**. It may have been common knowledge that Paul received gifts from Philippi. This may have led some to conclude that he had come to Thessalonica hoping for some more of the same (cf. Phil. 4:15f.). Later, this same motive is suggested again with reference to his collection for the Judean churches, and again Paul denied it (2 Cor. 9:5; 12:17f.). But in this letter, the denial may have referred to more than money. *Pleonexia* is greed for anything, not only for what one does not have, but for what belongs to others. It amounts to self-aggrandizement, the making of an idol of oneself (cf. Eph. 5:5; Col. 3:5). Paul denies that he has done this. Elsewhere he joins with others in roundly condemning *pleonexia*, which is so contrary to what we see in Christ (Rom. 1:29; Eph. 4:19; cf. Mark 7:22; Luke 12:15; also 1 Cor. 5:10f.; 6:10). He calls God to witness (again, see disc. on 2:4) that greed plays no part in their missionary service.

His third denial concerns a charge that they had looked for **praise from men**, whether from the Thessalonians (**you**) **or anyone else** (cf. 2:4). The gospel that they preached, or rather, the Christ of their gospel alone, deserved praise (cf. 2 Cor. 3:7–11; 4:7). For them, the Baptist's words would have been a fitting motto: "He must increase, but I must decrease" (RSV John 3:30). The missionaries were concerned not with their own image but only with imaging Christ in their ministry.

2:6b–7 / It is debatable whether the opening statement of this verse should be read with what follows or with the previous verse. The decision rests on what we make of its meaning. *Baros*, the Greek word translated **burden** in NIV, can also mean "dignity" or "authority," so that Paul could have been saying, "We were not looking for praise from men (v. 6), although, as apostles of Christ, we could have expected it" (lit. "we could have been with authority"). But if we accept the NIV translation as the more likely, the statement forms a fitting introduction to what follows, where Paul reminds the Thessalonians that the missionaries were not a burden (see disc. on 2:9).

The verb "to be able" (*dynamai*), NIV **we could have been**, expresses Paul's conviction that the **apostles of Christ** have the right to be maintained by their churches. But it is a right that he chooses not to exercise, perhaps for a number of reasons including the desire to set an example (cf. 1:5; 1 Cor. 9:3–18; 2 Cor. 11:7–11; 2 Thess. 3:7–9; see also Matt. 10:5–15 par.; Luke 10:1–12). Notice that he includes his colleagues, Silas and Timothy, in this reference to apostles. Evidently he is using the term in the more general sense of "messenger." Nevertheless, they were messengers of Christ, the genitive expressing an appointment in no sense inferior to that of the Twelve (for Christ, see note on 1:1).

So they had come as apostles of Christ to the Thessalonians and had been **gentle** among them, as Paul puts it, **like a mother caring for her little children**. The weight of MSS evidence is in favor of the reading which has them coming as "babes" among the Thessalonians. The two possible readings differ only by one letter in the Greek text (the letter *nu*), which happens to be the last letter of the previous word. Thus, that letter was either accidentally repeated, giving *nepioi*, "babes," or accidentally omitted because it had just been written, giving *epioi*, "gentle." When we remember that ancient writing ran all words together, we can see how easily such an accident, either way, could have happened. The question is, What is Paul most likely to have said? "Gentle" is consistent with his metaphor of a mother caring for children, but Paul was quite capable of mixing his metaphors and, indeed, of employing such a striking mixture as this, likening himself and his colleagues first to babes and then to a mother (see S. Fowl, "A Metaphor in Distress, A Reading of *nepioi* in 1 Thessalonians 2:7," *NTS* 36 [3, 1990], pp. 469–73). Within a few verses, he likens them also to a father (2:11), and in verse 17 to parents bereft of their children. In the end, by a happy coincidence, the meaning is much the same whether he wrote "babes" or "gentle." The one would imply the other, in the sense that they had gone out of their way to keep their message simple, "like a nurse among her children talking baby language" (Origen and Augustine, cited without reference by Morris). *Trophos*, in this verse, is "nurse" rather than "mother," but the reflexive pronoun suggests that the image is of a nurse caring not for someone else's children, but for her own. In short, the metaphor is of a nursing mother—as tender an image as one could find to represent the pastor and his/her people (cf. Gal. 4:19; also Num. 11:12; see W. A. Meeks, *The Moral World of the First Christians* [Philadelphia: Westminster Press, 1986], pp. 125–30). The verb, *thalpō*, means strictly, "to warm," but carries its secondary sense, "to care for," "to cherish" (cf. Eph. 5:29).

2:8 / **We loved you so much**, Paul adds, and the verse ends as it begins on this note, **that we were delighted to share with you not only the gospel of God but our lives as well**. It is conjectured that the verb *homeiromai*, found only here in the NT, is "a term of endearment borrowed from the language of the nursery" (Wohlenberg, cited by Milligan) and that Paul is, therefore, sustaining the metaphor of the previous verse. In any case, the point of that verse is reinforced with this further assertion of the missionaries' affection for the Thessalonians, such that they were pleased "to spend and be spent" in their interest (2 Cor. 12:15). The divine origin of the gospel is again indicated by the subjective genitive, "of God" (see disc. on 1:5). To preach such a gospel is a demanding task, but nowhere nearly as demanding as sharing one's life with those to whom it is preached. But can the preacher do any less? "No servant is greater than his master," said Jesus, "nor is a messenger greater than the one who sent him"

(John 13:16). But our Master, Jesus, "did not come to be served, but to serve, and to give his life as a ransom for many" (Mark 10:45). As self-sacrifice lay at the heart of his ministry, so it does with all Christian ministry, whether it be preaching or any other.

2:9 / This was certainly the character of the service of Paul, Silas, and Timothy in Thessalonica, as Paul reminds his readers—or perhaps, he simply observes that they remembered (taking the verb, with NIV, to be indicative rather than imperative). But notice, he again calls them **brothers** (see disc. on 1:4), suggesting thereby that the burden of this service was lightened by love. He speaks of their **toil and hardship**. These words (*kopos*, see disc. on 1:3, and *mochthos*) mean much the same. Each speaks of hard work, and in combination, they underline the hardship that the missionaries endured. This is further emphasized by the statement, **we worked night and day**, whose word order reflects the fact that in the ancient world the working day started early, while it was still night (cf. Acts 20:31; 2 Thess. 3:8; also 1 Thess. 3:10). This was done, explains Paul, that we might **not be a burden to anyone while we preached the gospel of God to you**. These words may give some encouragement to those latter day missionaries who find that the only way into some communities is by using their technical skills. The verb "to be a burden" (*epibareō*, cf. 2 Thess. 3:8) derives from the same root as the noun in verse 7 and makes the same point as in that verse. The verb, "to preach" (*kēryssō*), commonly concerns the proclamation of the gospel. It denoted the work of a herald (*kēryx*; cf. 1 Tim. 2:7; 2 Tim. 1:11), who was not to entertain or to win approval, but to faithfully transmit the message that was entrusted to him, in this case, that message is "the gospel of God" (see disc. on 1:5).

2:10 / Again Paul calls on the Thessalonians (**you**, with some emphasis in the Greek) and on God to witness to the truth of what he says about the missionaries' conduct. The confidence with which he does this is impressive (see the comment on 1:6). He uses three adverbs, **holy, righteous and blameless**. On the basis of their meaning in classical Greek, the first two are thought by some to refer to their Godward and their manward conduct respectively, and the third to their faultless conduct in both respects. It is unlikely, however, that these distinctions held good by the time that Paul wrote. The dative case that follows must also be taken into account. NIV reads **among you**, but it may be better to take the dative as meaning "towards you," in which case the Thessalonians are exclusively in view, and the three adverbs are virtually synonymous. In short, the missionaries' conduct towards them was irreproachable. Proper conduct is an essential factor in any missionary enterprise, whether in Paul's world or in today's Western society which has equally lost sight of its ethical boundaries. As for their Thessalonian converts, Paul describes them as **you who believed**, a common description of Christians in the NT, not surprisingly, for faith (in Christ) is central to Christianity. It puts us into the way of salvation and is the key to our continuing relationship with God. The latter is especially in view here since Paul uses the present participle.

2:11–12 / Yet again he calls on the Thessalonians to witness to the truth of what he says (cf. vv. 1, 2, 5, 9, 10). **You know**, he says, and the Greek text joins this to verse 10 with the conjunction *kathaper*, "just as." That is, what the Thessalonians knew of the missionaries' conduct corresponded exactly with Paul's statement that they had been "holy, righteous, and blameless." **You know that we dealt with each of you**. NIV adds **we dealt** to supply the missing verb in the Greek—some such verb, of course, is understood. Its direct object, literally, **each of you** (cf. 2 Thess. 1:3), conveys emphasis in the Greek, and, being in the singular, it draws attention to the fact that they were concerned not merely with numbers ("how many were at the service today?"), but with their converts as individuals (cf. Col. 1:28 with its repeated "everyone"—again, the singular). These they care for as tenderly as a mother nurses her child (see disc. on 2:7) and **as a father deals with** (again understood in the Greek) **his own children**. Being like a father to the Thessalonians meant **encouraging** them (the Gk. verb, *parakaleō*, has a range of meanings, see disc. on 3:2, but most often in the NT it has the meaning given here, especially when coupled with **comforting**, *paramytheomai*, cf. 5:14). Being like a father also meant **urging** (*martyromai*) them **to live lives worthy of God**. The verb has a more authoritative nuance than the others. It had by this time lost its original sense of invoking witnesses (*martyrēs*), but it retained something of the sense of witnessing, "to solemnly affirm" and so "to make an urgent appeal." The appeal, in this case, was literally "to walk worthily of God." The Greek construction, *eis to* with the infinitive ("to walk") expresses the goal to which the missionaries urged their converts.

There is no higher purpose in life than this (for the same construction expressing purpose cf. 3:2, 10, 13; 4:9; 2 Thess. 2:2; and for the similar *pros to* with the infinitive, v. 9; see also disc. on v. 16).

The figure of walking (*peripateō*) with reference to conduct is a common one in the NT and especially in Paul (cf. 4:1, 12; 2 Thess. 3:6, 11; cf. also the use of "way" for manner of life, Acts 9:2; 19:9, 23; 24:14, 22; 1 Cor. 4:17). "Walking" can indicate good or bad conduct (cf. 2 Cor. 4:2; 10:2). Here, of course, it is good and, indeed, with the infinitive in the present tense, it indicates persistence in doing good. Specifically, Paul wanted their lives to persistently reflect the life of God—striving to be perfect because God is perfect (Matt. 5:48), to be loving because God is love (John 13:34; 1 John 4:16). This is "to walk worthily" of God and only such a life befits the people of God's kingdom.

Perhaps Paul arrived at his description of God as the one **who calls you into his kingdom and glory** via this train of thought. A variant reading, with the aorist participle, would hark back to God's "call" in Christ—"come to me" (Matt. 11:28 etc.)—or to that moment when the believer first responded to that call. But NIV accepts the better reading of the present participle, which reminds us that God goes on calling to the weary and the burdened. See also 5:24 where the present participle appears again: "the one who calls you is faithful" (cf. Rom. 8:30; 1 Cor. 1:9). It can still be said that, while this age continues, "now is the time of God's favor, now is the day of salvation" (2 Cor. 6:2). The two concepts of kingdom and of glory are drawn together in the phrase before us by the single preposition and article to give the sense, "God's glorious kingdom." This denotes that aspect of his kingdom that is yet to be revealed, when the restoration of God's rule to his rebellious creation will be completed. It began with Christ's coming and will be completed at his return (see note) in glory (see, e.g., Matt. 16:27; 19:28; 24:30; 25:31). Paul thereby discloses one of the major themes of these letters (cf. 2 Thess. 1:5). In 2 Thessalonians 2:14 the same thought of future glory is found, but what is here spoken of as God's is there ascribed to Jesus— "the glory of our Lord Jesus Christ." For Paul, the two are One (see disc. on 3:11 and 2 Thess. 2:16).

2:13 / Paul returns to his theme of thanksgiving (see disc. on 1:2–10). Using language similar to that in chapter 1, he tells his readers, **we also thank God continually** (cf. 1:2; 5:17). Prefaced in the Greek by the phrase, "because of this" (*dia touto*), this statement looks ahead to the explanatory clause, "because, when you received." The redundant phrase is wisely omitted by NIV. Whether "also" should be read with "thank" or with the pronoun "we" remains unclear. The Greek word order favors the latter. This reading gives the impression that Paul was responding to secondhand news or perhaps to an earlier letter that reported that the Thessalonians were giving thanks to God. Paul, Silas, and Timothy now echo this thanks to God. In chapter 1, the thanksgiving was for the coming of the gospel to their city; here it is for the Thessalonians' reception of it as the word of God. He speaks of this twice in the one verse: **you received the word of God . . . you accepted it.** Of the two different verbs, the first, *paralambanō*, apparently functioned almost as a technical term for the reception of the Christian faith (cf. 4:1; 2 Thess. 3:6 and its use with the correlative verb, *paradidomi*, "to hand down," in 1 Cor. 11:23; 15:3; see note on 2:13); the second, *dechomai* adds the thought that they had welcomed what they had received (cf. 1:6; 2 Thess. 2:10).

Emphasis is laid on the fact that what they received was **the word of God**. That phrase is repeated (at least, as NIV understands it; see note on 2:13) and Paul further underscores his point by stating that it was not **the word of men** (cf. Gal. 1:11f.) but was **actually** "just as" (*kathōs*) he had described it. Paul could not have expressed himself much more strongly than this. The strength of his conviction about the gospel explains his commitment to preaching it. On one occasion, Luke graphically describes Paul as being "seized by the word" (Acts 18:5), as though it had overpowered him, and he was no longer master of when he would preach but the servant of a gospel that would be preached "in season and out" (2 Tim. 4:2). But there had to be a preacher, and so he adds that it was the word of God **which you heard from us.** It was also the word **which is at work in you who believe.** Here another link is forged with the earlier thanksgiving, which spoke of the gospel coming to the Thessalonians with power (1:5). The changing lives of those who received it—the present tense of the verb *energeō*, "to be at work," implies that the work is still in process—verifies that the gospel is the word of God. The description of its recipients as those **who believe** reminds us once again that faith is the key that opens the door (from the inside) to God's word (cf. Acts 14:27; Rev. 3:20) and so puts us in the path of God's salvation.

2:14 / In 1:6 Paul remarks that the Thessalonians were their imitators, and imitators therefore of the Lord in terms of conduct. But the likeness to their mentors did not end there. They also suffered (as of necessity since they were Christians; the promise of Jesus to his followers is not popularity but persecution; see disc. on 3:3). Just like (*kathōs*) **God's churches in Judea**, said Paul, **you suffered from your own countrymen**. The churches in question comprised the original church in Jerusalem, which itself may have been made up of a number of different groups (see Acts 6:1), and those others which subsequently sprang up following the scattering of its members (like seed) through persecution (see Acts 8:1, 4; 11:19). In referring to the Judean churches, Paul uses the participle of the verb "to be"—"the churches being in, . . ." which appears to have been a quasi-technical term for the church in a particular place, as we would say, "the local church" (Acts 11:22; 13:1). But alongside this is another phrase that points to what all (true) churches have in common, and this constitutes them as part of the one church: they **are in Christ Jesus** (cf. Acts 9:31 where the daughter churches of Jerusalem are spoken of collectively as "the church [singular] throughout Judea, Galilee and Samaria"; with the phrase, "in Christ Jesus," cf. "in the Lord," 3:8 and for Christ, see note on 1:1). Paul could never forget his own part in persecuting God's churches, and this no doubt came to mind now as he wrote; but whether he was referring specifically to that persecution or to a later one (e.g., Acts 12:1) we cannot tell (see note on 2:14).

On the one hand, the point of comparison between the church in Thessalonica and God's churches in Judea may extend beyond their suffering to its cause: **the Jews** who killed the Lord Jesus (for Lord, see note on 1:1). From Luke's brief account of the mission in Thessalonica, it was evidently the Jews who instigated the riot that forced Paul, Silas, and Timothy to leave. On the other hand, Paul's use here of the word *symphyletēs*, **your own countrymen**, may argue against blaming the Jews for the Thessalonians' present troubles. If the Thessalonian church was now a predominantly Gentile church, the argument is even stronger, assuming, of course, that the Jews of Thessalonica were deemed by Paul to be foreigners. Others may have thought of them as such, but would Paul have done so? The condemnation of the Jews in verses 15 and 16 is general, extending beyond their activities in Judea to Paul's experience of their resistance to the gospel in the course of his missionary journeys, and could be understood to include Thessalonica. Even so, such a passage as this must always be set over against a passage like Romans 9–11, where we see the apostle anguishing for his fellow Jews, wishing that he himself could be "cursed and cut off from Christ" for their sake (Rom. 9:3). A frank recognition of guilt does not preclude love for the guilty—a point that ought not to be lost on us (cf. Rom. 5:8).

2:15–16 / These verses contain a fivefold condemnation of the Jews ranging from what they did to Jesus, to what they continued to do to prevent his followers from preaching the gospel. (1) It was they **who killed the Lord Jesus and the prophets**. Only here, in all his writings, does Paul explicitly lay this charge against his fellow Jews (cf. 1 Cor. 2:8; Col. 2:15). Moreover, the way he does it magnifies the enormity of what they had done. His unusual word order draws attention to the fact that the Jesus whom they killed was the Lord. The title stands at the front of the sentence—"the Lord they killed, even Jesus"—with all the implications of glory that that title could bear (cf. Acts 2:32–36 and see note on 1:1).

What they did to Jesus was the climax of a history in which they had done the same thing to the prophets "who predicted the coming of the Righteous One" (Acts 7:52; cf. Matt. 23:37; Luke 11:47–51; 13:33f.; Mart. Isa. 5:1–14; Tertullian, *Scorpiace* 8; Jerome, *Adversus Jovinianum* 2.37). (2) Now they were even persecuting Jesus' followers: (**and also drove us out**). The reference may be a general one, but it is more likely a specific allusion to what happened in Macedonia (Acts 17:1–14; cf. 13:50; 14:5, 19; 17:13; 18:6; 19:9).

(3) **They displease God** is a charge that Paul also leveled against Gentiles who were "controlled by [their] sinful nature" and, therefore, could not "please God" (Rom. 8:8; cf. 1 Thess. 4:1). Indeed, the charge is leveled not against the Jews as Jews, but against them as those who (like many Gentiles) rejected Christ. In this connection, Paul adds (4) that they **are hostile to all men**. This charge echoes what was widely said of the Jews at that time, as it was soon to be said of Christians (see Tacitus, *History* 5.5.2; Josephus, *Against Apion* 2.121, and, with reference to Christians, Tacitus, *Annals* 15.44.5). It must be asked whether Paul would have joined in condemning his fellow Jews in those terms. Not, perhaps, on the same grounds. But on the grounds of their

rejection of Christ out of their resistance to the gospel, he may well have used this language against them. The gospel was for the general good, so that any hindrance of it was an act of hostility **to all men**. So NIV interprets this charge, linking it to what follows: (5) they **keep us from speaking to the Gentiles**. The connection is not as explicit in the Greek as in our version, but it is implied in the train of thought by the present participle, which conveys the persistent attitude of the Jews: "They keep on (trying) to keep us from speaking" (see the passages in Acts listed above which bear this out). The speaking was to the end **that they** (the Gentiles) **may be saved**. Salvation is conceived of here in the broadest sense and includes the whole spectrum of God's grace. By resisting that grace and hindering it in others, the Jews, said Paul, **always heap up their sins to the limit**. This comment gathers up all the charges listed above.

The verb, *anaplēroō* perhaps suggests an image of a cup—to "fill up" might be better than "to heap up." The prefix *ana-* perhaps adds the thought that they had filled the cup of their sins to the full (cf. Matt. 23:32). The verb, an infinitive in a preposi-tional phrase with *eis*, expresses the purpose of those concerned (see disc. on 2:12), but in this instance, it must be understood as expressing the result. This leads to Paul's final declaration: **The wrath of God has come upon them at last** (see disc. on 1:10). The use and form of the verb *phthanō* raises two questions: First, what does the verb itself mean? Second, what is the significance of the tense? Strictly speaking, it means "to come before," "to antici-pate," and it bears this sense in 4:15. But generally, by the time that Paul wrote, it meant simply "to come." Its aorist tense (in the indicative mood) generally connotes past time, but in a prophetic context, it may depict something future but so certain that it can be spoken of as if past. The question is, Was Paul saying that God's wrath had come—that it had already manifested itself, in the strict sense of the verb, in anticipation of the eschatological judgment? Or was he speaking prophetically of the wrath that was yet to be revealed from heaven (Rom. 1:18)? And if the former, what had happened? The classic case (as we suppose) of a historical anticipation of the judgment is the fall of Jerusalem in A.D. 70 (see Mark 13), and assuming that this is in view here, some have held these verses to be a later interpolation (1 Thessalonians was written about A.D. 51; see Introduction). But there is nothing that compels us to identify this passage and, in particular, the

second half of verse 16 with that disaster. An alternative suggestion (always assuming that the reference is to something past and
not future) contends that Paul had in mind the series of disasters
in A.D. 49 involving Jews, including a massacre in the temple
(Josephus, *War* 2.224–227; *Ant.* 20.105–112) and their expulsion
from Rome (Suetonuis, *Claudius* 25.4; cf. Acts 18:2 and see further,
Williams, *Acts*, pp. 319f.). But in the context of this letter and in
the light of 1:10 especially, it may be best to understand the
reference as eschatological—the wrath is yet to come upon them.
In this case the aorist (past) tense would be functioning in the
prophetic manner to express what is future. The marginal reading of the NIV, "fully," is better than **at last** for *eis telos*, since the
thought is that the Jews, in common with all who reject Christ,
will in that day drink to the dregs the cup of God's wrath that is
filled by their sins.

Additional Notes   §3

2:2 / **Insulted in Philippi**: The insult lay not simply in their
being mistreated as Roman citizens, but in the treatment itself. They were
publicly stripped, evidently at the hands of the magistrates themselves
(not apparent in NIV), and beaten, without any inquiry into the charges
(Acts 16:22–24; see Williams, *Acts*, p. 288).

2:3 / **Impure motives**: Schmithals, p. 145, sees a reference here
to the collection for the relief of the Christian poor in Jerusalem (cf. Acts
24:17; Rom. 15:25–31; 1 Cor. 16:1–4; 2 Cor. 8–9), suggesting that Paul had
suddenly demanded a contribution from the Thessalonians after having
earlier refused to live at their expense. It is highly unlikely, however, that
he was already working on the collection at this time. The desperate
plight of the Judean Christians may have been borne in upon him only
on his fleeting visit to the city (as we suppose) in Acts 18:22, so that it was
not until his years in Ephesus (Acts 19) that he did anything to organize
for their relief. The epistles that stem from this period reflect this. See
Williams, *Acts*, pp. 323, 336.

2:6 / **Apostles of Christ**: Early use of the term "apostle" appears
to be restricted to the Twelve (Acts 1:2, 6, 12; 2:43; 4:35, 37; 5:2, 12, 18; 8:1)
or, at least, this is how Luke generally uses the term. Only twice, in Acts
14:4, 14, does he extend the category to include Paul and Barnabas. Paul,
though, readily applied the title to a wider group, which included James,
the Lord's brother (1 Cor. 15:7; Gal. 1:19), and Andronicus and Junia (not

Junias as NIV, Rom. 16:7). It is a question, however, whether he would have applied it so widely as to include Timothy, his own "true son in the faith" (1 Tim. 1:2). If 1 Corinthians 9:1 can be taken as a statement of apostolic criteria, namely, that he or she had "seen Jesus our Lord" (risen) (cf. Acts 1:21), this would rule out Timothy; and we must understand apostles here (supposing that Timothy is included in the reference) in the more general sense of messengers (cf. John 13:16; 2 Cor. 8:23; Phil. 2:25).

2:9 / **We worked night and day:** Paul appears committed to the principle of self-support (cf. 1 Cor. 9:6), which, in his case, meant making tents or, more generally, working in leather (see R. F. Hock, *The Social Context of Paul's Ministry: Tent Making and Apostleship* [Philadelphia: Fortress Press, 1980], p. 21). Rabbis were expected to learn and practice a trade (cf. *Pirqe 'Abot* 2.2), and Paul must have been glad of this in later life as he worked to support his ministry (cf. Acts 20:34; 1 Cor. 4:12; 9:3–19; 2 Cor. 11:7ff.; 2 Thess. 3:8). During his time at Thessalonica, more than once he received gifts from the church in Philippi to support his ministry (cf. Phil. 4:15f.). While the Thessalonians may have known this (see disc. on 2:5f.), rather than embarrass them, Paul may have chosen to not mention that outside help, since he had not accepted the support of the Thessalonians. In any case, the gifts from Philippi were probably not sufficient for keeping body and soul together and, therefore, they had no bearing on his point.

2:12 / **His kingdom and glory:** For a proper understanding of the term "the kingdom of God," note that both the Greek and the Hebrew or Aramaic words thus translated signify kingship rather than kingdom; rule rather than realm. Essentially, therefore, the kingdom of God "is not a community of Christians nor an inner life of the soul, nor yet an earthly paradise which mankind is bringing into being and which is in the process of development" (G. Lundstrom, *The Kingdom of God in the Teaching of Jesus* [Edinburgh: Oliver & Boyd, 1963], p. 232), though it might embrace all these notions. Rather, it is God acting in his kingly power, expressing sovereignty and, in particular, asserting his rule both for the overthrow of Satan (see note on 2:18) and for the restoration of humanity to a relationship with himself. But this was conceived of in various ways: sometimes in terms of God's eternal sovereignty and sometimes in terms of our present experience of him, but chiefly in terms of the kingdom's future manifestation. Its onset would be marked by the "day of the Lord" when God and/or his Messiah would appear (see note on 1:1), the dead would be raised, God would vindicate the righteous and judge the unrighteous (Joel 2:31; Amos 5:18–20; Mal. 4:5), and the new age would be ushered in. Then all would know God, from the least to the greatest, and he would forgive them (Jer. 31:34) and pour out his Spirit upon them (Joel 2:28).

For Jesus' contemporaries as for all generations before them, the kingdom conceived of in these terms was no more than a distant hope. With what astonishment, therefore, must they have heard Jesus' announcement of the kingdom's arrival (see, e.g., Mark 1:22, 27). "The time has come," he said (i.e., the anticipated time of its manifestation), "the kingdom of God" has arrived (Mark 1:15; cf., e.g., Luke 17:21). But, if Jesus was right (and the evidence of his life, his miracles, his resurrection, and the Pentecostal outpouring assure us that he was), then the kingdom clearly had not come in the manner expected. For the time being, it remained a personal and partial (though real) experience for those who submitted to God's rule in Jesus Christ (cf. 1 Cor. 13:12). Only when Jesus returns will the kingdom be fully established and God's rule become all in all (cf. 1 Cor. 15:24f.). Thus the day of the Lord that arrived with the coming of Jesus has been drawn out until his return. Much of the language of the OT describing the day of the Lord is applied by the NT to Jesus and to the day of his return—he is viewed as the Lord whose day it was. Hence, in addition to being called the day of the Lord (cf. 1 Cor. 5:5; 1 Thess. 5:2; 2 Thess. 2:2; 2 Pet. 3:10), it is called "the day of Christ" (Phil. 1:10; 2:16), "the day of Christ Jesus" (Phil. 1:6), "the day of the Lord Jesus" (2 Cor. 1:14), "the day of our Lord Jesus Christ" (1 Cor. 1:8), and sometimes simply as "the day" (Rom. 13:12; 1 Cor. 3:13; 1 Thess. 5:4; Heb. 10:25) or "that day" (2 Thess. 1:10 in Greek; not apparent in NIV). See further Williams, *Promise*, esp. pp. 19–35.

2:13 / When you received the word of God: As discussed above, the verb *paralambanō*, "to receive," and its correlative, *paradidomi*, "to hand down," were apparently almost technical terms for the reception and transmission of the Christian faith, "the tradition" (*paradosis*, see disc. on 2 Thess. 2:15). Broadly speaking, this tradition had three components: (1) a summary of the gospel story, (2) a rehearsal of the deeds and words of Jesus, and (3) an outline of how his followers should behave. The latter was apparently transmitted in an ordered form under subject headings such as "Put off (old vices)," "Put on (new virtues)," "Be subject (to those in authority and to one another)," " Watch and pray" (cf. Col. 3:5–4:6 for such a catechesis, and Rom. 6:17 for reference to the catechesis which was handed down [*paradidomi*] to the Roman Christians; both Jesus himself [Col. 2:6f.] and the apostles [Phil. 4:9; 2 Thess. 3:6–10] were "received" [*paralambanō*] as exemplars of this tradition).

The word of God which you heard from us (*logon akoēs par' hēmōn tou theou*): NIV takes *logon* closely with *tou theou*, "the word of God," and *akoēs* with *par' hēmōn*, "which you heard from us." This can be read differently, though to the same effect, by staying closer to the word order of the Greek: "you received the word of hearing (i.e., the word which you heard) from us, (but it was) God's (word)." *Tou theou* may be placed at the end for emphasis and intended, thereby, to stand in contrast to *par' hēmōn*, "from us"—"you heard us speaking, but in reality it was God's word that you heard, not a piece of interesting human wisdom, but the very word of God." That is the important thing. The gospel is God's word, not a human invention. For *logon akoēs*, cf. Heb. 4:2; see also Rom. 10:17; Gal. 3:2, 5.

2:14 / The ... things those (Judean) **churches suffered from the Jews**: We have already considered (see disc. on 1:6) the difficulty of identifying precisely what **things ... suffered** Paul had in mind. Perhaps it was the persecution in which he himself had played a part (cf. Acts

8:1–3; 9:1f.). On those occasions when he plainly referred to this persecution, however, he spoke explicitly of his own role. There is no hint of that here (cf. Gal. 1:22f.; 1 Tim. 1:12–14). That the persecution of Acts 12:1 was seemingly aimed chiefly at the apostles and not at the rank-and-file lends further weight against the view that it was the persecution in which Paul played a role. Bruce suggests that we should think here of a more recent persecution associated with the increase of Zealot activities in Judea around the time of Ventidius Cumanus' arrival as procurator in A.D. 48 (cf. Josephus, *Ant.* 20.105–135. See also R. Jewett, "The Agitators and the Galatian Congregation," *NTS* 17 [1970–71], pp. 198–212).

§4 Paul's Longing to See the Thessalonians (1 Thess. 2:17–3:5)

Paul reflects "the kindness and sternness" of God as he moves from denouncing the Jews and defending himself against their slanders (2:1–16) to revealing his concern for the Thessalonians. He opens his heart, telling them how much they (the missionaries)—and none more than himself—long to see them. But he had been prevented thus far from returning (2:17–20). Therefore, to set their mind at rest and to "strengthen and encourage " them in what he knew to be difficult and dangerous times, he sent Timothy from Athens (3:1–5). In a sense, in Timothy Paul was himself present (he was "torn away . . . in person, not in thought," v. 17), and through Timothy, Paul again exercised his apostolic ministry to them. The notion of Paul's coming through his emissary leads R. W. Funk to describe this section as "the apostolic parousia" (in *Christian History and Interpretation: Studies Presented to John Knox*, ed. W. R. Farmer, C. F. D. Moule, R. R. Niebuhr [Cambridge: Cambridge University Press, 1967], pp. 249–68). This letter was written in response to Timothy's subsequent report. Details supplied in 3:1–5 (see also disc. on 3:6–8) supplement the narrative of Acts 17.

2:17 / The events that had forced the missionaries to leave Thessalonica (Acts 17:5–10) are described by Paul in terms of a bereavement. Strictly, the verb *aporphanizō* expresses a parent's loss of a child: "we were bereft of you" (NIV **we were torn away from you**). Consequently, whether consciously or not, he is maintaining the parental metaphor of the previous section (2:7, 11). Their loss, he says, was **for a short time**—or so they hoped. In Paul's case, it would be some five years, as far as we can tell, before he would see them again (Acts 20:2f. by implication). Meanwhile, he was present with them at least **in thought**, if not **in person** (cf. 1 Cor. 5:3–5; also Gal. 4:20 for a similar paternal longing to be with his children). The Greek is literally, "in heart," and this, more than the rendering of NIV, captures Paul's affection for them (see disc. on 2:4). Paul's is the burning pastoral heart that marks the genuine servant of God. His deep concern is further conveyed in what follows: **out of our intense longing we made every effort to see you**. Words pile up, each reinforcing the other, as Paul attempts to share with his readers what he and the others felt for them. The verb *spoudazō* "combines the idea of speed and diligence, and conveys an impression of eagerness, of making a quick and serious effort" (Morris). To this is added the comparative *perissoterōs*, "more abundantly," underlining their eagerness, the more so as we recognize that the comparative in the NT had practically replaced the superlative, "most abundantly." And then, as if that were not enough, he adds, "with great desire" (*en pollē epithymia*). *Epithymia* speaks of passion, often in the sense of lust, but here of their passionate longing for their friends.

2:18 / **We wanted to come to you**, Paul explains. The conjunction **for** (*dioti*) links this verse to the last and explains their longing. He especially wanted to come **again and again** (this phrase is better taken with **I, Paul** than with "we wanted to come"), but Satan hindered both him and his colleagues from returning to Thessalonica. This is a general statement to which Timothy's return visit, mentioned in 3:1ff., was the exception that proved the rule (cf. Rom. 15:22; Gal. 5:7 for the *enkoptō* in this sense of "to hinder"; for the activity of Satan, cf. 1 Thess. 3:5; 2 Thess. 2:9; 3:3). In the NT, Satan's activities are spoken of only in relation to Christians and his attempts to hinder them in one way or another. But equally, Satan is presented as being always subject to the greater power of God. We need not doubt, then, that God overrules these hindrances. However we view the matter (and Paul was evidently frustrated and disappointed by what had happened in this case), God's purpose is set forward, and Satan cannot hinder that purpose. In what sense or by what means Satan had prevented the missionaries from returning to Thessalonica, we can only guess. Presumably the Thessalonians knew what Paul meant. The phrase "again and again" (*kai hapax kai dis*, "and once and twice," indicating "a plurality of occasions without exact specification," cf. Phil. 4:16) makes the guessing more difficult. Evidently something had consistently hindered their coming. This may rule out sickness, which is commonly attributed to Satan (see, e.g., 2 Cor. 12:7), since it is most unlikely that the three of them or, if we leave out Timothy, that Paul and Silas would have been so sick for so long that neither could go. More likely, the ban imposed by the Thessalonian magistrates on their preaching had prevented their return (Acts 17:9 and see Introduction on The Founding of the Church). Paul's reference to Satan as the real power behind "the coming of the lawless one" in 2 Thessalonians 2:9 may be reason for thinking that he viewed him also as the power behind the lawless rioting of Acts 17:5 and the consequent action of the magistrates (cf. Eph. 6:12). At least it is beyond any doubt that Paul longed intensely to see the Thessalonian Christians. The next verse explains why.

2:19 / We wanted to come to you, he declares, **for** (*gar*) **what is our hope, our joy, or the crown in which we will glory . . . ? Is it not you?** In a generally prosaic letter, Paul rises here to lyrical heights. He is proud of the Thessalonians, as a parent of his children. His hope is that "he who began a good work in (them) will carry it on to completion" (Phil. 1:6). That work is his joy, and its completion will be his crown. His metaphor is of the wreath awarded to the winner of an event in the games. Every game had a wreath distinctive to it—the olive wreath of the Olympian games, the laurel of the Pythian games, the parsley of the Nemean games, etc. In Paul's contest the Thessalonians were his crown—one that would last forever (cf. 1 Cor. 9:25) and would be lasting proof that he had not run in vain (cf. 3:5; Gal. 2:2; Phil. 2:16). In such a crown, he says, **we will glory**. Here the Greek simply asks, "What is our . . . crown of *kauchēsis*?" The word can sometimes mean "boasting" (cf., e.g., Rom. 3:27; 2 Cor. 11:10, 17) but in this context is best translated "glory." Paul is maintaining the metaphor of the games and sees himself like an athlete, boasting, in the sense of glorying in his victory before the president's podium, that is, **in the presence of our Lord Jesus when he comes**. Only then, in that presence, will his achievement be truly assessed (cf. 1 Cor. 3:11–15; 4:3–5; for the phrase, "in the presence of" cf. 3:9, 13)—not now, not by others, not even by himself, but only by Jesus *en te autou parousia*, "in his *parousia*." The metaphor continues. Games were often held in honor of a visiting dignitary, whose arrival would be spoken of as his *parousia*, his "coming," or his "being present" (see A. Deissmann, *Light from the Ancient*

East [London: Hodder & Stoughton, 1927], p. 372, and the disc. on 4:17 of *apantēsis*, the word used of welcoming the new arrival). In a religious connection, *parousia* also depicted the coming of a god (Josephus applies it in this way to the God of Israel [*Ant.* 3.80, 203; 9.55]). This adds further color to Paul's application of the word to Jesus' coming (six times in the Thessalonian letters: here and in 3:13; 4:15; 5:23; 2 Thess. 2:1, 8 and elsewhere only in 1 Cor. 15:23; cf. also Matt. 24:3, 27, 37, 39; James 5:7f.; 1 John 2:28; 2 Pet. 1:16; 3:4, 12; the word had also a mundane application, cf. e.g., 1 Cor. 16:17; 2 Cor. 7:6).

2:20 / This verse offers the answer to the question of verse 19, "Is it not you?" **Indeed,** says Paul (indicating the affirmative by the interrogative *ouchi*), it is you. You are our crown because (*gar*) **you are our glory** (*doxa*) **and joy.** *Kauchēsis* (2:19) indicates the activity, *doxa* the grounds of his glorying in the Thessalonians. As we might say, "They did him credit." (For a similar use of *doxa*, cf. 1 Cor. 11:7; 2 Cor. 8:23). The Thessalonians are his pride; they are also his joy. This is why he sends Timothy to them.

3:1–3 / The chapter division interrupts the connection between 2:20 (or rather 2:17–20) and 3:1–3, the latter verses expressing the outcome of the former. Our text has **we sent.** The use of the plural pronoun is awkward throughout the letter and never more so than in these verses. The letter carries all the hallmarks of a Pauline epistle, removing any doubt who wrote the letter (see Introduction on The Authenticity of 1 Thessalonians). But since Paul names his colleagues in the address, that dictates the use of "we" throughout the letter. But in the events described here, Silas was apparently still in Berea (Acts 17:14f.), and although Timothy may have been consulted when he rejoined Paul in Athens, it was Paul's own decision to send him back to Thessalonica, thus leaving the apostle on his own until they were all reunited in Corinth (Acts 18:5). Events may be more complex than Luke's narrative in Acts would have us believe. Perhaps on one occasion all three were together in Athens, in which case the "we" of this passage represents a decision taken by Paul and Silas together. The difficulty may be resolved in verse 5 where Paul chooses the singular, "I sent." However, some interpret that verse as Paul's emphasizing his own feelings as distinct from those of his colleagues and their joint decision in verse 1. If verse 5 is a reiteration of verse 1 as we suppose it is, and if the decision to send Timothy back was Paul's alone, we must understand the "we" of verse 1 as editorial. That is, it was Paul who **could stand** his separation from the Thessalonians **no longer**. The verb *stegō* means "to keep watertight" and so "to contain," and then "to endure" (cf. 3:5; 1 Cor. 9:12; 13:7)—he could contain himself no longer, with the present participle underlining the intensity of his feeling. So desperately does he want to be in touch with the Thessalonians that he is prepared "to be abandoned" (the sense of *kataleipō*, NIV **to be left**). This word helps us feel something of Paul's apprehension at being left alone in these foreign cities (cf. 1 Cor. 2:3). One writer describes Paul's experience as a "kind of widowhood." But it was not too great a price to pay to find out how his children were faring.

His emissary Timothy receives a twofold description. Whatever his probably subordinate role was in the missionary team, he is nevertheless their **brother** in Christ. This is more than merely a recognition of Timothy's status: it is a term of endearment. He is also **God's fellow worker**. There are a number of variants to this text, but the very boldness of the reading accepted by NIV is the best proof of its authenticity. But even accepting this reading, differences of interpretation remain. Was Timothy a fellow worker with the others in God's work? Or was he God's fellow worker? From time to time, Paul speaks of others as his (or our) fellow worker(s) (Rom. 16:3, 9, 21; Phil. 2:25; Philem. 1, 24), whose qualifying genitive indicates with whom they worked. On that analogy, the qualifying genitive, "of God," indicates with whom Timothy worked. He and God were in partnership! Compare this description with the report in Acts 14:27 of how God worked with Paul and Barnabas (cf. Acts 15:4; NIV misses the point in both references). To speak of our working with God or of God with us (rather than simply through us) draws attention to the importance of the human agent in mission. At the same time, it acknowledges that no missionary enterprise can succeed without God. Consider Acts 16:14: Paul spoke to Lydia, and God opened her heart (cf. also Acts 2:47). But not any speaking will do to achieve such a result. Thus Timothy was God's fellow worker **in . . . the gospel of Christ**. The genitive is objective (for Christ, see note on 1:1). It is the gospel of which Christ is the content (see disc. on 1:5). By no other "gospel" can we—God working with us—open hearts.

Paul's purpose (see disc. on 2:12) in sending Timothy, apart from expressing his own longing to be in touch with them, is **to strengthen and encourage** them (cf. 4:1 for the emphasis given by doubling up verbs). Timothy could do so in his own right, but as Paul's emissary, he assures the Thessalonians of Paul's continuing concern. *Sterizō* means "to fix," "to make fast" (from *sterinx*, "a support") and expresses precisely what converts need—the kind of support that fixes them securely in the faith. "To encourage" (*parakaleō*) shares this sense. Strictly, it means "to call to one's side," with the implication of giving aid, hence specifically, "to encourage" or "to comfort," or "to appeal" to someone, or "to urge" someone to action (cf. 2:12; 3:7; 4:1, 10, 18; 5:11, 14; 2 Thess. 2:17; 3:12; the noun *paraklēsis* shares the same range of meanings as the verb; cf. 2:3; 2 Thess. 2:16). The verb is qualified by **in your faith**, where the Greek has the preposition *hyper*, "for the sake of your faith." Faith here might be subjective or objective, either their trust—Timothy encouraging them to go on trusting God and Christ to bring them to God—or the body of teaching, the faith, that was the basis of that trust. Thus Timothy encourages them to remain true to that faith (for faith, *pistis*, cf. 1:3, 8; 3:5, 6, 7, 10; 5:8; 2 Thess. 1:3, 4, 11; 2:13; 3:2).

A further purpose in sending Timothy is **so that no one would be unsettled by these trials**. The verb, *sainō*, occurs only here in the NT. It is used of dogs, "to wag the tail," but it has several derived meanings including the one adopted by NIV, "to unsettle" (attested in the papyri). The trials (*thlipsis*, lit. "pressures") are those referred to in 1:6 and 2:14—the pressures of persecution. **You know quite well**, Paul adds, **that we were destined for them**—the verb *keimai*, "to be laid down," "destined," suggests something fixed: there is an inevitability about trials. Like Jesus before him, Paul spells out the truth that trials are part of the package of being a Christian. They come with the world in which we live, but in addition, they are the product of the prince of this world's special targeting of the Christian (cf. 2:18; 3:5). "In this world," Jesus warned, "you will have trouble. But take heart! I have overcome this world"—and its prince (John 16:33; cf. Matt. 5:11f.; Mark 8:34ff.; John 12:31; 14:30; 15:18–21; 16:11; Acts 14:22; Phil. 1:29). Believers will share in that victory and, in a sense, they already have. But as long as this age lasts, they must not expect an easy life. But Paul is saying something more than this. Trials are a part of God's purpose for us. Why, we do not know, but acceptance of the proposition that "we were destined for them" does put meaning into life when difficult and dark days overtake us (see disc. on 1:6 for the positive outcome of suffering in building character).

3:4 / Paul had warned the Thessalonians along these lines before. **When we were with you** (for *pros* with the accusative in the sense of "with," cf. Mark 6:3; John 1:1) **we kept telling you** (impf.), he reminds them (*prolegō* means "to tell beforehand," "to tell plainly"), **that we would be persecuted**. For the sake of variety NIV employs this word, but the Greek word is the same as before, only now in the verbal form, "to suffer trials" (*thlibō*, cf. 2 Thess. 1:6f.). In this context it means persecution. Instead of using the verb in the simple future, Paul strengthens the statement by using *mellō* and making the verb an infinitive, "to be about to suffer" (present infinitive for an ongoing suffering). This also reinforces the notion that these trials are inevitable (cf. 3:3). **And it turned out that way**, literally "just as (*kathōs*) it happened"—there was an exact correspondence between his prediction and its outcome. To which he adds, as though quashing any lingering doubts on the matter, **as you well know**.

3:5 / This verse reiterates 3:1 (see disc. above), and the editorial "we" of that verse now becomes the singular pronoun "I." **For this reason** (*dia touto*), he says (and the phrase points to what follows and gives it some weight; cf. 3:7), **when I could stand it** (i.e., his intense longing for the Thessalonians, cf. 2:17) **no longer, I sent to find out about your faith**. Here there can be little doubt that "faith" (*pistis*) means their trust in God and in Christ (see disc. on 3:2). It has been suggested that *pistis* in this verse means "faithfulness." That meaning is possible, but there is no compelling reason to accept it. He was anxious about their faith on two grounds. **I was afraid that in some way the tempter might have tempted you**. In such a sentence (in the Greek), we might expect Paul to use the subjunctive mood, but he uses the indicative, showing his awareness that they had indeed been tempted (*peirazō*, "to test," cf. *dokimazō*, 2:4, etc.) by Satan, the same malignant being who had thwarted his attempts to come to them (cf. 2:18; also Matt. 4:3; 1 Cor. 7:5) and who stood behind whatever human agents may have been the immediate cause of their trials. But in stating the second reason for his anxiety, namely, that **our efforts might have been useless**, he does use the subjunctive, for here there was no ground for concern. The Thessalonians had not succumbed to Satan's temptation. They had not abandoned their faith. The missionaries' hard work (*kopos*, see disc. on 1:3) in preaching the gospel to them had not been empty (*kenos*, see disc. on 2:1) in terms of its lasting results. Satan could not hinder God's purpose (see disc. on 2:18).

Additional Notes   §4

2:18 / Satan, Heb. *Satan*, Gk. *Satanas*, meaning basically "adversary" (the word is so rendered, e.g., in Num. 22:22): The OT references to Satan are few, but in them he is consistently represented as working against the best interests of men and women (see, e.g., 1 Chron. 21:1; Job 1:7–2:9; Ps. 109:6; Zech. 3:1f.). This characterization is more distinct in the NT, where he is found to be the adversary not only of men and women but of God. Jesus expressly comes to overthrow Satan (cf. 1 John 3:8; Heb. 2:14 and see note on 2:12). This role of the Savior permeates the whole of the NT. In the Thessalonian letters, Paul calls the adversary Satan (cf. 2 Cor. 2:11; 11:14; also Matt. 16:23; Luke 22:3; John 13:27; Acts 5:3), the tempter (3:5), and probably the evil one (2 Thess. 3:3, see disc.). Elsewhere, Paul refers to him as the devil (Eph. 4:27; 6:11; 1 Tim. 3:7; 2 Tim. 2:26; cf. Matt. 4:1–11; John 8:44; Acts 13:10; James 4:7; 1 Pet. 5:8), the god of this age (2 Cor. 4:4), and the ruler of the kingdom of the air (Eph. 2:2). Like other NT writers, Paul thought of him as having real existence—as a personal, malevolent being (cf. also Matt. 10:25; 12:24, 27 where he is called Beelzebub, and John 14:30, where he is called the prince of this world).

§5 Timothy's Encouraging Report
(1 Thess. 3:6–13)

The somber note on which the previous section ended now gives way to joy at the news brought to Paul at Corinth by Timothy. The Thessalonians were standing firm in the faith and still held the missionaries dear. In view of the missionaries' intense longing for the Thessalonians (2:17), this news is like a breath of life to them—"now we really live" (vv. 6–9). On the strength of it, Paul reports, they pray night and day that they may see them again (v. 10). An actual prayer to that end follows in verses 11 to 13, with prayer also for the Thessalonians that they may grow in love and in holiness. This is "the first of the two main wish-prayers to be found in the epistle," the second being in 5:23 (G. P. Wiles, *Paul's Intercessory Prayers* [Cambridge: Cambridge University Press, 1974], p. 52; see also 2 Thess. 2:16f. and 3:16). It is called a wish-prayer because it is expressed in the optative (may it be . . .) rather than in the imperative mood (let it be . . .). The distinction between these two forms of expression is one of style only (cf. also 2 Thess. 2:16f.; 3:16).

3:6–8 / At the center of these verses stands the statement, **we were encouraged** (cf. 3:2). All the rest is added by way of explanation, starting with Timothy's report. **Timothy**, says Paul, **has just now come to us from you and has brought good news**. Evidently this letter was written soon after his arrival. In the NT, *euangelizō* especially refers to preaching the gospel, but here it describes good news in a more general sense (cf. Luke 1:19). It touches on three things: their **faith**, again in the sense of their trust in God (see disc. on 3:2); their **love**, the outworking of that faith which had been evident in them from the outset (cf. 1:3; Gal. 5:6); and their **pleasant memories** of the missionaries. "Pleasant" captures well what Paul means here by *agathē*. It means "good," not in the sense that the Thessalonians had a good recall of events, but that what they recalled of the past, when the missionaries were with them, was good. So much so that the longing the Thessalonians experienced for the missionaries matched the missionaries' own intense longing to return (cf. 2:17). The verb, *epipotheō*, is a strong one, and the present tense of the participle (ongoing action), and the adverb, *pantote*, "always," further strengthen it. The Thessalonians' longing was no less intense than that of the missionaries.

In verse 5, the phrase *dia touto*, "for this reason," points to what follows. Here, in verse 7, it looks back to what was just said. Addressing them again as **brothers** (see disc. on 1:4), and with their faith, love, and longing for the missionaries in mind ("for this reason" NIV **therefore**), Paul tells them that he and his colleagues are encouraged, adding four more points to fill out that statement. First, their encouragement came during all their own **distress and persecution**. The preposition *epi* with the dative has a range of meanings but is best understood here (with NIV) as having a temporal sense. Of the two nouns in this phrase, we have already met the second, *thlipsis* (see disc. on 1:6). Like *thlipsis*, *anankē* implies pressure from without, so that there is no clear distinction between the two, and together they simply underscore the point. In the earlier references, the context showed that thlipsis meant persecution, but that meaning is less certain here. Rather, it may describe the missionaries' mental state—their anxiety for the Thessalonians as well as their anxiety for themselves and for their mission generally (cf. Acts 18:9f.; 1 Cor. 2:3). Persecution, of course, cannot be ruled out of this reference. Acts suggests that Paul did suffer persecution in Corinth (Acts 18:6, 12ff.).

Second, the encouragement, he says, was **about you**. The preposition is again *epi* with the dative, but in the sense now of "resting upon"—the Thessalonians were the basis of their encouragement (cf. 3:9). This phrase resumes the thought of verse 6. So too does the third qualification, **because of your faith**, which expresses more explicitly what was so encouraging about the Thessalonians. The preposition *dia* with the genitive strictly denotes "through." The thought is, then, that their faith—and what Paul really means is the news of their faith—was the means through which the encouragement came to them.

The fourth qualification, comprising verse 8, builds upon that last point. It is added as an explanation and is structured as a conditional sentence. "We were encouraged," he says, "because

(*hoti*, NIV **for**) if you stand . . . we live." They were, of course,
"standing," otherwise none of this would have been written, and
this explains the construction of the Greek. *Ean*, "if," would normally be used with the verb in the subjunctive mood, but here it
occurs with the indicative. The difference is between what might
be and what is the case—they were in fact standing. The verb
stēkō is a late form developed from the perfect of *histēmi*, serving
better than *histēmi* to express the thought of **standing firm**, which
they did, says Paul, **in the Lord** (*en kyriō*, cf. 4:1 and see note on
1:1). There may be no difference of meaning between this phrase
and the more common "in Christ" or "in Christ Jesus" (cf. 2:14),
although C. F. D. Moule, *The Origin of Christology* (Cambridge:
Cambridge University Press, 1977), pp. 58–62, does discern a
tendency for the latter to be "associated with the *fait accompli* of
God's saving work," and the former "with its implementation
and its working out in human conduct." If that distinction does
indeed hold true, the thought expressed in the statement that the
Thessalonians were standing firm in the Lord would sit well with
Paul's earlier remembrance of their work produced by faith (1:3).

On the condition that the Thessalonians were standing
firm, the missionaries lived. The verb is in the present tense, **we
. . . live**, and the adverb **now** (*nyn*) probably refers to the time of
writing. Clearly, there was a lot at stake for Paul in Thessalonica.
Part of the explanation may be that he saw the mission there as
something of a test case. It was the first large city in which he had
worked since he left Antioch in Syria (Acts 13:1ff.) and certainly
the first large city in Grecian lands. Athens seems not to have
produced many converts, and now he had come to Corinth.
Would there be converts there? Could a church be established in
a city like Corinth? If the Thessalonians were standing firm, the
chances were that it could, and in that sense the missionaries
"lived"—their ministry in Corinth was potentially viable. But this
is only part of the explanation. Surely they "lived" not simply in
terms of the ongoing mission, but because of the Thessalonians
themselves. What happens to the Thessalonians matters intensely to Paul, and if they fall, something in him and the others
would die. It is no accident that this passage leads into prayer, for
the more we care for others, the more we pray.

3:9 / Paul's immediate response to the news from Thessalonica is to ask, "**How can we thank God enough?**" Timothy's

report confirmed that the work had been well done, much had been achieved, and this might easily have become for Paul a source of pride. But he knew that, whatever he and his colleagues had done, it was God who had opened the hearts (see disc. on 3:2). It is to God, therefore, that thanks must be returned. The Greek reads literally, "What thanks can we pay back to God?" where the verb *antapodidomi*, here in the aorist infinitive (cf. 2 Thess. 1:6), has the sense, "to pay back what is due." His thanks are *peri hymōn*, "in reference to you," i.e., the Thessalonians (NIV **for you)** and are offered "on the basis of (*epi* with the dat., see disc. on 3:7) all the joy" (NIV **for all the joy**). But now, having introduced the theme of joy, Paul cannot let it pass without comment. This is **the joy**, he explains, that **we have** (lit. the joy that we rejoice) **in the presence of our God because of you**, and with this the verse returns full cycle to where it began. For it is thanks to God that they have something to rejoice in, and the phrase, "in the presence of our God," is Paul's recognition of that fact (cf. 2:19 and 3:13 where the same or a similar phrase has an eschatological reference). Throughout this letter, there is a consciousness of God, which in this instance leads naturally to prayer (cf. 1:3 and see on 5:18).

3:10 / Paul and the others express their joy in the context of prayer (note the present participle, we rejoice . . . praying) **night and day** (for the order of the words, see disc. on 2:9). This phrase emphasizes the centrality of prayer in their lives; *hyperekperissou* intensifies this even more. This adverb is a double compound of an already strong word, creating what Findlay described as "a triple Pauline intensive" with the sense "beyond— exceedingly—abundantly" (cf. 5:13). Pauline style typically features such compounds (cf. Rom. 5:20; 2 Cor. 7:4), but he almost certainly uses it deliberately here "to express a feeling too deep for words" (Morris). Paul poured out his heart in prayer **most earnestly** for the Thessalonian Christians. Of a number of verbs that he might have chosen to relay the idea, "to pray," Paul adopts one in particular, *deomai*, that conveys his sense of dependence on God. What follows relates both the content and the purpose (see disc. on 2:12) of his prayer. It was twofold: First, **that we may see you again**—the longing for the Thessalonians already mentioned several times in this epistle (cf. 2:17f.; 3:5f.)—and second, that we may **supply what is lacking in your faith**. That is, Paul has a pastoral as well as a personal interest in his prayer. "Notice how Paul understands ministry as a mutual act between pastor and people. It is a giving and receiving on both sides, a ministering and a being ministered to. What comfort and joy they had given him (vv. 7, 9); what new strength he wants to give them (v. 10)" (Saunders). Nothing in the letter thus far suggests that there is any serious problem within the church. On the contrary, in the fundamentals of faith and love, the Thessalonians are a model for others (cf. 1:3, 7; 3:6). But clearly, there are some areas of the faith—in the sense of the body of Christian teaching (see disc. on 3:2)—in which they do need further instruction (*katartizō* means "to make complete"). The nature of these areas emerges from chapters 4 and 5. Paul must have realized that he would not be able to come to them in the short term and decided, therefore, that his written instructions must substitute for face-to-face teaching. Notice how he emphasizes the positive, giving thanks for what has been achieved before mentioning what remains to be done.

3:11 / From a rhetorical question about prayer, which in the Greek includes both verse 9 and verse 10, Paul turns to an actual prayer (cf. 5:23, where he prays again for the Thessalonians). Broadly there are two petitions: one for the missionaries, the other for the Thessalonians. **Now may our God and Father himself and our Lord Jesus clear the way for us to come to you**. The emphatic pronoun, "himself" (*autos*), which in the Greek stands at the beginning of the prayer as also in the other wish-prayers of 5:23 and 2 Thessalonians 2:16f. and 3:16, is not easy to explain. Some see it as marking a contrast with their own attempts at returning or with Satan's hindrance of those attempts, while others regard it as simply marking a new section of the letter. In view of the similar construction elsewhere, Bruce may be right to see it as an echo of "the language of the synagogue liturgy, where the address would be in the second person; this goes back in turn to the language of the Psalter, as for example in Ps. 22:19, 'But thou, O Lord.' " Particularly striking is the coupling of Jesus with the Father both in the address and in the ascription of the right to determine in what way they should go (cf. 1:1 and Ps. 32:8; 37:23; 40:2; Prov. 3:6; 4:26; 16:9). Nowhere more plainly than in these early Christian prayers do we see how high a status Jesus had in the minds of his followers as a result of their experience of him, especially of his resurrection (see disc. on 1:1). People like

Paul were nurtured on the truth that there is one God (Deut. 6:4). Without ceasing to believe that truth, they now prayed to him as Father and Son. The singular verb could be taken as further evidence of Paul's belief that Father and Son are one. However, Greek regularly requires the verb to take its number from the first or the nearest of its subjects if there is more than one. Thus the evidence is inconclusive. The fact remains, however, that Jesus is petitioned, no less than God, and indeed, as God, "to clear the way," i.e., to remove the hindrances to their return (*kateuthynō*, strictly, "to make or keep straight," also "to direct," cf. 2 Thess. 3:5; see note on 1:1 for God as Father and Jesus as Lord, and the further disc. on 2 Thess. 2:16f. of the significance of prayer addressed to Jesus and to God).

3:12 / The second petition, for the Thessalonians, is as follows: **May the Lord make your love increase and overflow**. The two petitions of verses 11 and 12 are united by "but" (*de*), and the Greek word order in the second has "you" (the direct object of the verbs) at the beginning for emphasis. This shows that whatever God has in store for the missionaries—whether to clear the way for them or not (cf. "not what I will, but what you will," Mark 14:36)—the Thessalonians are foremost in their mind, and this remains their prayer for them. Because Jesus is called "Lord" in verse 11, we must assume that he is the Lord of this verse (see note on 1:1). Thus the prayer is now addressed to him alone. It is for the enlargement of the Thessalonians' love, love being the hallmark of true Christianity (*pleonazō*, "to abound," or "to make to abound," cf. 2 Thess. 1:3; *perisseuō*, "to abound," "to excel," or "to make to excel," cf. 1 Thess. 4:1, 10, also 2 Cor. 6:11, 13). The prayer is that it might extend beyond the love that they have for **each other** (church members) to **everyone else** (those outside the church; JB, "the whole human race"; cf. 5:15 and Luke 6:32–36, Gal. 6:10, etc. for the same universality). That Paul so prays reminds us that love is a gift of God: he gives both the motive and the model in his own love for us, and he provides the means—the ability to love—by his Spirit. Since God loves everyone (John 3:16), his gift of love to us is to the same end. That end (in some measure at least) had been realized in Paul's own and his colleagues' lives, for he adds, **just as ours** i.e., our love, overflows **for you**. Paul not only practiced what he preached, but he practiced what he prayed!

3:13 / NIV presents this verse as a separate petition, but in fact, in the Greek it is part of the petition of verse 12, expressing what is the goal of this enlargement of their love (see disc. on 2:12); namely, that their "hearts might be established blameless in holiness" (NIV, that he may **strengthen** [their] **hearts so that** [they] **will be blameless and holy**). For "heart," see disc. on 2:4. What Paul is getting at is that love (*agapē*) is unselfish, and its practice develops the unselfishness which is the basis of holiness. He can, therefore, speak of love as the means to that end. *Hagiosynē*, "holiness," refers exclusively to God in the Greek OT (cf. Rom. 1:4 where it concerns the Spirit of God). Against this background, Paul's use implies that the holiness of God must be the measure of whether a believer is "blameless in holiness"—"Be perfect, therefore, as your heavenly Father is perfect" (Matt. 5:48). This implication is reinforced by the addition of the words: **in the presence of our God and Father** (see disc. on 3:9). In Christ, believers are already holy in terms of *status*. God accepts them as blameless (cf. 1 Cor. 1:30). But this prayer has to do with *practice*. Their practice should match their status—that they might "be who they are" (see J. F. Kilner, "A Pauline Approach to Ethical Decision-Making," *Interp* 43 [4, 1989] p. 373)—and that, in fact, they might be "blameless in holiness" **when our Lord Jesus comes with all his holy ones** (see note on 1:1 for the titles and the disc. on 2:19 for the Parousia). The Parousia is both the goal of our Christian life, for only then will God's work of salvation be completed, and an incentive for us to work (God being our helper) towards that goal (see disc. on 4:3ff. and 2 Thess. 2:13f. for *hagiasmos*, the process of becoming holy). The identity of **his holy ones** (*hoi hagioi*), who accompany Jesus, is uncertain. A number of OT passages suggest angels are in view (cf. Deut. 33:2; Ps. 89:5, 7; Dan. 7:10; Zech. 14:5; cf. also Matt. 13:41; 25:31; Mark 8:38; 13:26f.; Luke 9:26; 2 Thess. 1:7; Jude 14f.; Rev. 19:14). But in the NT, "the holy ones," does not appear to be used of angels. Rather, the term is commonly applied to believers. In 2 Thessalonians 1:10, "holy ones" (NIV "his holy people") and "those who have believed" are synonymous. In the light of this and 4:14 (see also Rom. 8:19; 1 Cor. 6:2), we should understand Paul to be at least including believers who have died, even he is not exclusively referring to them (note that Paul speaks of **all** his holy ones).

Additional Notes   §5

3:13 / When our Lord Jesus comes with all his holy ones: One scenario of the end time embraced by many Christians today sees a twofold return of Jesus: the first in secret to gather up the church, the second openly, following the tribulation (which, on this theory, only the world will endure) to judge the world. The first return is called the Rapture, the second the Revelation. The Greek word from whose Latin equivalent (*rapere*) our word "rapture" is derived, is actually used by Paul in 4:17, "we . . . will be caught up" (but not, we believe in the sense of the modern theory; see disc. on 4:17 and 2 Thess. 2:1). The theory rests largely on a conclusion drawn from the verse before us. If Jesus is to come **with** his saints, it is argued, as this verse says he will, he must first have come *for* them. A number of other passages are enlisted to corroborate this scenario (e.g., Mark 13:27; Rev. 11:11f.), but none of them, and least of all 1 Thessalonians 3:13, can bear the weight of this interpretation.

Some would even doubt that *the holy ones* refers to his saints; but allowing that it does (see the disc.), what more is Paul saying here than he says, for example, in 4:14? Paul wants to assure the Thessalonians that their dead will not be disadvantaged. They will be raised, the living will be transformed, and together, the living and the dead will "meet the Lord" and be "with the Lord forever" (4:16f.). The "all" of 3:13 is important. In anticipation of his fuller treatment in chapter 4, Paul casually indicates that all will be involved in the Parousia, but he says nothing more than that. Besides reading too much into a passage dealing with other matters, the whole idea of the Rapture founders (1) on the fact that the church's hope—based, we may believe, on Jesus' own teaching—has from the outset been fixed upon his *visible* return (cf. 1 Cor. 1:7; Titus 2:13); and (2) on the language of 2 Thessalonians 2:1, where Paul speaks of "the coming of our Lord Jesus Christ and our being gathered to him." Paul used two nouns governed by the one definite article, which shows beyond question that he thought of the "coming" and the "gathering" as two facets of the one event. In short, Christ's Revelation is at one and the same time our Rapture (see Williams, *Promise*, pp. 112–14).

§6   *Living to Please God (1 Thess. 4:1–12)*

The first three chapters of this letter are largely personal and historical in character, the last two practical and doctrinal. They are joined in the Greek by the conjunction *oun*, which sometimes expresses a logical connection, as in Romans 12:1 where the exhortation arises out of the doctrinal exposition (cf. also Eph. 4:1; Col. 3:5). But not here. The *oun* is simply transitional. In his report, Timothy may have noted a tendency, or at least a temptation, for the Thessalonians to slip back into heathen conduct. There is always the pressure to conform—the downward pull of society. Paul exhorts them, therefore, to holiness (vv. 1–8; cf. 5:22f.), and to love (vv. 9f.), taking up the themes of the prayer of 3:11–13. He also pleads that they live quiet and industrious lives (vv. 11f.). Bruce suggests that the urgency of the exhortation betrays some resistance on the part of the Thessalonians. In the light of verse 1, however, this should not be overstated. But there may have been a tendency to think that Christian liberty meant Christian license: that Christ had set them free from codes and taboos, leading them to ask, therefore, why they should now be expected to submit to a new set of rules. What they needed to learn was that their liberty was to enable them to live a Christ-like life, a life with a positive ethical content which some rules might help them to achieve. In terms of its form, the exhortation (or parenesis) of these verses falls into a pattern found elsewhere, both in these and in other Pauline epistles (in the Greek, not always discernible in the English). In its fullest form, this pattern comprises a verb of exhortation, a vocative such as "brothers," a prepositional phrase such as "in the Lord Jesus " (which puts the exhortation into context), and an injunction expressed by *hina* with the verb in the subjunctive, by an imperative, or by an infinitive (cf. 5:12, 14; 2 Thess. 3:6, 12).

4:1 / **Finally** (*loipon*) seems strange in the middle of the letter and has occasioned much discussion. A number of commentators see the word as simply marking a transition (e.g., Milligan; Lightfoot; J. W. Bailey, *The First and Second Epistles to the Thessalonians* [New York: Abingdon, 1955]), but others accept the rendering, "finally," as appropriate at this point (e.g., C. F. D. Moule, *Idiom Book of New Testament Greek* [Cambridge: Cambridge University Press, 1959], p. 161). Morris comments that Paul can use "finally" quite early in a letter (1 Cor. 1:16; 4:2; Phil. 3:1; 4:8), but in this instance "it seems to mean that the main argument has been concluded, though other, not unimportant, matters are now to be dealt with." The teaching of this section builds on what the missionaries had told the Thessalonians while they were still with them. **We instructed you**, says Paul (Gk. "just as," *kathōs*, "you received from us," *paralambanō;* see disc. and note on 2:13), **how to live in order to please God**. "To live" is, literally, "to walk" (see disc. on 2:12). The figure suggests that the Christian life should be marked by progress (i.e., spiritual growth); it is "itinerant, always on the march." That thought is now enhanced by the present tense of the infinitive. The instruction was "to go on walking"—to persist in their efforts towards perfection; that is, to be like Christ—and so "to go on pleasing God" (another present infinitive). The phrase in Greek is stronger than it appears in NIV, for the Greek uses *dei*, "must." The instruction was that they "must go on walking and pleasing." There is no question of its being a matter of choice. It is part of what it means to be a Christian. In receiving Christ, we take on the obligation to be like him. Paul acknowledges that the Thessalonians had done this: **as in fact you are living** (i.e., "walking"). But there was no room for complacency. The urgency of the appeal is verified by the doubling of the verbs (cf. 3:2, "to strengthen and encourage"): **We ask you and urge you . . . to do this more and more** (cf. 4:10). *Erōtaō*, used in classical Greek only of asking a question, acquired by this time the additional sense of making a request (cf. 5:12; 2 Thess. 2:1). But "request" is too weak a term, and so the other is added (*parakaleō*, see disc. on 3:2). Added also is the phrase, **in the Lord Jesus**, which puts the appeal into context. It could be read as an assertion by the missionaries of their authority to lay down the rules, but it is better read as indicative of their consciousness of the presence of Christ (for Lord, see note on 1:1). They speak simply as Christians to Christians (but cf. the authoritative tone of the phrase, "in the name of the Lord" in 2 Thess. 3:6). Their authority is, however, asserted in the next verse.

4:2 / Paul reminds his Thessalonian readers of what they had been told earlier: **You know what instructions we gave you**. The authoritative tone is unmistakable, sounded in the word, *parangelia*, which signifies an order passed from one to another, often in a military context (cf. Acts 5:28; 16:24; 1 Tim. 1:5, 18). Paul is referring, then, to instructions that have come "down the line" from God, "through the Lord Jesus" (*dia tou kyriou Iēsou;* see note on 1:1). Some uncertainty exists as to how best to render the preposition *dia* in this phrase. It may be, as we have suggested, that it denotes agency: Jesus acts for God in the transmission. Or it may mean something like "in the name of the Lord Jesus." Cf. NIV **by the authority of**. . . . In any case, the instructions come from the highest authority and must, therefore, be obeyed (for the oneness of the Father and Son, see disc. on 3:11 and 2 Thess. 2:16).

4:3 / These orders are **that you should be sanctified**. The Greek runs, "This is God's will; [namely,] your sanctification." In 3:13, *hagiosynē* is holiness itself; now the related word, *hagiasmos*, is rather the process that results in that state. Strictly the word means to be set apart for God, but what is set apart for God must be worthy of him, and so *hagiasmos* acquires an ethical meaning. It is the process of becoming holy in the sense of good, of bringing Christian practice into line with Christian status (cf. vv. 4, 7; 2 Thess. 2:13, but see comment on that verse; for the corresponding verb, *hagiazō*, "to sanctify," cf. 1 Thess. 5:23). Sanctification in this sense requires the work of a lifetime and will be completed only at the Parousia (cf. Phil. 3:12, 21). It covers the whole range of Christian living, but on this occasion Paul deals specifically with sexual matters, detailing three areas in particular in which the Thessalonians were to look to their present practice. First, he says, God's will is **that you should avoid sexual immorality**. The language resembles the apostolic decree in Acts 15:20, 29; 21:25, with which both Paul and Silas would have been familiar. The word rendered "sexual immorality" is *porneia*, which regularly means to have dealings with a prostitute (*pornē*), but it was also used of any form of illicit sex—illicit from the Jewish/Christian point of view—that is, of any sexual relationship outside of marriage and sometimes of those marriage relationships forbidden by Jewish law. It may have been to the latter especially that the apostolic decree was referring (cf. also Matt. 5:32; 19:9; 1 Cor. 5:1). This restriction of sex to marriage struck the pagan world of that day as odd, for it tolerated and even encouraged, at least in the case of men, various forms of extramarital sexual activity. But the lives of believers are to be governed not by the general level of morality in the community, but by the will of God.

4:4–5 / God's will is, second, **that each of you should learn to control his own body**. Paul changes from the plural "you" of the previous verse to the singular, and from the negative "avoid" to the positive "control." The object of that control is understood by NIV to be the body, but it must be acknowledged that this is not the most common meaning of *skeuos*, the word thus translated. *Skeuos* usually means "a vessel" or "an implement." It does, however, function metaphorically of people, including Paul himself, in a number of places (cf. Acts 9:15; Rom. 9:22f.; 2 Tim. 2:21) and in 1 Peter 3:7 with reference to the marriage relationship, of wives in particular. Peter describes the wife as the weaker vessel. On the basis of that passage, some suppose that Paul is also speaking of wives—"that each of you should learn to control his own wife." But it should be observed that Peter does not call the wife the husband's vessel, but rather implies that both the husband and wife are the vessels of God. In any case, if that were Paul's meaning here, it would imply such a low view of marriage as would make nonsense of his use of marriage elsewhere as a model of mutual love and esteem (e.g., Eph. 5:21–23). Some support for the meaning of *skeuos* as "body" occurs in 2 Corinthians 4:7, where Paul highlights the weakness, including the physical weakness, of the ministers of the gospel by describing them literally as "vessels of clay." But the best support surfaces in 1 Samuel 21:5, where David assures the priest of Nob that his young men have kept themselves from women. Their "vessels (LXX *skēnē*) are holy," he said. The reference is, broadly, to their bodies and, perhaps, specifically to their genitalia. How specific Paul may have intended to be is open to question, but it does seem highly likely that he meant "body" by *skeuos*, not "wife." Accordingly, he also intended this to be a general instruction, like that which precedes it in verse 3 and follows it in verse 6, addressed to both men and women (see further notes).

Further difficulty arises with the verb *ktaomai*, which usually means "to acquire" and would make good sense here with that meaning: "that each of you should acquire his own wife." But given that "wife" is a less likely meaning of *skeuos* than "body," we should take *ktaomai* to mean "to possess." In classical usage, this sense is restricted to the perfect and pluperfect tenses, but Moulton-Milligan cite evidence that this restriction no longer applied in NT Greek. Here Paul uses the verb in the present tense (of the infinitive) with the sense, "to be in the process of gaining possession, i.e., control." He was realistic enough to know that we are not made into saints (in the popular sense) overnight and that we must work at it, especially with regard to our bodies. Sex is a good thing, but our proclivity to illicit sex must be controlled. Nor is this discipline merely for discipline's sake. It is for God's sake.

This whole discussion centers on doing God's will. Thus the "possession" of the body must be achieved **in a way that is holy and honorable**. Again we have the word *hagiasmos*. In verse 3 it meant sanctification, the process of making holy. In this passage it draws closer to the meaning of *hagiosynē*, the resultant state. Paul wants each of them to control his or her body in a way that accords with their consecration to God (to be holy means [1] to be separate, set apart for God, and [2] to be worthy of God). Their self-control should be honorable (*timē*) in the sense of honoring God (cf. 1 Cor. 6:20), in contrast with the sexual excesses of others which involve the "dishonoring (*atimazō*) of their bodies with one another" (Rom. 1:24). So he adds, **not in passionate lust like the heathen**. *Pathos* generally has a neutral sense, "experience," "emotion," but in the NT it consistently carries the bad sense of "passion," not a violent emotion as we think of passion but rather as an over-mastering emotion. "It denotes the passive side of a vice" (Morris). *Epithymia*, though, is concerned with its active side, generally also in a bad sense: desiring what is forbidden. The combination of the two words (*en pathei epithymias*, "in a passion of desire") suggests the idea of total surrender to illicit sex, which, says Paul, typifies the heathen **who do not know God**. Their behavior is explained by their ignorance but is not excused by it. In Romans 1:28, the heathens' ignorance of God is due not to any lack of data but to their deliberately ignoring God (cf. 2 Thess. 1:8).

4:6 / Third (in detailing three areas in which the Thessalonians were to be sanctified), God's will is **that in this matter**, i.e., in respect to sex, **no one should wrong his brother or take advantage of him**. Some dispute that Paul's theme was still sex and see this as a general warning (see, e.g., RSV marg., "defraud his brother in business"). But in the Greek, verses 3 to 6 are one sentence in which three phrases (expressed by infinitives) stand in apposition with *hagiasmos* in verse 3, defining it. This being so, it is more likely that Paul would maintain the one theme throughout the sentence than change it in the last phrase. In any case, "in this matter" (*en tō pragmati*) clearly refers to the matter already under discussion. Specifically then with respect to sex, "no one should wrong his brother." The verb *hyperbainō*, which is found only here in the NT, means "to go beyond" and thus "to go beyond the bounds," "to trespass," and here, "to have illicit sex"; that is, to enter into a sexual relationship outside of marriage. "Brother" probably means one's fellow Christian, whether male or female, although the same prohibition would apply were the other party a pagan. The second infinitive in this phrase, "to take advantage" (from the verb *pleonekteō*), connotes greed, "to want to have more than one should," and here, "to want the spouse of another."

The sentence (vv. 3 to 6) ends with an explanation (not apparent in NIV) which is at the same time a warning: "because (*dioti*) the Lord is an avenger in (*peri*, 'concerning') all these (matters)." From the apparent change of subject in verse 7 to God (*theos*), we can assume that the "Lord" of this verse is Jesus (see note on 1:1) and that he is the *endikos*, the avenger. The only other instance of this word in the NT concerns the civil magistrates in Romans 13:4. It would appear, then, that Paul envisions a trial in which Jesus is the judge (cf. Acts 10:42; 17:31; 1 Cor. 4:5; 2 Thess. 1:8). His thought is probably of the Parousia, although the NT, and indeed Paul himself, is not unfamiliar with the idea of divine judgment taking place even now (cf. John 3:18; Rom. 1:24, 26, 28). And this judgment will take account of, among other things, sexual morality. Earlier, the missionaries warned the Thessalonians about this. Christians, no less than others, will be judged, although in their case the judgment will not be a matter of life and death. As far as that is concerned, they have already been acquitted of the "capital offense" of sin; that is, they are already justified. But they will still be called to give an account of themselves as Christians, and Timothy's report may indicate that their earlier warning along these lines could do with repetition (for Christians being judged, see Williams, *Promise*, pp. 93–96).

4:7–8 / A further explanation is added: **For God did not call us to be impure, but to live a holy life**. The tense of the verb (aorist) dates this call from conversion (see disc. on 2 Thess. 2:14). The mention of impurity (*akatharsia*, cf. 2:3) confirms that the subject of verse 6 is sexual rather than general behavior. The construction in the Greek, with this noun in the dative case governed by the preposition *epi*, denotes purpose. But the construction changes in the second half of the verse to *en* with the dative. The noun is once again *hagiasmos* (see disc. on 4:3 and 4:4f.), and once again the thought is of believers being called to be "in the process of becoming holy." They are consecrated to God, and consecration demands sanctification. To fail to appreciate this has serious consequences, as indicated by what follows.

Therefore (*toigaroun*, an emphatic and somewhat portentous conjunction) **he who rejects this instruction does not reject man but God**. NIV supplies "this instruction" (from 4:2), the Greek being only "he who rejects does not reject man." The verb "to reject" (*atheteō*) means "to do away with what has been laid down." It was sometimes used with regard to documents, such as a will (cf. Gal. 3:15), in which case it means "to annul." Where people are concerned, it means "to treat as of no account," and that is the sense here. Whoever regards sexual sin as a matter of little consequence is guilty of discounting God. "Man" lacks a definite article and therefore includes any who might have instructed them or might do so again in the future. But the human teacher is incidental; the instruction is God's, and the sin of disregarding it is against God. The seriousness of such sin, or rather, the ingratitude it exemplifies, is brought home by the description of God as the one **who gives you his Holy Spirit**. That he "gives" demonstrates his grace and demands our gratitude, not disregard; that he gives his *Holy* Spirit (where the adjective is deliberately employed as indicated by its emphatic position in the Greek) indicates his concern that his grace should issue in our holiness. And in this context, the reference to God's Spirit will remind Paul's later readers who are familiar with his Corinthian correspondence, that the very "vessel" with which sexual sin might be committed, is the dwelling place of the God who forbids it (cf. 1 Cor. 3:16; 6:18f.).

4:9 / The opening words of this verse, **Now about brotherly love**, employ the same formula (*peri* with the gen. case)
found in 1 Corinthians, where it signals Paul's answers to the
Corinthians' questions (cf. 1 Cor. 7:1; 8:1; 12:1; 16:1, 12; cf. also
1 Thess. 5:1). It is unlikely, however, that the Thessalonians had
asked his advice about brotherly love. It is not the kind of specific
subject on which advice would be sought, and, in any case, Paul
acknowledges that there was no need for him to write on the
subject. He comments several times on the love that characterized
the Thessalonian church (1:3; 3:6, 12). Brotherly love (*philadelphia*)
is a particular instance of the love (*agapē*) that Christians should
have for all people (see disc. on 3:12). It is their love for each other
as members of the one family. Sadly, it is not always obvious, but
in this case it is. **You yourselves**, Paul declares, **have been taught
by God to love** (*agapaō*) **each other**. In saying this, Paul employs
a word unique to this passage in the NT and, indeed, in the whole
of the Greek literature to that time—*theodidaktos*, "God-taught."
He may have coined it himself. It picks up the promise of the OT
that the day would come when God would teach his people (Isa.
54:13; Jer. 31:33f.). That day had now come, but how precisely had
God's people been taught? They had been taught by Jesus: by the
precepts that he had given them reaffirming the law of love (Mark
12:31; John 13:34; cf. Lev. 19:18; Rom. 13:8–10), by his own practice of that law (John 13:1), and by the Spirit who imprints that
law of love on our hearts (Rom. 5:5; Gal. 5:22). The juxtaposition
of this verse with the reference to the Spirit in verse 8 suggests
that the Holy Spirit is especially in Paul's mind as the one by
whom the Thessalonians were instructed.

4:10 / **And in fact**, he adds, **you do love all the brothers
throughout Macedonia** (cf. 1:7f.). But Paul's attitude to his own
sanctification is "Not that I have . . . already been made perfect,
but I press on" (Phil. 3:12). Showing the same attitude to the Thessalonians and their sanctification, he acknowledges their progress (cf. 3:7), but urges them to press on toward that goal of
perfection to which he also strove. The language is almost identical with that of verse 1, but the reference is now specifically to
their love for each other: **we urge you, brothers, to do so more
and more** (for *parakaleō*, "to urge," see disc. on 3:2 and for *perisseuō*, "to abound," see disc. on 3:12 and for the present infinitive,
see disc. on vv. 11–12 below).

4:11–12 / These verses continue the sentence (in Gk.) begun at the end of verse 10. Paul urges the Thessalonians to abound in love and "to be ambitious" in specific areas relating to conduct. These two objectives are closely connected, in that the bad conduct of individuals can unsettle the church or bring the church into disrepute and so become an offense against brotherly love. *Philotimeomai*, "to be ambitious," acquired the sense "to seek restlessly after one's objective" (for the present infinitive, see below), which presents us with the paradoxical instruction that the Thessalonians are "to seek restlessly to be quiet." The point, however, is clear. They are to make every effort **to lead a quiet life** (cf. 5:13). What is not so apparent is what prompts Paul to give this advice. It is commonly thought that an "undue eschatological excitement had induced a restless tendency in some of the Thessalonian Christians and made them disinclined to attend to their ordinary business" (Bruce); but there may have been some other local sociological reason (see further disc. and note on 2 Thess. 3:6–12; cf. the plea for quietness in v. 12 of that passage with the similar plea here in v. 11). To be quiet is the first of the three goals on which Paul would have them set their ambition. The second is **to mind your own business** and the third **to work with your own hands**. Each of these is expressed by a present infinitive, underscoring that this is to be their practice (this applies also to the infinitives "to abound" and "to be ambitious"). The injunction to work with your own hands must be read against a background in which manual labor was little esteemed by the Greeks, but its dignity was affirmed by the Jews. In this matter, Paul held true to his Jewish origins. Free-loaders had no place in Paul's concept of Christian community, which called for shared work (Gal. 6:2) in a context of personal responsibility (Gal. 6:5). Had he not himself, many times, with "these hands" worked to support himself and his friends (cf. 2:9; 2 Thess. 3:7–10; Acts 20:34; also Eph. 4:28)? The missionaries had already given the Thessalonians instruction on the importance of work—**just as we told you**. The verb behind **told** (*parangellō*) has a distinctively military ring, "to command" (cf. 2 Thess. 3:4, 6, 10, 12). But Paul reminds them of work's significance now because it has implications for their witness—**that your daily life may win the respect of outsiders**. Literally, this is "that you might walk fittingly towards those outside" (cf. Col. 4:5 for the same idea and disc. on 2:12 for the idea of walking). See the discussion on 5:14 for a further treatment of this theme of the work ethic as a factor in promoting well-being both of the church and of society. Alone among NT writers, Paul insists that one of the criteria of Christian action of any kind is its effect on the world at large (cf. 1 Cor. 14:16, 23f.)—and on the well-being of themselves and the church. Those who could, should work so as **not to be dependent on anybody** or "not to need anything." The Greek can be rendered either way, although the latter is more likely since the Greek word for "need" (*chreia*) is usually followed by a thing, not a person. There was no question, however, that those who could not work, whether through lack of opportunity or because of age or infirmity, should look to the church for their support. This is specifically mentioned in Ephesians 4:28 as a reason for the Christian's "doing something useful with his own hands"; namely, "that he may have something to share with those in need" (cf. 1 Tim. 5:3–8).

Additional Notes §6

4:3 / It is God's will that you should be sanctified: For a literal rendering of the Greek, see above. The word for "will," *thelēma*, lacks any definite article, and, although qualified by "of God," it should be regarded as indefinite (a gen. qualification sometimes appears to make an anarthrous noun definite). This indicates that while sanctification is a part of God's will—and that fact must be given all the importance it deserves—it is not the whole of it. God's will, even if we restrict the reference to ourselves, concerns much more than this.

4:4 / Each of you should learn to control his own body: The debate on how this admonition should be understood has a long and complex history. For a full discussion of that history, cf. B. Rigaux, *Les Epîtres aux Thessaloniciens* (Paris: Gabalda, 1956) pp. 502–7, and for the scholarship since Rigaux, see R. F. Collins, *Studies on the First Letter to the Thessalonians* (Leuven: Leuven University, 1984) pp. 299–325, to which should be added J. Whitton, "A Neglected Meaning for *Skeuos* in 1 Thessalonians 4:4," *NTS* 28 (1982) pp. 142–43, and O. L. Yarbrough, *Not Like the Gentiles: Marriage Rules in the Letters of Paul* (Atlanta: Scholars Press, 1985) p. 7. Michael McGehee offers a critique of both Yarbrough and Collins in "A Rejoiner to Two Recent Studies Dealing with 1 Thess. 4:4," *CBQ* 51 (1989) pp. 82–89. In this article McGehee draws attention especially to the social setting of the letter, which provides further support for the position that this is not an instruction as to how a man should acquire a wife, but a general instruction to both men and women as to how they should conduct themselves sexually. McGehee points out that at the society level to which most church members would have belonged, there would be very few men of "independent means who could make social decisions on their own without reference to parents, masters, or other family members." Moreover, since marriages were usually arranged, the opportunity to choose a wife was even further restricted.

§7 *The Coming of the Lord (1 Thess. 4:13–5:11)*

Although the formula, "Now about . . . " (*peri de*), which sometimes appears to have marked Paul's answers to questions (see disc. on 4:9) does not occur, 4:13–18 is probably his answer to a question about the fate of deceased believers. From the teaching the missionaries gave while they were still with them, the Thessalonians would have known the general eschatological scenario that Paul unfolds in these verses, but at least some of them were still unsure where the Christian dead fitted into it. They may have understood that all believers would live to see the Parousia; and, now that some had died, they were anxious for their sake. Would they be disadvantaged? Or worse, would they be disqualified from sharing in the glory of that day? Paul answers that question in verse 17.

But one thing leads to another, and from this discussion of the events of the Day, Paul goes on to speak of its "times and dates." This is the subject of 5:1–11. Paul makes two points: (1) the time of the Parousia is unpredictable (vv. 1–3). The Lord will indeed come, it is only a question of when. (2) Therefore, it is essential to always be prepared (vv. 4–10). The subsection ends, as does 4:13–18, with an exhortation to mutual encouragement (5:11). Perhaps the most striking feature of the whole section, whose authenticity has at times been questioned, is the number of parallels with the eschatological teaching of the Synoptic tradition. These parallels include material peculiar to Matthew (cf. esp. 1 Thess. 4:16f. with Matt. 24:31) and to Luke (cf. esp. 1 Thess. 5:8–11 with Luke 21:34–36). If by reference to this teaching we can show that it is early, we have taken an important step towards establishing its authenticity, which is to say that it had its origin in Jesus' teaching (see disc. on v. 15).

4:13 / **Brothers**—the familiar affectionate address of these letters (see disc. on 1:4)—**we do not want you to be ignorant**—

another familiar Pauline phrase: his way of saying, "We want you to know (cf. Rom. 1:13; 11:25; 1 Cor. 10:1; 12:1; 2 Cor. 1:8; see also Col. 2:1). There is no need to suppose, as some do, that Paul is countering external false teaching, such as an early form of Gnosticism, that denied the resurrection hope. Even less should we think that he is correcting his own teaching. The question of what happened to the Christian dead may never have been raised during the missionaries' stay in Thessalonica, or if it was, some may have missed or misunderstood what was said. But the question is now raised, and Paul replies. The description of the dead as **those who . . . sleep** (*koimaō*, see disc. on 5:6) is not peculiar to Christians (see, e.g., 1 Kings 2:10; Homer, *Iliad*, 11.241), but it is the characteristic way in which the NT speaks of the Christian dead and a most apt expression on the lips of those who believe in the resurrection of the dead. Without that hope, people must view death only as a sleep from which there is no awakening— "one unending night to be slept through" (Catullus 5.4–6), "one unbroken night of sleep" (Aeschylus, *Eumenides* 651). Such hopelessness in the face of death permeated pagan society. Bruce cites Theocritus: "hopes are for the living; the dead are without hope." But the Thessalonian Christians had no cause **to grieve like the rest of men, who have no hope** (for the Christian idea of hope, see disc. on 1:3) and for whom the fear of death was pervasive (Heb. 2:14f.).

4:14 / This verse, introduced in the Greek by the conjunction *gar*, "because," explains the confidence expressed in verse 13. It rests on the events of Jesus' life: **We believe that Jesus died and rose again** (cf. 1 Cor. 15:3f.), and on the conviction that in those events the hand of God could be discerned. If God acted in the past to raise Jesus from the dead, he could be relied upon to act again along those lines and to **bring with Jesus those who have fallen asleep in him** (cf. 1 Cor. 15:23). The verb *anistēmi* is used here, with reference to Jesus, in an intransitive form (second aorist active), "he rose." But Scripture also testifies that God raised Jesus, and we should understand this reference in those terms (see, e.g., Acts 3:15; Rom. 8:11; 2 Cor. 13:4; Eph. 1:20; Col. 2:12; also 2 Cor. 1:9). Significantly, while Paul describes the Christian dead as sleeping, he nowhere uses that expression of Jesus. On the contrary, Jesus is always said to have died (cf. 5:10). The stark truth of that statement puts the miracle of the resurrection into perspective. At the same time it emphasizes that only because he endured the full horror of the wages of sin (Rom. 6:23) can we now "sleep" and expect to "awake." This understanding is implied in Paul's reference to believers sleeping **in him** (in Jesus). The Greek is literally "through" (*dia*)—through him and what he has done for us (the *dia* of attendant circumstances). We may merely "sleep" because he has spared us the necessity of dying in the sense of being separated, cut off from the presence of God— "(our) death has been swallowed up in (his) victory" (1 Cor. 15:54)— by virtue of his death and resurrection. Thus the resurrection of believers is not a separate event, but they participate in Jesus' resurrection: they will be raised up "with Jesus" (2 Cor. 4:14). This thought underlies Paul's statement that those who sleep through Jesus, God will bring from death with Jesus. The focus here, however, is not so much on that, as on its sequel: their participation in his Parousia.

4:15 / Paul explains the confidence expressed in verse 14. It is because (*gar*), **according to the Lord's own word**, certain events including the resurrection of the dead are to take place. In short, this verse and those that follow (vv. 15–17) provide the context of verse 14, and the whole is guaranteed by the word of the Lord (Jesus). But there is a difficulty here in that not all the details of these verses, and specifically those relating to the resurrection of the dead, can be paralleled in the recorded words of Jesus. Either Paul is referring to some otherwise unrecorded saying of Jesus, or these are the words of the risen Lord given to him or to Silas as his prophets (cf. Acts 13:1; 15:32; for an example of such words, see Rev. 16:15, which, however, is based on a Gospel saying; cf. Matt. 24:43; Luke 12:39; 1 Thess. 5:2; see further disc. on 2 Thess. 2:2). The traditions of Jesus' teaching were far more extensive than the written records we possess (cf. John 20:30, Acts 20:35). Thus Paul may have had access to teaching not found in our Gospels. We should also keep in mind that elsewhere Paul took pains to distinguish between his teaching and that of Jesus (1 Cor. 7:10–12). If then, he calls this teaching "the Lord's own word," we may be sure that Paul had reason to think it was (for Lord, see note on 1:1).

The teaching was **that we who are still alive, who are left till the coming of the Lord** (see disc. on 2:19 and v. 16 below) **will certainly not precede those who have fallen asleep**. On the basis of Paul's use of the first person, "we" in reporting this word, some suppose that he expects to be among the living at the time of the Coming. That may be so, but we should note that he always refuses to put a time to the Parousia (e.g., 5:1f.); and, as far as he was concerned, he sometimes seems to expect that he will be among the dead (1 Cor. 6:14; 2 Cor. 4:14). Of course, he may later have changed his mind, but more likely the pronoun simply means "us Christians," without particular reference to himself (as in 1 Cor. 6:4; 15:52). Paul keeps an open mind on whether he will be among the living or the dead. Long ago, Lightfoot noted that Paul's words could be paraphrased as "When I say 'we,' I mean those who are living, those who survive to that day."

The Thessalonians may have been unsure as to how the resurrection related to the coming of the Lord. Would it be before or after? If after, then surely those living would have the advantage of witnessing what the dead would not. But "the Lord's own word" was quite explicit on this matter: the living will not have the advantage (the verb is *phthanō*, "to come before" another, with the emphatic negative *ou mē*; see disc. on 2:16). The living and the dead will be on an equal footing for the reason (4:16, *hoti*, "because") set out in the verses that follow.

4:16 / There will be an order in the events of the Parousia. First, **the Lord himself will come down from heaven**. The reference is to Jesus (see note on 1:1). Jesus' divine role is indicated by the phrase, "from heaven" (*ap' ouranou*, cf. 2 Thess. 1:7, also 1 Thess. 1:10, *ek tōn ouranōn*). That he personally plays that role and does not send a representative is highlighted by the emphatic pronoun *autos* "himself." The verse recalls some of Jesus' Son of Man sayings (cf. Mark 13:26; Luke 17:24). His coming will be **with a loud command, with the voice of the archangel and with the trumpet call of God**. J. B. Phillips captures something of the impact of the Greek: "One word of command, one shout from the Archangel, one blast from the trumpet of God and God in Person will come down from Heaven!" *Keleusma* is primarily a military word denoting "command." Always there is a ring of authority about it and a note of urgency. Who will issue the command, we are not told. Paul writes more for effect than for precision. But were the question put to him, no doubt he would answer, "the Lord" (cf. John 5:28). **The voice of the archangel** is literally, "a voice of an archangel." No specific archangel is meant and perhaps no archangel at all is in view (Michael is the only one named in the NT, Jude 9; Gabriel is mentioned in Luke 1:26 but not as an archangel). Paul might only mean "with a voice like the voice of an archangel." **The trumpet call of God** harks back to several OT passages (Exod. 19:16; Isa. 27:13; Joel 2:1, 15; Zech. 9:14) and is mentioned three times in the NT: Matthew 24:31, 1 Corinthians 15:52, and Revelation 11:15. The association of angels with the trumpet call in two of these three passages suggests that the call and the voice of the archangel and, indeed, the loud command, are simply different ways—figurative ways—of expressing the one thought that Jesus' coming will be with irresistible authority and indescribable grandeur (cf. Rev. 1:10; 4:1 for reference to a voice like the sound of a trumpet).

Then **the dead in Christ will rise** (cf. 1 Cor. 15:52 for similar teaching, and see note on 1:1 for the title **Christ**). The verb is again *anistēmi*, in an intransitive form (future middle), "they will rise," but it should be understood in the sense, "God will raise them" (see disc. on 4:14). Notice that those who live "in Christ," in death remain "in Christ" (cf. 1 Cor. 15:18; Rev. 14:13). Paul offers no account of an intermediate state between private death and the public event of the Parousia, except to assert that every Christian is somewhere in Christ's care (see further Williams, *Promise*, pp. 114–19). Nothing, not even death, can "separate us from the love of God that is in Christ Jesus our Lord" (Rom. 8:39). Apollo's lament in *The Eumenides* is that "the life once lost can live no more. For death my Father [Zeus] has ordained no healing spell" (651); to which the Christian joyfully replies, "Not so! We are with the Lord for ever" (4:17). Some identify the "rising" spoken of in this verse with "the first resurrection" of Revelation 20:5, but that reference is best understood in a spiritual rather than a bodily sense, in the sense of the new life of the believer (cf. John 5:24–27). The adverb, **first**, which qualifies this statement, must be read in conjunction with the "after that," *epeita*, of verse 17. Will the living have an advantage over the dead? They will not. If anything, it might be argued, the dead have the advantage in that their resurrection will take place first, but that is not the point. The only point is that they will not be disadvantaged.

4:17 / **After that, we who are still alive and are left** (this repeats the wording of verse 15) **will be caught up together with them**. The verb *harpazō* expresses what will happen in terms of a sudden and almost violent action (cf. Acts 8:39; 23:10). Those who are caught up will be subject to the irresistible power of God. While Paul struggles to show that the dead will not be disadvantaged, by the same token this "word of the Lord" shows that neither will the living. They will be caught up **with them,** i.e., with the dead, where the preceding *hama,* "together with," reinforces the preposition *syn,* "with," and the whole phrase, **together with them,** is emphasized by placing it early in the sentence before the verb. Thus for all practical purposes, the resurrection of the dead and the Rapture of the living (as this incident of the Parousia is sometimes called) will be simultaneous (see note on 3:13 and the further disc. on 2 Thess. 2:1). As for the transformation of the latter to equip them for their new condition, that subject must await Paul's later treatment in 1 Corinthians 15:50–53.

Two qualifying phrases are added. First, they will be **caught up . . . in the clouds. Clouds** symbolize divine glory (cf. Exod. 19:16; 24:15–18; 40:34; 1 Kings 8:10f.; Ps. 97:2) and from the NT perspective have an important association (derived from Dan. 7:13; see also 2 Enoch 3:1ff.) with Jesus' teaching about the coming of the Son of Man (Mark 13:26; 14:62). This association of clouds with the Coming has passed from Jesus to Paul (cf. also Mark 9:7; Acts 1:9–11; Rev. 1:7; 11:12; 14:14–16). Second, the living and the dead will together **meet the Lord in the air.** The Greek (and, indeed NIV) presents this as the purpose (*eis apantēsin,* "for meeting") of their being caught up, while the imagery is drawn from the practice of the day. Moulton and Milligan observe that "the word (*apantēsis*) seems to have been a kind of technical term for the official welcome of a newly arrived dignity" (p. 53; cf., e.g., Cicero, *Ad Att.* 8.16.2; 16.11.6; Matt. 25:6; Acts 28:15; the term used for the arrival was *parousia;* see disc. on 2:19). The air was deemed to be the abode of evil spirits (Eph. 2:2), and its mention now as the meeting place of Christ and his saints may suggest Christ's victory over them (so Morris), but that point cannot be pressed. We are not told what will follow that meeting in the air, but the imagery suggested by *apantēsis* (see above) points to the earth as their final destination (the citizens, who had gone out to meet him, escorting the new arrival back to their city). Paul, however, is not concerned to answer our questions as to what will follow, except to say that the saints **will be with** [*syn*] **the Lord forever** (cf. 2 Cor. 13:4; Phil. 1:23 for the same use of *syn* to mark our eternal companionship with Christ). Christ is central to all the blessings that God has for us—in a sense we might say that he is those blessings—and this will never be more true than at the consummation of our salvation. The Christian's final state of blessedness is to be with Christ (for Lord as a reference to Jesus Christ, see note on 1:1).

4:18 / **Therefore encourage each other with these words**. The same expression appears later in 5:11 but with a different connotation. The word *parakaleō* (see disc. on 3:2) has a range of meanings. One of its most common meanings, "comfort," is especially suitable here, since the Thessalonians were anxious about their dead. Bruce cites a letter of condolence from the papyri that ends in precisely the words, "encourage each other" (P. Oxy. 115). As Bruce observes, however, Paul could give the Thessalonians more solid grounds for comfort than that writer could.

5:1 / This verse begins in much the same way as 4:9, where we have already observed that, contrary to Paul's use in 1 Corinthians, the formula, **now about, . . .** is probably not a signal that he is answering the Thessalonian's questions. As in 4:9, he specifically states that he does not need to write to them on the subject concerned and does so only to reinforce what they already know. In this instance, the subject was the **times and dates** of the Lord's return. We cannot be certain whether Paul's choice of these two words over a simple expression and their use in the plural have any significance. It may have been a conventional phrase like our own "times and seasons" (cf. Acts 1:7). If there is any distinction between the words, "times" (*chronoi*) is chronological time, i.e., time measured by days, months, and years, while "dates" (*kairoi*) is qualitative time. This word is often translated "seasons," and the thought may have been of the nature of the times, with perhaps a reference to the hard times that lie ahead (cf. 2 Thess. 2:3).

5:2 / **The day** of the Lord's return **will come like a thief in the night**. Teaching on the Parousia and, in particular, on the impossibility of predicting when it would occur was evidently part of the missionaries' instruction. If this metaphor of the thief in the night is any guide, their instruction was based on Jesus' own teaching (cf. Matt. 24:43; Luke 12:39; Rev. 3:3; 16:15). The expression **the day of the Lord**, used of Jesus' return, originated in the OT, where it refers to the day when God would intervene in history to bring "the present evil age" to an end (cf. Gal. 1:4) and to inaugurate "the age to come," the age of his kingdom (rule) in the final and fullest sense of that term. The day of the Lord would see the salvation of the just and the judgment of the unjust. It would be a day of high drama, which is often described in terms of nature itself being involved in the event (cf. Joel 2:31; Amos 5:18; Mal. 4:5). In a sense, this day arrived with the advent of Jesus, for he inaugurated the kingdom, and salvation and judgment have begun. But the high drama awaits his return (at the end of the day, so to speak), which for Christians becomes "the day of the Lord (Jesus)" (see note on 1:1 for Jesus as Lord and on 2:12 for kingdom). In the Greek, neither "day" nor "Lord" has the definite article. This may indicate that this, like "times and dates," was a conventional phrase in the Christian vocabulary. The verb translated by NIV as the future "will come" is actually a present tense, "is coming," adding a note of certainty and a vividness to the statement.

5:3 / Concerning the Parousia, Jesus taught that it could, and very likely would, take people unaware. For that reason, they needed always to be ready, not by calculating from their calendars when it might be, for that cannot be done (cf. Mark 13:32), but by doing what is pleasing to God ("it is God's will that you should be sanctified," 4:3; cf. Luke 12:39f.; 17:24–32; 21:34–36). The history of the church should be sufficient warning against attempting to count the days or months or years to his coming— so many have guessed incorrectly. If we forget this, we become like athletes on the starting line, always breaking before the gun and never running the race. We run looking to Jesus but, for the present, the race is all that matters (cf. Heb. 12:1f.). Like Jesus, Paul warns that the **destruction** awaiting some in the Parousia **will come on them suddenly**, unaware (*aiphnidios*, found only here and in Luke 21:34 in the NT). This destruction should probably be understood in terms of separation from God rather than of annihilation by God. The word *olethros* can mean "deprivation" or "ruin" (NIV translates it in this way in 1 Tim. 6:9) as well as "destruction." This sense should be compared to its use in 2 Thessalonians 1:9 where it is qualified by the preposition *apo*, "*away from* the presence of the Lord." If this is how the word should be understood, it only heightens the stakes (annihilation would surely be a mercy compared with an eternity of conscious separation).

With so much at stake, therefore, beware, says Paul, of false reas-
surance, **Peace and safety**. Paul's language appears to be drawn
from the OT denunciations of those who cried, "Peace," when
there was no peace (cf. Jer. 6:14; Ezek. 13:10; for "peace," see disc.
on 1:1). The metaphor of labor pains finds parallels in both the OT
and NT (Isa. 13:6–8; 21:3; 37:3; Jer. 4:31; 6:24; Mark 13:8; John
16:21). Sometimes the emphasis is on the pain; sometimes, as
here, on the suddenness of its onset and its inevitability. **They
will not escape**, Paul declares, with reference to the unprepared
and to the terror of that day (see further disc. on 2 Thess. 1:9).
Believers, however, are instructed (not here but elsewhere) to
watch and to pray that they "may be able to escape (the terror)
. . . and . . . to stand before the Son of Man" (Luke 21:36).

5:4 / In contrast to the unprepared who will be overtaken by the Parousia, Paul can confidently assert of his Christian
readers: **But you, brothers, are not in darkness so that this day**
(see disc. on 5:2 and note on 2:12) **should surprise you like a thief**.
This verse recalls the metaphor of verse 2, which may also have
suggested the figure of darkness and light, night and day, that is
developed in what follows.

5:5 / "You don't know when, but you do know what," is
the line that Paul is taking in these verses. "And what you know
is quite enough!" **You** (the believers) **are all sons of light**. The
expression "son of" is a semitism characterizing the person by the
thing referred to. In this case believers are characterized by light
and day (cf. Luke 16:8; John 12:36; Eph. 5:8), where light has an
association with God and day with the "appearing of our great
God and Savior, Jesus Christ" (Titus 2:13). Put another way, believers are already in touch with God, they already have some
experience of him and have been touched by the first light of the
day. They already know something of the blessings of the kingdom. In modern theological terms, Paul is teaching both realized
and future eschatology—he intimates of the "now" and the "not
yet" character of the kingdom. And to reinforce his point, what
he said positively in the first half of the verse, he repeats in a
negative form in the second, changing the pronoun from "you"
to "we" to highlight that this holds true for all believers: **we do
not belong to the night or to the darkness**. The Greek reads
literally, "we are not of night and not of darkness." Perhaps we
should read into this, "sons of night . . . sons of darkness," main-

taining the structure of the first half of the verse, although the meaning is the same either way.

5:6 / The exhortations and explanations of this and the following verses rest on the truth expressed in verse 5. Believers are "sons of the light and sons of the day," **so then** (*ara oun*, introducing "an inescapable conclusion") **let us not be like others, who are asleep** (lit. "let us not sleep as the rest [of humankind] do"). The verb "to sleep" (*katheudō*) differs from the verb in 4:13ff. (*koimaō*). Elsewhere it describes moral indifference (Mark 13:36; Eph. 5:14), and that is clearly the meaning here (also in 5:7, but in 5:10 it is synonymous with *koimaō*). The believer's status as a son of light demands a morality, a holiness, in keeping with him who is the light (cf. John 8:12; 11:9f.; 12:46; 1 John 1:5f.). The image of sleeping maintains the metaphor of the thief in the night (5:2, 4) and resides in Jesus' use of the same metaphor (cf. Matt. 24:43; Luke 12:39). In that connection, moreover, Jesus explicitly urges his disciples to be watchful (cf. also Rev. 16:15), just as does Paul: **let us be alert** (*gregoreō*, cf. 5:10) **and self-controlled**. Watchfulness in this instance particularly concerns the Parousia. This should result in the believer's living a sane, sensible, and holy life (cf. Luke 21:34–36; 1 Pet. 5:8). The verb *nephō* (cf. 5:8) can mean "sober" as opposed to "drunk," but the thought in this case is probably of a more general sobriety. Nevertheless, the association of ideas leads to what follows.

5:7–8 / Paul explains the exhortation of verse 6 by characterizing the conduct of "the rest" (*hoi loipoi*, 5:6). He speaks metaphorically. Activities associated with the night become images of the moral condition of those "without hope and without God in the world" (Eph. 2:12). In that sense, they are sons of darkness, **For those who sleep, sleep at night**, where the verb is again *katheudō* (see disc. on 5:6), **and those who get drunk, get drunk at night**. In contrast with such activities (and Paul now returns to the exhortation of v. 6 and develops it), **since we** (the believers) **belong to the day, let us be self-controlled** (*nephō*, again see disc. on 5:6), **putting on faith and love as a breastplate, and the hope of salvation as a helmet** (cf. Rom. 13:12; 2 Cor. 6:7; 10:4; Eph. 6:11–17). The familiar metaphor of armor might have been suggested by a glimpse of armor catching and reflecting the first light of day. But equally the image might have been suggested by Isaiah 59:17, where God himself is said to be decked in the breastplate of righteousness and the helmet of salvation. At all events, Paul invites his readers, by means of this metaphor, to appreciate and to practice what is theirs (for the triad of Christian graces, see the disc. on 1:3, and for the close association of faith and love, see Gal. 5:6). The general term salvation embraces the whole work of God in Christ on our behalf. It becomes ours by faith (see disc. on 1:3 and 3:2f; cf. also 2 Thess. 2:13). But in speaking of the **hope of salvation**, Paul focuses especially on that part of the work that remains to be completed at the return of Christ. The awareness that God has begun a good work in us and that he will complete it (see Phil. 1:6) is our best protection (armor) against the contingencies of an uncertain world. It is also our best incentive to holiness.

5:9 / We have this hope (i.e., certainty, see disc. on 1:3) of future salvation, not through any merit of our own, but through the grace of God, or as Paul puts it, because (*hoti*) **God did not appoint us to suffer wrath** (see disc. on 1:10) **but to receive salvation** (lit. "for the obtaining of salvation," *eis peripoiēsin sōtērias;* see note). The initiative lies with God. Because he acted as he did, we can be saved—not *will be*, but *can be*. Salvation is only potential until our response of faith realizes the potential to make it actual. But our role is only reactive to his action. The initiative is God's. Further, it is as much a matter of salvation *from* as it is of salvation *to*. The wrath of God and its consequences, from which we need to be rescued, are as much a factor to be reckoned with as his love. Without that reckoning, we cannot begin "to grasp how wide and long and high and deep" is the love (Eph. 3:18) that has sought us and brought us home **through our Lord Jesus Christ** (cf. Luke 15:3–10). Christ is the agent of salvation (*dia*, "through"), God the loving author, to which proposition the next verse adds that Christ is also the goal of our salvation (for the titles Lord and Christ, see note on 1:1).

5:10 / The words **he died for us** explain how God brought us home through our Lord Jesus Christ. In the Greek, this is a participial phrase, the equivalent of a relative clause, "who died for us." The form of this description, as indeed, its content, may point to a pre-Pauline credal statement (see note on 4:14). This is the only place in the Thessalonian letters where Christ is said to have died "for us." But the way in which it is said, without defense or debate, leaves little doubt that it was an established understanding of the meaning of his death (cf. 1 Cor. 15:3 where the statement that "Christ died for our sins" is attributed to the tradition which Paul himself had received; again, see note 4:14 and cf. Acts 17:2–3). The preposition *hyper* should be noted in particular. It expresses the view that, in dying, Christ did so on our behalf— that his life was given for ours, as in Irenaeus' dictum: "He became what we are not, in order that we might become what he is" (*Adv. Haer.* 5; for this use of *hyper*, see, e.g., Rom. 5:6, 8; 8:32; 14:15; 1 Cor. 15:3; 2 Cor. 5:15, 21). His goal (*hina*) in giving his life was **that, whether we are awake or asleep,** "alive," as we would say, or "dead" (in terms of our physical condition), **we may live together with him.** Cf. 5:6 where the same verbs are found: *grēgoreō,* "to be awake, alert," *katheudō,* "to sleep." But the moral sense that they have in that verse no longer applies (against M. Lautenschlage, "*Eite grēgōremen eite katheudōmen.* Zum Verhältnis von Heilgung und Heil in 1 Thess. 5,10, " *ZNW* 81 (1–2, 1990), pp. 39–59, who maintains that Paul is expressing exactly the same thought as in v. 6, namely, the contrast of holy and unholy lives). It is inconceivable that Paul should suggest that whether we are morally alert or moribund will make no difference in the end. *Katheudō* is here synonymous with *koimaō* in 4:13ff. (for this sense of *katheudō* as physical death, cf. Mark 5:39; also LXX Ps. 87:6; Dan. 12:2; for similar statements concerning Christ's death and its outcome, see Rom. 14:8f.; 2 Cor. 5:15, 21; Gal. 1:4; 2:20). Paul ends as he began the section by assuring the Thessalonians that in whatever their physical condition at the Parousia, whether dead or alive, they will not be disadvantaged. The outcome for all believers will be the same: they will be with Christ. He is both the agent and the goal of their salvation. One detects almost a touch of impatience in this summing up—"Let's not waste time discussing whether it is better to be alive or dead. Let's get on with the job at hand." The aorist (subj.) verb translated "that . . . we may live" suggests that Paul viewed that life as something altogether new, rather than as the extension of the life that we now have. But in the light of his analogy of the seed in 1 Corinthians 15:37f., that distinction should not be pressed. There will be both continuity and discontinuity between what we are and what we will be. See further Williams, *Promise*, pp. 119–21.

5:11 / As in 4:18, with the prospect of the Parousia as his premise and using the same words as before, Paul demands:

Therefore, encourage one another (for *parakaleō*, "to encourage," see disc. on 3:2) **and build each other up** (in the Christian life). In Ephesians 4:13, he expresses this in terms of each helping the other to "become mature, attaining to the whole measure of the fullness of Christ." This figure of building up is a familiar one in the NT and a favorite of Paul, expressing what should be the goal both for our own life and for the lives of others (cf. Rom. 15:20; 1 Cor. 8:1; 10:23; 14:4, 17). With his usual sensitivity, Paul hastens to add that this was, in fact, what the Thessalonians were doing already.

Additional Notes   §7

4:14 / **We believe that Jesus died and rose again**: This should be compared with 1 Corinthians 15:3f., where Paul makes much the same statement, claiming in doing so that he was passing on to the Corinthians a tradition that he himself had received. This establishes the centrality of the death and resurrection of Jesus to Christian belief from earliest times. That Paul is similarly citing in Thessalonians an accepted credal statement is suggested by his use of the name Jesus rather than Christ (which is more usual in Paul) and by the verb *anistēmi* rather than *egeirō* (Paul's normal word for resurrection). *Anistēmi* is found in Paul's letters only in 1 Thessalonians 4:14, 16, and in Ephesians 5:14. It is noteworthy, perhaps, in the light of this, that it appears in Luke's summary of Paul's preaching at Thessalonica (Acts 17:3).

God will bring with Jesus those who have fallen asleep in him: Following NIV, we have construed the phrase "in him" (lit. "through Jesus," *dia tou Iēsou*) with the participle "those who sleep." RSV and several other versions and commentaries, however, take this phrase as qualifying the verb, "will bring": "through Jesus, God will bring with him those who have fallen asleep." The Greek can be read either way, but we accept Bruce's argument that if both phrases, "through Jesus" and "with him," qualify the verb, there is a certain imbalance in the sentence, while it is difficult to see what further meaning is added to the verb by the second phrase.

5:4 / **That this day should surprise you like a thief**: Some manuscripts (A B bohairic [at least 5 mss]) have a reading accepted by a number of commentators which means "as day surprises thieves" (*kleptas* instead of *kleptēs*). If this reading is accepted, we must suppose that, while the echo of the word (*kleptēs*) is still in Paul's mind from verse 2, he changes it to avoid repetition. Instances may be cited from Plutarch (e.g., *Vit. Crassi*

29) and others of nocturnal activities being overtaken by the dawn, so that the thought of the day surprising thieves is not out of the question. However, the weight of manuscript evidence, the argument for consistency with verse 2, and the use of the same figure in the teaching of Jesus, support the reading accepted by NIV.

5:9 / **To receive salvation**: The noun, *peripoiēsis*, can mean among other things, "the acquisition or obtaining" of something (in this case, salvation; cf. 2 Thess. 2:14; Heb. 10:39). Taken in isolation, this could imply that, to some extent, salvation is a matter of human endeavor—that it is something for which we must strive. This has prompted the suggestion that *peripoiēsis* should be understood passively rather than actively (as in Eph. 1:14; 1 Pet. 2:9) and the phrase rendered, "for the adoption of salvation" (Lightfoot)—i.e., "for our adoption (by God), which consists of our salvation." Such a rendering, however, is both strained and unnecessary, for Paul immediately goes on to say that our salvation is "through our Lord Jesus Christ." There is no question but that we are saved by grace and not by human endeavor.

§8   Final Instructions (1 Thess. 5:12–28)

Generally speaking, the report brought by Timothy concerning the church in Thessalonica was most heartening, and when Paul heard it, he offered thanks to God for their faith and love, for their hard work and hope. But in some respects there was room for improvement. Of particular concern was the relationship between the leaders of the church and the other members. Due perhaps to a restlessness provoked by uncertainty about the Parousia or by some other factor (see disc. on 4:11; 5:14; 2 Thess. 3:6–13 and note), some of the members' conduct called for rebuke by the leaders, but the leaders did not handle the situation as tactfully as they might have, and tensions resulted. Paul's advice to remedy this situation is found in verses 12 and 13 (on the form of this parenesis, see disc. on 4:1–12 but note that it does not conform fully to the pattern set out there, in that it has no prepositional phrase). The remaining verses of the section present us with a triple series of brief instructions. The first instruction consists of five pastoral exhortations, the last occurring in both a negative and a positive form (vv. 14f., again see disc. on 4:1–12 for the parenetic structure of these verses; and see A. J. Malherbe, "'Pastoral Care' in the Thessalonian Church," *NTS* 36 [3, 1990], pp. 375–91, for Paul's use of methods and traditions derived from the moral philosophers). The second consists of three directions for working out the will of God in one's life (vv. 16–18). The third contains five injunctions relating to the prophetic ministry (vv. 19–22). The letter ends with a prayer reminding the Thessalonians of God's grace and of the dignity that is theirs because of it. Every aspect of their lives is now important ("spirit, soul, and body"), and the prayer is that, in every way ("through and through"), they might be sanctified and found to be so at the coming of our Lord Jesus Christ (v. 23). Confident that God will answer this prayer (v. 24), Paul asks for prayer for himself and his colleagues (v. 25;

cf. 2 Thess. 3:1–5). The final greeting (v. 26) is followed by an instruction that this letter be read to the whole church (v. 27). He then pronounces the grace (v. 28).

5:12 / **Now we ask you, brothers** (for *erōtaō*, "to ask," see disc. on 4:1). The tone is respectful as he asks the Thessalonians **to** show **respect** for their leaders. The Greek is literally "to know" them in the sense "to know their worth." There follows a three-fold description of the leaders. The one definite article governing the three participles of this description makes it clear that Paul has in mind one group only and not three. They are described in terms of their functions (the present tense indicating that this is their characteristic role): they **work hard among you**, where the Greek implies laborious toil (*kopiaō;* see 1:3 for the corresponding noun); they **are over you in the Lord**, where, of the three participles, this one distinctly marked them out for what they were. But the qualifying phrase reminds us that Christian leaders are themselves under the Lord's authority (Jesus' authority; see note on 1:1) and that the style of their leadership must reflect that authority—"Be shepherds of God's flock . . . not greedy for money, but eager to serve; not lording it over those entrusted to you, but being examples to the flock" (1 Pet. 5:2f.). The verb itself illustrates this. *Proistēmi's* meaning ranges from having authority over others (cf. Rom. 12:8; 1 Tim. 5:17) to caring for others (cf. 1 Tim. 3:4, 5, 12 and Titus 3:8, 14, for the thought that this care will be expressed in action—in doing good works). A noun from the same root, *prostatis*, describes Phoebe, the deacon of Cenchreae, as having been "a great help" to many, including Paul (Rom. 16:2). And (returning to the description of the Thessalonian leaders) **they admonish you**. Like the hard work mentioned above, this was another aspect of their care. The verb *noutheteō* is peculiar to Paul in the NT and carries the sense of blame for wrongdoing, though more in the nature of a friendly than of a hostile warning (cf. 5:14; 2 Thess. 3:15).

5:13 / Paul asks two things of the Thessalonians concerning their leaders: First, as we have seen in verse 12, that they should know their worth and thus respect them, and second, that they should **hold them in the highest regard in love**. The verb *hēgeomai* usually means "to consider" or "to regard," in the neutral sense of that word (cf. 2 Thess. 3:15), but here it has a more positive content dictated both by the adverb, *hyperekperissōs* (see disc. on 3:10), and by the adverbial phrase, "in love." The church members are asked to regard their leaders thus, not for any personal qualities they might have, but **because of their work**, in the sense that their work will go better, whether within the church or in extending the church, if they can be made to feel that they are loved.

Commentators debate whether the final injunction of verse 13 belongs with the preceding or not. It probably does and is Paul's way of rounding off the discussion. It is important to note that it is a general injunction. Evidently, fault existed on both sides (leaders and members), and the whole church had to be told to make it their practice (note the present imperative) to **live in peace with each other** (cf. 4:11). This is a common Christian instruction (cf. Rom. 12:18; 14:19; 2 Cor. 13:11; Eph. 4:3; Col. 3:15; 2 Tim. 2:22; Heb. 12:14) going back to the instruction given by Jesus himself (Mark 9:50; cf. Ps. 34:14), for it goes to the heart of what we as Christians are called to be and to do: "Be imitators of God . . . and live a life of love" (Eph. 5:1f.).

5:14–15 / Again, it is important to note that the instruction contained in these verses is general, addressed to the whole church and not simply to the leaders, although it obviously applies to them in particular. The introductory formula, **we urge you, brothers** (for *parakaleō*, "to urge," see disc. on 3:2) is parallel to that in 4:1, 10 and 5:12, where the whole church is addressed, so that, as Paul understands it, every member of the brotherhood has a pastoral responsibility however much that may be the particular role of the leaders.

First they must **warn those who are idle**. Brotherhood does not mean turning a blind eye to the faults of others. Rather, it means being concerned for their welfare, reminding them, if need be, of the standards expected of Christians. The verb is again that of verse 12, *noutheteō*, while the word "idle" (*ataktos*, cf. 2 Thess. 3:6, 11 for the adverb *ataktōs*, and 2 Thess. 3:7 for the verb *atakteō*) is, strictly, a military term, signifying the soldier who does not hold the line in the pressure of battle but breaks ranks (*taxis*). Thus the word comes to describe the undisciplined who act in a disorderly manner. The precise nature of the "disorderliness" of the Thessalonian offenders is indicated by the context both here and, more importantly, in 2 Thessalonians 3:6–12. It was idleness. Apparently there were a number of people within the Thessalonian church who were not merely out of work (*argos,* Matt. 20:3, 6; 1 Tim. 5:13; Titus 1:12) but who refused to work (cf. 2 Thess. 3:10, who *"will* not work"), thus breaking ranks and undermining the good order both of the church and of society (for the tradition, *paradosis,* of work as a part of the Christian ethic, see disc. on 2 Thess. 3:6; cf. Rom. 13:13; 1 Cor. 14:33, 39f.; Eph. 5:3 where "greed," improper for Christians, could be countered by the manual work mentioned earlier in 4:28; for Paul's concern for the church's role in civil order, see disc. on 4:12, cf. Rom. 13:1–7; Col. 3:18–4:1). This phenomenon of culpable idleness is sometimes thought to have been the product of mistaken ideas about the Parousia, either that it was near or had come (see disc. on 2 Thess. 2:2). On the one hand, this view receives some support in the fact that Paul moves from an allusion to the idle in 4:11f., to eschatology in 4:13–5:11, and then back to the problem of idleness in 5:14. But, on the other hand, we notice that the missionaries had already warned against idleness when they were in Thessalonica, before there was any confusion, as far as we know, about the Parousia (cf. 2 Thess. 3:6). Perhaps then, the problem stemmed not from a mistaken eschatology but from social factors within that society (see note on 2 Thess. 3:6).

The second injunction is to **encourage** (or "comfort" or "console," see disc. on 2:12 for *paramytheomai*) **the timid**. "The timid" (*oligopsychos,* found only here in the NT) may refer to those who by nature are diffident, or to those who in terms of their Christian faith have lost heart. Perhaps the fear of some of the Thessalonians that their dead loved ones might miss the Parousia had caused them to lose heart.

Third they are to **help the weak**. The verb *antechomai* means "to hold fast to" (cf. Matt. 6:24; Luke 16:13; Titus 1:9), and here church members are told to hold fast to the weak in the sense of supporting them, helping them. "The weak" are the weak in faith (Rom. 14:1). The train of thought leading from the second to the third injunction is clear, and Paul is still requiring this pastoral concern of his readers in Romans 15:1 when he wrote, "we who are strong ought to bear with the failings of the weak and not please ourselves."

Fourth, they are to **be patient** (*makrothymeō*) **with everyone**. In Galatians 5:22, patience (*makrothymia*) is a fruit of the Spirit (cf. also 1 Cor. 13:4; Eph. 4:2; Col. 1:11; 3:12), reproducing in us a characteristic of God who is himself "patient (*makrothymos,*

NIV 'compassionate') and gracious" (Exod. 34:6; Ps. 103:8). The word implies an enduring patience, a patience that lasts the distance (the sense of *makro-*) no matter how trying the circumstances. Some people are easy to be patient with; others are not. But Paul says "be patient with **everyone**" (*pros pantas*, "towards all" including, we suppose, those outside the church; see disc. on 3:12). An enduring patience even with the most difficult of people is a real test of Christian character. It is a product both of God's grace (the fruit of the Spirit) and of our own discipline and determination (hence this injunction).

The last injunction is described first negatively and then positively: **Make sure that nobody pays back wrong for wrong, but always try to be kind to each other and to everyone else**. A change from the plural throughout these verses (vv. 13–15), including the imperative of this verse, "make sure" (lit. "you [pl.] see to it"), to the third person singular in the noun clause, "that **nobody** pays back wrong for wrong," makes the point that individually as well as corporately we have a responsibility in this matter. This was a theme of Jesus' teaching (cf. Matt. 5:44–48; Luke 6:27–36; cf. Prov. 25:21) as it was elsewhere of Paul's (cf. Rom. 12:17, which uses the same verb, *apodidōmi* and the same expression *kakon anti kakou*, "wrong for wrong"), in the face of a society which, then as now, accepted retaliation as the norm. Injustice done, injustice returned. Dirty tricks done, dirty tricks done in return. Violence suffered, revenge paid back in kind. The Christian norm, however, is to do good. A Christian congregation that tolerates the harboring of grudges or the intention to retaliate is a contradiction in terms. In the second half of the verse Paul reverts to the plural, making the complementary point to the singular noted above, that we are all expected to act in this way. The command is general to all Christians, literally "pursue the good" (*to agathon diōkete*), that is, make the best interest of others our aim and work constantly at achieving it (the force of the present imperative and of the adverb, *pantote*, "always"). The "try to be kind" of NIV is too feeble. Paul throws down a tremendous challenge to Christians to be Christlike (for that is what the injunction amounts to) both within the church in our dealings with each other (*eis allēlous*), and outside in our dealings with everyone else (*eis pantas*). Remember, the Thessalonians were a persecuted church, but for all that, they were not to return wrong for wrong, but rather, they were to work constantly for the good of the very people who were doing them harm. Not an easy assignment! Impossible, indeed, apart from God's grace. Yet something required of us no less than of them.

5:16–18 / Some things vary in the Christian experience; they come and go. But some things have an "always" attached to them. These verses name three, for the explanatory clause at the end of these verses almost certainly refers to them all (despite the singular "this" of v. 18 which might appear to refer only to the last of the three). Thus it was **God's will for** them first, that they should learn to face all that comes with irrepressible joy (NIV **be joyful always**). Paul's intent is explained more fully in Philippians 4:4, where he has "rejoice *in the Lord* always." We might have little in the world to be glad about (cf. 1:6), but in the Lord we have much, and the world cannot take that joy from us (cf. John 16:22). The phrase "in the Lord" points to the objective grounds for our rejoicing in what God has done for us in Christ: "God so loved ... that he gave ... " (John 3:16). But this is linked with a subjective capacity to rejoice, which is no less God-given: once again a part of the fruit of the Spirit (Gal. 5:22; cf. Acts 13:52; Rom. 14:17). In short, joy lies at the heart of the gospel—a truth echoed in the common root, in Greek, of two words, grace and joy (*charis, chara*). It is God's joy to be gracious to us, while our joy has its grounds in his grace.

Second, they should face all that comes with prayer—**pray continually**, that is, live always in the spirit of prayer. Prayer acknowledges our utter dependence upon God and the utter dependability of God in all circumstances. Prayer as much as joy is the product of God's grace. For the adverb, "continually," *adialeiptōs*, cf. 1:2 and 2:13, and for the injunction to pray continually, compare Jesus' intention in telling the parable of the Persistent Widow: "that they (the disciples) should always pray and not give up" (Luke 18:1). See also Romans 12:12, where the thought is again of persistence in prayer. Paul's own letters are a case in point. They are full of prayers for his readers, and their picture of Paul as a man of prayer is corroborated by Luke's account of him in Acts (cf. Acts 9:11; 13:2f.; 14:23; 16:25; 20:36; 21:5; 22:17–21; 27:35; 28:8).

Third, God's will for them was that they should **give thanks in all circumstances**. This is not a stoical indifference to all that comes. Paul regards the Christian as vulnerable. He or she can be hurt, disappointed, confused, or defeated, but never driven to total despair, never forsaken, never destroyed (2 Cor. 4:8–11), for God is always there. As in verse 17, so here, there is the implied qualification: "to the Lord." Compare Paul's thanksgiving for joy "in the presence of our God" in 3:9. His love and his power give the strength to meet every situation in life. The thanks are not for the circumstances but for the fact that in all circumstances the Lord is there. The same association of thanksgiving with prayer in these verses occurred earlier in 1:2 and reappears in Philippians 4:6. According to Romans 1:21, the failure to give thanks is a mark of human sinfulness, and elsewhere Paul urges those whose sins have been forgiven to "overflow with thankfulness" (Col. 2:7; cf. also Eph. 5:4, 20; Col. 3:15, 17; 4:2). To be able to give thanks in all circumstances presupposes a recognition of God's sovereignty, that in all these circumstances (whatever the appearance might be) he is working "for the good of those who love him, who have been called according to his purpose" (Rom. 8:28).

Finally, we note that God's will is said to be **in Christ Jesus**. In these particular matters, as in all others (for God's will includes far more than is mentioned here; note that "will" in the Greek lacks the definite article—"a will of God for you is . . . "), his will is made known to us in Christ, whether in his practice or in his precepts, whether in the days of his flesh or through his Spirit. Moreover, only as we are "in Christ" are we empowered through that same Spirit to do what God's will demands (for Christ, see note on 1:1, and for his oneness with the Father, see disc. on 3:11 and 2 Thess. 2:16).

5:19–22 / Verse 20 may be the key to the interpretation of all five injunctions in these verses; they may all have to do with the prophetic gift. The prophet spoke for the risen Lord; he or she could declare, "Thus says the Lord," and in that capacity the prophet's ministry comprised both preaching and prediction. This ministry was a gift of the Spirit (cf. Acts 11:28; 21:11; 1 Cor. 12:10f., 28; 14:1, 39; Eph. 4:11; see also Eph. 2:20; 3:5 for the ranking of prophets next to apostles) and in that connection especially, though the same would apply to any aspect of the Spirit's work, Paul warned, **Do not put out the Spirit's fire** (v. 19, lit., "do not extinguish the Spirit"). The figure of fire variously denotes the Spirit or the work of the Spirit (cf. Matt. 3:11; Luke 3:16; 12:49; Acts 2:3). This particular prohibition is expressed in the Greek by the negative of the present imperative (as also v. 20, **do not treat prophecies with contempt**), which may imply that the Thessalonians were extinguishing the fire of the Spirit as manifested in the voice of prophecy and were being told by Paul to put an end to such practice. But the present tense may only mean that they should not make it their habit to extinguish the Spirit, whether or not they were doing so now (the three positive injunctions of vv. 21, 22 are all in the present imperative, giving the same sense that believers should make the thing commanded their practice).

The voice of prophecy might be extinguished either by the prophet's refusing to speak (cf. Jer. 20:9) or by others' refusing to listen or obstructing the speaker (cf. Amos 2:12; Mic. 2:6). The particular issue may have been prophecies concerning the coming of Christ, which some members, overreacting against the enthusiasm of others, rejected. But no prophecy should be rejected out of hand, any more than should all that purports to be prophecy be accepted uncritically. Rather, Paul instructs, **Test everything** (the neuter *panta* indicates that it is the substance, not the speaker, which is to be tested; for the verb, *dokimazō*, see disc. on 2:4). No criterion is offered for testing what the prophet said, but elsewhere we learn of two tests of genuine prophecy: how it measures up against what other prophets said (1 Cor. 14:29) and how it measures up against "the Lord's command" (1 Cor. 14:37f.). The latter reference implies that the *kerygma*—the gospel—central to which is the proclamation of Jesus as Lord (cf. Acts 2:36; 1 Cor. 12:3) is the ultimate criterion of genuine prophecy. This comes as a warning, then, that prophets are not the source of new truth insofar as they are preachers, but they are expositors of truth that has already been revealed. In this connection, another gift, founded upon and fostered by a knowledge of Scripture, of "distinguishing between spirits," is much to be prized (1 Cor. 12:10).

Out of such a gift will come the church's ability to **hold on to the good** in what the prophet may utter (for the verb *katechō*, cf. 2 Thess. 2:6) and to **avoid every kind of evil**. If it is right that all five of these injunctions concern prophecy, it may be better to treat "evil" as an attributive adjective and to translate this injunction, "avoid every evil kind (of utterance)," which would be every utterance that ran counter to the *kerygma*. It must be conceded, however, that Paul's thought may have moved beyond prophecy to more general considerations in verse 22 and even in verse 21, and that his instruction in these verses is that in all matters the Thessalonians should "hold on to the good" and "avoid every kind of evil" (cf. Isa. 1:16f., also 1 Thess. 4:3). This expression is sometimes understood in the sense of "every *appearance* of evil" (cf. AV). The word concerned (*eidos*) does sometimes have that meaning. If it were taken in that sense, it would mean the evil that outwardly reflects the inner character. But NIV has probably expressed the sense that Paul intended.

5:23–24 / Paul prays again for the Thessalonians. Earlier he prayed that their "hearts might be established blameless in holiness" (3:13), and he defined holiness both as consecration to God and as separation from the world and its ways (4:3–8). Here he stresses that the consecration must be total, "through and through . . . spirit, soul and body." For the expression, **God himself**, using the emphatic pronoun, see disc. on 3:11. The description **the God of peace** is echoed in 2 Thessalonians 3:16 (the Lord of peace) and later in Romans 15:33; 16:20; 2 Corinthians 13:11 (the God of love and peace) and Philippians 4:9 (cf. also Heb. 13:20 and Rom. 14:17 for peace as a characteristic of God's kingdom). Peace, as we have seen (1:1), signifies well-being in the widest sense, but Paul has in mind spiritual well-being, peace with God. That peace originates with God himself, not the person concerned. God takes the initiative in salvation (see disc. on 1:4; 5:9). The point is reinforced by the conjunction *de*, "but" (not shown in NIV), which sets this prayer over against the injunctions of the preceding verses. They speak of what we must do; this prayer concerns what God has done and will do on our behalf. God could not acquiesce in a state of affairs in which sinners were at enmity with himself. In Christ, therefore, he took the initiative to put them at peace (cf. Rom. 5:6ff.; Eph. 2:13ff.). To those who respond to his initiative, he gives a new status, a new start; and now Paul prays, in effect, that he who began this good work in them might "carry it on to completion until the day of Christ Jesus" (Phil. 1:6). That is, he prays that God might **sanctify** them **through and through**. The latter expression renders the word, *holotelēs*, unique to this passage in the NT. It is comprised of two words, the one signifying wholeness, the other completion. Paul was never afraid to aim high in his prayers (see, e.g., Eph. 3:19). His prayer for the Thessalonians was for their total sanctification (see disc. on 4:3). We have seen that there is a human role in this process, hence the exhortations above; but even that is largely a matter of letting God do the work, and this prayer focuses on that work of God in shaping their lives.

The second half of the prayer (**may your whole spirit, soul and body be kept blameless**) is essentially the same as the first (and as the prayer of 3:11–13 where Paul also prays that they "will be blameless," *amemptos*). Again praying for their complete sanctification, Paul now uses the adjective "whole," *holoklēron* (lit. "complete in all its parts," cf. James 1:4, and Acts 3:16 for the equivalent noun), but the sense is the same as that of *holotelēs* (the "through and through") in the first half of the prayer. "Clearly Paul is stretching his vocabulary . . . to bring out the truth that he is looking for the Thessalonian Christians to live on the highest plane" (Morris, *Themes*, p. 61). *Holoklēron* qualifies the three nouns, **spirit, soul and body.**

Paul's use of these three nouns should not be pressed as a basis of his anthropology. The piling up of the nouns functions only to emphasize the completeness of the sanctification—it is to touch every aspect of their lives. One would be hard pressed indeed to draw a distinction between spirit and soul; and, while it may be easier to distinguish between spirit and body, the biblical notion of the wholeness of our being must be kept in view. Aspects of our being can be referred to as spirit, soul, or body, but our being is indivisible. It is a whole. We are one.

Paul is confident that God will sanctify the Thessalonians and keep them blameless, not because he has prayed, but because the God to whom he has prayed is faithful—**the one who calls you is faithful and he will do it**. The faithfulness of God, i.e., his utter dependability, is a favorite Pauline theme (see disc. on 2 Thess. 3:3; cf. 1 Cor. 1:9; 10:13; 2 Cor. 1:18; 2 Tim. 2:13; also Heb. 10:23; 11:11). As for God's calling the Thessalonians, Paul referred to this earlier in connection with both their salvation (2:12) and their sanctification (4:7). The present tense of the participle, "who calls," suggests that God goes on calling—he calls the unbeliever to faith and the believer to holiness. Paul's prayer concerns the latter and is offered with an eye to **the coming of our Lord Jesus Christ** (for *parousia*, see disc. on 2:19, and on 3:13 for the Coming as an incentive to Christian practice; see note on 1:1 for the titles Lord and Christ).

5:25 / In the same confidence that God will answer his prayer for them, Paul asks the Thessalonians to pray for him and his colleagues—to pray constantly, if we can again press the present tense of the imperative. Notice the mutuality of ministry implied in this request—his to them and theirs to him. "The church at prayer is a church where pastor and people are praying for others, where pastors pray for their people, and where people are praying for their pastors who, like them, are standing in the need of prayer" (Saunders). Paul was certainly conscious of that need, ever aware of his own weakness and of his utter dependence on God. Similar requests for prayer are found in 2 Thessalonians 3:1f.; Romans 15:30; Ephesians 6:19; Colossians 4:3f. (cf. also Heb. 13:18). See also 2 Corinthians 1:11 and Philippians 1:19 for the acknowledgement that others were praying for him. If his request shows an awareness of the weakness of his humanity, his calling the Thessalonians **brothers** evinces its warmth. See the discussion on 1:4 for this address as a measure of his affection for the Thessalonians.

5:26 / The instruction **Greet all the brothers with a holy kiss** means, "Give them all a kiss from me" (cf. Rom. 16:16; 1 Cor. 16:20; 2 Cor. 13:12; in 1 Pet. 5:14 it is called the "kiss of love" and, with this, cf. 1 Cor. 16:24, "my love to all of you"). Kissing was a common form of salutation in the ancient world, indicating affection and sometimes homage (1 Sam. 10:1) and sometimes, in that sense, it became an act of worship (1 Kings 19:18; Job 31:27; Hos. 13:2). By the time of Justin Martyr (ca. A.D. 100–165), the kiss had become an accepted part of the Christian liturgy and was exchanged after the prayers and before the presentation of the bread and wine (*First Apol.* 65.2). Hippolytus (d. ca. A.D. 236) called it the "kiss of peace," and in the *Apostolic Constitutions* (fourth century) its practice was regulated: men were to kiss only men, and women only women (2.57.17). Whether the kiss was formalized in the liturgy in Paul's day is open to question. It is also a moot point whether "all" should be given particular emphasis. Is Paul stressing that all should be greeted in a situation where there was dissension? Or should we treat "all" as no different from "one another," the expression he employs elsewhere?

5:27 / As evidence of dissension and even of division within the church, some commentators appeal to this verse, where the very strength of Paul's language, **I charge you before the Lord to have this letter read to all the brothers**, might hint at his fear that it would not be read at all (cf. the milder request of

Col. 4:16, "see that it is . . . read"). But nothing in the letter thus far indicates that the situation in Thessalonica is nearly as serious as this suggests. On the contrary, such is the general tenor of the letter (cf. e.g., 1:2f.; 2:19f.; 3:7–9) that this church seems to have been free from any serious problems of division. It would be unwise, therefore, to build too much on the strength of the language. Rather, it probably reflects his love for the Thessalonians. He longed to be with them and, for the time being, this letter was the closest he could come to satisfying that longing. Therefore he wanted them all to hear it read. Notice the first person singular, "I charge you. "This is Paul speaking for himself, from his own heart and perhaps, at this point, holding the pen in his own hand (see disc. on 5:28; cf. also 2 Thess. 2:5). The expression is a strong one (*enorkizō*), "I put you on oath." He is not swearing by the Lord (cf. Matt. 5:34) but appealing to his readers to act as though, in this matter, they were on oath to the Lord. Almost certainly the Lord is Jesus, as in verses 23 and 28, and that Paul should invoke him in this way is "another indication of the stature of the Lord as Paul saw him" (Morris, *Themes*, p. 33; see disc. on 3:11 and 2 Thess. 2:16).

5:28 / The letter ends much as it began (1:1) and in a manner that would soon become the trademark of the apostle. He commends his readers to **the grace of our Lord Jesus Christ** (for an expanded form of this grace, see 2 Cor. 13:14, and for a shortened form, Col. 4:18; 1 Tim. 6:21; 2 Tim. 4:22; Titus 3:15; for the titles Lord and Christ, see note on 1:1). Paul typically links grace with the Lord Jesus Christ (2 Thess. 1:2, 12; 2:16; 3:18). He also customarily employed an amanuensis to transcribe his letters, but at about this point he would seize the pen and write the final words in his own hand (cf. 2 Thess. 3:17; Gal. 6:11). The first person singular of verse 27 may signal that change.

Additional Notes   §8

5:20 / **Do not treat prophecies with contempt**: If 1 Corinthians is any guide, it may not have been unusual to find men and women exercising the gift of prophecy during a worship service (see 1 Cor. 11:4f.;

14:29; cf. also Acts 13:1). But besides these, others, such as the "prophets" referred to in the list of charismata (1 Cor. 12:28f.; Eph. 4:11; cf. Eph. 2:20; 3:5), exercised this gift more widely. To this group belonged Agabus and the others mentioned in Acts 11:27 (cf. also Acts 21:10). In their capacity as preachers, the prophets offered edification, comfort, and encouragement (Acts 15:32; 1 Cor. 14:2f.). The reaction of unbelievers to their ministry (1 Cor. 14:24f.) shows that they preached "the whole will of God" (Acts 20:27). In the context of the church meeting, their ministry is described as a "revelation" (1 Cor. 14:26ff.), which appears to mean that it was usually a spontaneous utterance in response to a distinct moving of the Spirit. The utterances of the prophets communicated intelligently (unlike the gift of tongues) to those who heard them.

5:21–22 / Test everything. Hold on to the good. Avoid every kind of evil: Early Christian writers invariably quote these words as a comment on a logion attributed to Jesus: "Be approved money changers" (see J. Jeremias, *Unknown Sayings of Jesus* [London: S.P.C.K., 1964], pp. 100–104). The connection between Paul's injunction and the logion was found in the word *eidos*, which early writers understood in the sense of "kind of money," i.e., Latin *species*. On this basis, Paul extended Jesus' metaphor, "Be like good money changers; test every coin that comes across your table; keep the good, reject the bad." However, "kind of money" is not attested for *eidos*, and the connection is, therefore, a tenuous one.

2 Thessalonians

§1 Address and Greeting (2 Thess. 1:1–2)

1:1–2 / The wording resembles the first letter's address (see comment there) except for the addition of "our" in the phrase, **in God our Father**. This clarifies that God is being presented, not as the Father of Jesus but as the Father of his people and, specifically, of **the church of the Thessalonians**. The greeting also parallels the first letter's (again, see the comment there), but it is expanded by the addition of **from God the Father and the Lord Jesus Christ**, which becomes Paul's regular form of greeting in later letters (cf. Rom. 1:7; 1 Cor. 1:3; 2 Cor. 1:2; Gal. 1:3; Eph. 1:2; Phil. 1:2; Col. 1:2 and for variants, cf. 1 Tim. 1:2; 2 Tim. 1:2; Titus 1:4; Philem. 3). It makes explicit what is implicit in the simpler form: God (as author) and the Lord Jesus (as agent) are together the source of our salvation, which is entirely of **grace** ("the extravagant goodness of God," see disc. on 1 Thess. 1:1) and which results in our **peace**. God himself (Father and Son) puts us at peace with himself. For the implication of Jesus' divine status in his being linked by the one preposition with God the Father as both the "place" (*en*) in which the church has its rest and the source (*apo*) from which come grace and peace, see the discussion on 1 Thessalonians 1:1. For the titles Lord and Christ, see the note on 1 Thessalonians 1:1.

§2   *Thanksgiving and Prayer (2 Thess. 1:3–12)*

This section divides into three subdivisions marked in NIV by the paragraphs. The subdivisions, however, are not as obvious in the Greek as in NIV. In the Greek, verses 1 to 10 form a single (complex) sentence. Nevertheless, this sentence exhibits a definite movement in the thought from thanksgiving to encouragement. Some have suggested that, compared with the earlier letter, this epistle's thanksgiving reflects a certain coolness (vv. 3–4). Such a charge, however, must be offset by the affectionate address of verse 3 ("brothers") and the boast in verse 4 about the Thessalonians' perseverance and faith. What appears to be aloofness might be better explained in terms of the formality of the language, perhaps influenced by liturgical language (see R. D. Aus, "The Liturgical Background of the Necessity and Propriety of Giving Thanks According to 2 Thessalonians 1:3," *JBL* 92 [1973], pp. 432–38). In verses 5 to 10, Paul encourages his readers by reference to "the day" (of Jesus' return). These verses, and more specifically verses 7 to 10, reveal a poetic structure such that A. S. Way, *The Letters of St. Paul* (London: Macmillan, 1921), describes them as the "Hymn of the Second Coming." This might be Paul's own composition or an earlier work, either Christian or Jewish, on which he draws. Either way, the hymn owes much to the language and style of the Septuagint (LXX). The remaining verses in this section (vv. 11–12) constitute not so much a prayer as a report of prayer, although the difference is more stylistic than real. Effectively these verses are Paul's prayer for his readers.

1:3 / It is possible that the Thessalonians had demurred at the praise heaped upon them in the earlier letter. They would not have been the first to find it difficult to accept a compliment, and this may account for Paul's words, **we ought always to thank God** (but see above for a possible liturgical influence). The word

ought (*opheilō*) expresses the idea of a personal obligation, "we owe it," to which he adds the phrase, **and rightly so**. Thanksgiving is fitting because it is warranted—"we owe it because it is appropriate." Christian leaders are not always as quick to acknowledge the pluses in the lives of their people. The thanksgiving is, of course, to God, for God made them what they were. It is *to* God *for* them. The present tense of the infinitive "to thank" suggests an ongoing activity that is reinforced by the adverb "always" (*pantote*).

Paul's two reasons (*hoti*) for this thanksgiving each refer to two of the three traditional Christian graces (see disc. on 1 Thess. 1:3). Only the word "hope" is omitted; nonetheless, the theme of the Parousia, which lies at the center of the Christian hope, pervades the letter, while the "endurance inspired by hope," mentioned in 1 Thessalonians 1:3, is the subject of the next verse. Thus the thought of hope, if not the actual word, belongs to this thanksgiving. Paul offers thanksgiving for their faith, **because your faith is growing more and more**. Faith can be understood either subjectively as trust, or objectively as the body of teaching, "the faith" (see disc. on 1 Thess. 3:2). In 1 Thessalonians 3:10, Paul spoke of their deficiency of faith in the latter sense—in some areas they needed further instruction—and he may be speaking of faith in that sense again—they were now better instructed. But the two meanings merge. A better grasp of *the* faith leads (or should lead) to a greater trust in the one with whom the faith is concerned. The verb (*hyperauxanō*), a "classical compound" (Bruce), is striking and occurs only here in the NT. It means "to increase beyond measure." The hyperbole reflects Paul's delight in their progress.

Second, the thanksgiving is for their love. We ought always to thank God, he says, because **the love every one of you has for each other is increasing**. Again this picks up something from the earlier letter. In 1 Thessalonians 3:12, Paul prayed that their love might "increase (*pleonazō*, the same verb as in this verse) and overflow for each other and for everyone else." He could now give thanks because that prayer had been answered. These references to the satisfactory outcome of earlier matters of concern and prayer are compelling evidence that both letters were addressed to the same people and written in their present sequence (see Introduction on The Authenticity of 2 Thessalonians and The Sequence of the Letters). In speaking of their love, Paul puts the matter most emphatically: literally, "the love of each one of you all" (stronger, e.g., than "each one of you," 1 Thess. 2:11). Clearly from this, love in particular stood out as a characteristic of this church, even though some of its members' conduct left something to be desired (see disc. on 3:11f.). Both verbs in this verse are in the present tense, indicating that their faith and love were still growing.

1:4 / As a result (*hōste*) of their growth, Paul and the others could boast about the Thessalonians **among God's** other **churches**, here presumably the churches of Achaia (see note). "We ourselves boast," he says, giving unusual emphasis to the pronoun and thus, perhaps, making the point that although their habit was not to boast of their converts (in 1 Thess. 1:9 it is others who boast about them), in this case they could not keep silent about the men and women who were their "glory and joy" (1 Thess. 2:20). The compound verb *enkauchaomai*, more forceful perhaps than the simple verb which Paul commonly employs, is unique to this passage in the NT. "We ourselves glory in" might better capture the sense. The grounds of that glorying were stated earlier: the Thessalonians' increasing faith and love. But Paul restates those grounds with a difference. He speaks now of their **perseverance** (*hypomonēs*, see disc. on 1 Thess. 1:3) **and faith**, which in this context undoubtedly means trust. This hints at the circumstances in which they had trusted God and persevered; namely, **in all the persecutions and trials** they were **enduring**. The present tense (*anechesthe*) compared with the aorist (*epathēte*) of 1 Thessalonians 2:14 indicates that persecution was a recurring problem for this church (see Introduction on The Sequence of the Letters). The more general word "trials" (*thlipsis*; see disc. on 1 Thess. 1:6) means "pressures" and can refer to any of the pressures to which we as human beings are subject in this "present evil age" (Gal. 1:4). "Persecutions" is more specific. The noun derives from a verb meaning "to put to flight," "to pursue," and refers in particular to trials that come to us as Christians (cf. Matt. 13:21; Mark 4:17; 10:30; Acts 8:1; 13:50; Rom. 8:35; 2 Cor. 12:10; 2 Tim. 3:11).

1:5 / From thanksgiving, Paul turns to encouragement. In introducing this theme, he appears (in the Gk.; see BDF §480 [6] for the syntax concerned) to set the word *endeigma*, a "token" or "proof" (found only here in the NT; but cf. Rom. 3:25f.; 2 Cor. 8:24; Phil. 1:28 for the similar *endeixis*), in apposition to "the persecutions and trials." This identifies the latter as **evidence that God's judgment is right**, perhaps in the sense that their suffering proved the genuineness of their faith, i.e., God had indeed adjudged them his own (cf. 1 Thess. 2:14; 3:3f.). Had it not been genuine they would not have been suffering as they were. But it may be, as Morris suggests, that the evidence lay not so much in their suffering as in the way the Thessalonians bore it—their "perseverance and faith" (v. 4; see Morris, *Themes*, p. 18). At all events, the final proof of the rightness of God's judgment would be furnished, as we see in the next verse, in his vindication of the sufferers and wreaking vengeance on their oppressors (cf. Phil. 1:28 for similar teaching). That theme of vindication is anticipated in v. 5, where the Greek appears to express the purpose of the judgment in the Thessalonians' being **counted worthy of the kingdom of God** (*eis to* with the infinitive; see disc. on 1 Thess. 2:12; NIV takes the Gk. construction as expressing result—outcome rather than the intention; see disc. on 1 Thess. 2:16). Suffering is not instigated by God (cf. James 1:13), but he turns it to his purpose (cf. Rom. 8:28). As for that purpose, it should be noted that the verb *kataxioō* (only here, Luke 20:35, and Acts 5:41 in the NT) means "to deem" or "to count worthy," not "to make worthy" (cf. the other great Pauline word, *dikaioō*, not "to make just" but "to deem just"). It is not God's purpose that, by suffering, we should be made worthy to enter his kingdom, but that, having entered by grace, we should be counted worthy to be there (cf. Matt. 5:10). This is just another way of saying that suffering is part of the package of being a Christian (see disc. on 1 Thess. 3:3). Paul puts the same thought into different words at the end of the verse when he speaks of suffering "on behalf of" (*hyper* with the gen. in the causal sense "for the sake of"; for other uses see disc. on 2:1 and 1 Thess. 5:10) the kingdom of God. In this context, the kingdom means the final phase of God's rule, which will be inaugurated at the coming of Christ (see disc. and note on 1 Thess. 2:12).

1:6–7 / The statements of verse 5 are based upon the general principle expressed in verse 6 that **God is just**. In the Greek this is a conditional clause, "if to pay back (*antapodidomi*, see disc. on 1 Thess. 3:9) . . . and to give relief . . . is just with God." But this is simply a literary form ("a rhetorical understatement," Morris; cf. Rom. 8:9; 1 Cor. 8:5), and there is no question that God's justice is concerned with condemnation and vindication, with the giving of relief, and with retribution in kind to the troublemakers. Some are uncomfortable with this proposition. They can accept that God is love but not that he is just and will condemn. And yet God's justice as much as his love saves us; only as we refuse his salvation do we see the other side of the coin. As in the parable, if we will not have him as king, we will have him as judge (cf. Luke 19:27 and see disc. on 1 Thess. 1:10). **Trouble** translates the Greek word rendered "trials" in verse 4 (*thlipsis*, see disc. on 1 Thess. 1:6), suggesting that there is an element of *quid pro quo* in God's justice, people getting what they deserve. But, if this is true of his condemnation, it is not true of his salvation, for in salvation he gives far more than we deserve. But that is not Paul's point. Paul mentions only the negative benefit of **relief to you who are troubled** (for the verb *thlibō*, here as a participle, see disc. on 1 Thess. 3:4). The noun *anesis* is often used by Paul as the antithesis of *thlipsis*—relief from trouble (cf. 2 Cor. 2:13; 7:5; 8:13). He and his colleagues looked forward to sharing this respite with the Thessalonians—**and to us as well**. "When we are thinking of the great apostle as bringing consolation and encouragement to his persecuted friends, it is easy to think of him as living in a different atmosphere. We tend to forget that he shared the same world as that inhabited by the Thessalonians; he, too, was afflicted (2 Cor. 11:23–29)" (Morris, *Themes*, p. 53). Relief will come **when the Lord Jesus is revealed**—the word is *apokalypsis*, literally, "in the revelation," and implies that Jesus is already crowned with glory as Lord (Acts 2:36 and see note on 1:1). But it awaits his return (*parousia*, see disc. on 1 Thess. 2:19) for his glory to be revealed. The phrase is qualified in three ways: (1) he will be revealed **from heaven**, signifying his divinity (cf. 1 Thess. 1:10; 4:16); (2) **with his powerful angels**, literally, "angels of power," but according to the semitic idiom the genitive may be understood as adjectival, characterizing them in the manner indicated (cf. 2:9f.; and see 1 Thess. 5:5 for the similar construction, "sons of"; for "mighty angels," cf. Ps. 103:20). But the focus of this passage is on Jesus. It may be better, therefore, to understand the power as his, and the angels as those attendants appropriate to his position and power (cf. JB, "the angels of his power," and see disc. on 1 Thess. 3:13 for the angels' attending him); and (3) **in blazing fire** (cf. Rev. 1:13–16; for the association of fire with theophanies, see Exod. 3:2; 19:18; Lev. 9:24; Ps. 18:8; Ezek. 1:13, 27;

and for its association with divine judgment, see Isa. 66:15f.; Dan. 7:9f., Matt. 3:11f.).

1:8 / From the revelation of Jesus, Paul turns to a description of what God will do, echoing the note of judgment sounded in the earlier verses (see also disc. on 1 Thess. 4:6). **He will punish**, says Paul. In the Greek this is not a separate statement but a description, going back to verse 7, of the Lord Jesus as "giving vengeance (upon)." His punishment is directed to those earlier referred to as "those who trouble you" and here as **those who do not know God and do not obey the gospel of our Lord Jesus**. In repeating the Greek definite article with the second participle, Paul may have in view two distinct groups of people. If this is the case, we should suppose that the Gentiles are "those who do not know God" and the Jews are "those who do not obey the gospel." The fact that in the OT "those who do not know God" are the Gentiles adds weight to this interpretation (Ps. 9:17; 79:6 and see disc. on 1 Thess. 4:5). But most commentators reject it as reading too much into the passage, preferring to take the "and" (*kai*) as epexegetical and the second participle as a particular case of the first (as indeed is the earlier phrase, "those who trouble you"; the style reflects the parallelism of OT poetry). Not to know God is culpable ignorance. It is also a fatal ignorance, for life in the ultimate sense, eternal life, lies only in knowing God (John 17:3)—knowing, not in the sense of possessing information about him, but of being in a personal relationship with him. This life and the way to it are set forward in **the gospel of our Lord Jesus** (the gospel of which he is the content; see disc. on 1 Thess. 1:5 and, for title Lord, the note on 1 Thess. 1:1). In nothing, then, are these people more culpable than in not obeying the gospel (cf. Rom. 10:16, lit. "not all obeyed the gospel"). Paul is referring not to people who never experienced the opportunity of hearing, but to those who had the opportunity and did not respond. Later, in Romans, he casts the net wider and condemns even those who had not heard. They could have seen something of God in his creation, he argues, but they "did not think it worthwhile to retain (lit. 'did not approve to have') the knowledge of God" (Rom. 1:28). The point remains: some respond to God's revelation and others do not. The latter must bear the consequences of their own choice.

1:9 / **They will be punished**, literally, "pay the penalty."
Penalty represents the Greek *dikē*, from the same root as *dikaios*,
"just." Theirs is a just punishment; they get the penalty they
deserve. The verb, "to pay," (*tinō*) only occurs here in the NT. In
the Greek this verse, together with verse 10, forms a relative
clause, adding a further description to those referred to in verse
8. Strictly, the introductory pronoun is the relative of quality:
"who are of such a kind as to," underlining the fitness of these
people to be punished in this way. We cannot be certain, however, that Paul used the pronoun in the strict sense. In apposition
with "penalty," giving content to their punishment, is the phrase,
everlasting destruction (*olethron aiōnion*, "destruction of the age,"
i.e., destruction in relation to the age to come; cf. 4 Macc. 10:15).
This is the counterpart of God's gift of eternal life (*zōē aiōnios*, life
in relation to the age to come; cf. Rom. 2:7; 5:21; 6:22f.; Gal. 6:8).
There is a sense of finality about both the gift and the punishment.
Neither will be revoked (cf. 1 Thess. 5:3). As to what "destruction
of the age" means, we are not told except in negative terms that
it is **from the presence** (*prosōpon*, "face") **of the Lord and from the
majesty** (*doxa*, "glory") **of his power**. The **Lord** is Jesus, as the next
verse makes plain, whereas in the OT passages echoed here, it is
God who is the Lord (cf. Isa. 2:10, 19, 21, and see disc. and note
on 1 Thess. 1:1 for the divine status of Jesus). As eternal life lies
in knowing God and of necessity Jesus Christ through whom
alone he can be known (Matt. 11:27), so eternal destruction lies
in being "separate from Christ . . . and (therefore in being) without
God" (Eph. 2:12; cf. Rom. 6:23). It would seem that separation,
not annihilation, is intended by this destruction (*olethros*, see disc.
on 1 Thess. 5:3). It is destruction in the sense of deprivation "away
from" (*apo*) the face of the Lord, depicted in NIV as being **shut out
from** his presence. The two expressions, "the face of the Lord"
and "his glory" mean much the same, for glory signifies what may
be seen of Christ. In this connection, having in mind perhaps how
oppressed the church was in Thessalonica and how impotent it
must have seemed in the face of its oppressors, Paul singles out
what may be seen of Christ, namely, his power. In effect, he is
declaring as Elisha did in similar circumstances that, contrary to
appearances, "those who are with us are more than those who
are with them" (2 Kings 6:16). But this thought, if it is present at
all, is only incidental to his main thought concerning the ruin that
awaits those who "do not obey the gospel of our Lord Jesus."

1:10 / Their "wages" will be "paid" **on the day he comes** (cf. Rom. 6:23 and see disc. on 1 Thess. 2:12 and note). The temporal conjunction in the Greek "whenever he comes" is indefinite, but the indefiniteness lies not in the event but only in the *time* of the event. He will come, but we do not know when (see disc. on 1 Thess. 5:2). "The day" (lit. "that day") is "the day of the Lord" (cf. 2:2; Isa. 2:11, 17, a passage echoed in v. 9 above; 1 Thess. 5:2). The implications of his coming are far-reaching, including, as we have seen, the punishment of those who do not know God. But now Paul focuses on what it will mean for Jesus himself. Jesus will come **to be glorified in his holy people**. The verb is a compound, *endoxazō*, "to be glorified in" (only here and in 1:12 in the NT), and the preposition is repeated in the phrase, "in (*en*) his holy people." This unusual expression in this precise form occurs only here in the NT. Its effect is to bring home what an important, though essentially passive, role the people of God play in the scheme of things, for they are "God's workmanship, created in Christ Jesus" (Eph. 2:10). In God's design, "nobodies" become "somebodies." What they are will be made known in that day to all, including "the rulers and authorities in the heavenly realms (Eph. 3:10), and what they are will redound in that day to the glory of their creator (cf. Gal. 1:24; 1 John 3:2). For the presence of the *hagioi*, "the holy ones," at the Parousia, see the discussion on 1 Thessalonians 3:13. In another context, they could be understood to be angels, but the parallelism of the following phrase, **to be marveled at among all those who have believed**, illumines that they are the saints or at least include the saints. Moreover, the preposition employed in the second half of the verse is the same as that in the first half, repeating the thought that Christ will be glorified "in" them, not "by" as NIV implies with its "among"(it would be an unusual use of *en* if Paul had meant "by" them; in that case we should have expected *hypo*). The sense is, then, that Christ will be "marveled at (by others, unspecified, because of what they see) in those who have believed." The use of the aorist participle looks back to the decisive moment when these men and women first put their trust in Christ and became a new creation (cf. 2 Cor. 5:17). And notice the word "all." No believer is excluded from this role. It is the privilege of all of God's people to be the ground of the glory of Christ.

An explanation follows (*hoti*) that, in the Greek, stands awkwardly with the rest of the verse, unless we understand some such ellipsis as NIV has supplied: **This includes you**, i.e., among all those who have believed, **because you believed our testimony to you** (cf., our gospel, 2:14; our preaching, 1 Cor. 15:14; and see disc. on 1 Thess. 1:5).

1:11 / **With this in mind**, literally, "to this end" (*eis ho*), namely, the Coming and its outcome in the lives of believers, **we constantly pray for you**. This assurance of prayer for the Thessalonians is the other side of the missionaries' confidence that at the Coming the Thessalonians would prove to be the crown in which they would glory in the presence of the Lord (1 Thess. 2:19). As often, the conjunction *hina* introduces both the content and the purpose of the twofold prayer (cf. 1 Thess. 4:1; for a similar effect with the infinitive, see 1 Thess. 2:12): First, **that our God may count you worthy of his calling**. The only assessment of our lives that matters in the end is God's, and it will rest on what we have made of our lives (or on what we have allowed him to make of them; see disc. on 1 Thess. 5:23). "Calling" (*klēsis*) generally refers to the initial act whereby God calls us to himself, but the question raised by this petition is, What sort of Christians have we now become? Have we "become mature, attaining to the whole measure of the fullness of Christ" (Eph. 4:13)? Have we, in terms of Paul's metaphor, built upon the foundation which is Christ (1 Cor. 3:11)? The fundamental question for Christians is: "Since everything will be destroyed . . . , what kind of people ought you to be? You ought to live holy and godly lives," says Peter, answering his own question, "as you look forward to the day" (2 Pet. 3:11f.). Paul agrees, hence this prayer for his readers. Most of the calls to holiness in the NT are made in the light of the coming judgment. For Christians this will not be a matter of life or death (they have already been acquitted on the capital charge—justified), but it will entail an assessment of how they have done and will have a bearing on their future glory (see disc. on 1 Thess. 2:4 for the judgment of those who believe, and on 1 Thess. 3:13 and 5:23 for the Parousia as an incentive to holiness; see further Williams, *Promise*, pp. 93–96). This prayer exhorts the Thessalonians to live lives worthy of their calling (cf. Eph. 4:1).

Second, Paul prays **that by** God's **power, he may fulfill every good purpose . . . and every act prompted by your faith**. Nothing in the Greek corresponds to **of yours** as found in NIV. It is possible then, that the good purpose is not the Thessalonians', but God's, as in Philippians 2:13. But NIV is probably correct in its interpretation. The expression is literally, "good pleasure of goodness." Morris notes that the noun "goodness" (*agathosynē*) is never used of God elsewhere in the NT, and Milligan adds that it would be more natural to have the article before "good pleasure" (*eudokia*), if Paul were referring to God's purpose. But even allowing that "every good purpose" is the Thessalonians', clearly the inspiration is God's, and so Paul looks to God to complete their good intentions along with "every act prompted by (their) faith" (lit. "a work of faith"; see disc. on 1 Thess. 1:3 and, for faith, on 1 Thess. 3:2).

1:12 / The section ends with a partial return to the thought of verse 10. The missionaries' prayer of the previous verse is to the end (*hopos*), says Paul, **that the name of our Lord Jesus may be glorified in you**. The **name** signifies the person; the purpose of their prayer, then, is that the Lord Jesus himself may be glorified by the holy and godly lives of his people. The difference between this and verse 10 is that, where the latter refers to the Parousia, this concerns (typically of the NT) the present. Even now, despite the restriction of a mortal body and a hostile environment (cf. Rom. 8:22f.; 1 John 3:2), enough should be seen of Christ in us to redound to his glory and, in a secondary sense, to our own: **and you in him** (—should be, but is it?). Paul intends, however, not to emphasize our glorification as such, but rather to disclose what is ours in Christ (cf. John 17:10, 21–23). The final phrase leaves no doubt where Paul's emphasis lies. Even if in a reflected sense we have a glory, there is no room for self-satisfaction, for all that we have is **according to the grace of our God and the Lord Jesus Christ**. The NIV marginal reading, "Our God and Lord, Jesus Christ," is possible in terms of the Greek, where the one definite article governs both "God" and "Lord," but it is unlikely in terms of Paul's style. The one article should be seen rather as drawing the two persons of the Godhead together in the grace that has saved us (see disc. on 1 Thess. 1:1 and 5:28, and for the titles Lord and Christ, the note on 1 Thess. 1:1).

Additional Notes §2

1:4 / **God's churches**: This phrase in 1 Thessalonians 2:14 concerned the churches of Judea that sprang up after the scattering of the members of the original church in Jerusalem. Primarily, the Jerusalem church is meant by "the church of God" in Paul's references to his persecution of the church in 1 Corinthians 15:9; Galatians 1:13; cf. Philippians 3:6. But now other "churches of God" existed, especially, from Paul's point of view, "the churches of the Gentiles" (Rom. 16:4). Thus, for example, the believers in Corinth constituted "the church of God in Corinth" (1 Cor. 1:2; 2 Cor. 1:1; cf. 1 Cor. 10:32; 11:22). The sum of such local churches constitutes "the churches of God" in the broadest sense, an entity that might also be referred to in the singular as simply "the church" (cf. Acts 9:31 where the daughter churches of Jerusalem are spoken of collectively as "the church throughout Judea, Galilee, and Samaria"; see also Eph. 1:22; 3:10, 21; 5:23ff.). The genitive in the phrase, the churches of God, marks their special nature. Just as they are "in God" (1 Thess. 1:1), so they belong to God. They are not merely assemblies of like-minded people, but are people "who are God's possession—to the praise of his glory" (Eph. 1:14). Moreover, the assemblies as such belong to God. That is, there is both an individual and a corporate relationship with him.

§3   *The Man of Lawlessness (2 Thess. 2:1–12)*

We come now to the heart of the letter, where Paul attempts to put right some wrong ideas about the Parousia (see Introduction). How Paul learned about the problem we are not told. In 3:11 he speaks of having heard a report that some in the church were idle. If this report were more recent than the one brought by Timothy, it might have included the issues dealt with in this section (see Introduction on The Sequence of the Letters). This is one of the most difficult passages of the NT to interpret, largely because it presupposes Paul's oral teaching (cf. v. 5 "don't you remember," v. 6 "you know"), which gave his Thessalonian readers the key to unlock its meaning. That key now being lost, his later readers must approach the passage with caution. Augustine's comment in *The City of God* is apposite:

> Since Paul said that they knew, he was unwilling to say this openly. And thus we, who do not know what they knew, desire and yet are unable even with effort to get at what the apostle meant, especially as the things which he adds makes his meaning obscure . . . I frankly confess I do not know what he means (20.19).

As in 1:5–10, we see that the author owes a debt to the language and style of the OT, especially in verses 3–4 and 8–12. This may be Paul himself or an earlier source. Bruce sees these verses as "part of the common stock of primitive Christian eschatology," while he regards the intervening and more prosaic verses 5–7 to be possibly Paul's own "contribution to the account of the rise and fall of Antichrist" (p. 163).

2:1 / The section begins with a plea couched in terms identical with those of 1 Thessalonians 5:12 and not unlike those of 4:1: **We ask you, brothers. . . .** In this instance, the plea is **concerning the coming of our Lord Jesus Christ and our being gathered to him**. The word translated **concerning** (*hyper*) usually means, "on behalf of," and if something of that usual meaning is retained here (and *hyper* is not simply the equivalent of *peri*), the sense may be, "on behalf of" or "in the interest of the truth concerning. . . ." The two nouns, **coming** (*parousia*, see disc. on 1 Thess. 2:19) and **being gathered** (*episynagogē*), are governed by the one article and are thus depicted as the one (complex) event. The gathering is that spoken of in 1 Thessalonians 4:17. Therefore, those who use this verse to make a distinction between the time of the so-called Rapture of the saints and the Parousia, do so in defiance of the syntax (see note on 1 Thess. 3:13). A single event comprises the return of Jesus (visibly, in glory, cf. 1:10) and the Rapture of the saints. The use of the full, formal title, **our Lord Jesus Christ** (see note on 1 Thess. 1:1), underlines the solemnity of the occasion.

2:2 / The construction *eis to* with the infinitive expresses both the content and the purpose of the plea (cf. 1 Thess. 2:12 and for the similar use of *hina*, 1 Thess. 4:1; 2 Thess. 1:11). They should not **become easily unsettled or alarmed. Unsettled** renders the Greek word *saleuō* which often describes the action of wind and wave, a restless tossing as of a ship, wind-blown and wave-tossed in a storm (for the same image differently expressed, see Eph. 4:14). The aorist tense of the infinitive conveys the idea of a sudden shock to which is added the qualifying phrase (not apparent in NIV), "from the mind" (*apo tou noos*), where "mind" indicates the mental balance of those concerned. Our expression, "to blow the mind," is akin to Paul's, who did not want the Thessalonians' minds blown "quickly," in the sense of hastily (NIV **easily**). J. B. Phillips' translation puts it this way: "Don't be thrown off your balance," which is apt, since balance is one thing that is needed in any discussion of the Parousia. Nor did Paul want them to be **alarmed** (*throeō*). Here the infinitive changes to the present tense to suggest a continuing state of agitation (cf. its similar use in an eschatological context in Mark 13:7).

Three things might unsettle or alarm the Thessalonians: **some prophecy, report or letter. Some prophecy** is literally, "through Spirit," meaning a revelation from the Spirit of God to which the prophet gives utterance. Paul himself encouraged prophecy in this church (1 Thess. 5:19f.), and "the Lord's own word" of 1 Thessalonians 4:15 may have been just such an utterance. But care had to be exercised. "Test everything" advised Paul (1 Thess. 5:21f.), especially, as in this case, where the prophecy related to the future. This sound advice applied no less to the **report** (*logos*), the non-prophetic utterance which might be a word of wisdom (as in 1 Cor. 12:8), or a word of authority (as in 2:15), or simply a report as we would understand it. As for the **letter**, the qualifying phrase (which could attach to all three nouns but is best taken with this alone) shows some uncertainty on Paul's part as to what exactly he was up against. The literal Greek, "as through us" (NIV, **supposed to have come from us**), is sufficiently vague that it could refer either to a genuine letter of Paul or to a forgery purporting to be from him. If to a genuine letter, it presumably means 1 Thessalonians, and the problem in that case becomes one of misunderstanding something Paul said, perhaps his warning about the unexpectedness of **the day of the Lord** (1 Thess. 5:1–11; for this term, see disc. and note on 1 Thess. 2:12; and for the title Lord, see the note on 1 Thess. 1:1). "Sudden" (see disc. on 1 Thess. 5:3) may somehow have become "soon" and soon "now," and so rumors spread that it had **already come** (*enestēken*, the perfect of *enistēmi*, is commonly employed to mean, "to be present as distinct from future"; cf. Rom. 8:38; 1 Cor. 3:22; 7:26; Gal. 1:4; Heb. 9:9, and see Moulton-Milligan). The combination in the Greek of the two conjunctions *hōs* and *hoti*, where either would have served on its own, "may here impart a subjective flavor to the clause thus introduced" (Bruce); as we would say, " . . . that the day of the Lord has *allegedly* come," the writer wishing to dissociate himself from the report. Clearly, the Lord had not returned visibly in the manner anticipated in 1 Thessalonians 4:16f., but his coming comprised a complex of events, and it is not beyond imagination that some in Thessalonica should think that the Day had begun (see note).

2:3–4 / **Don't let anyone deceive you in any way** sums up what has been said in the previous verses. Having made this plea, Paul intends to give an explanation, but, since all that he actually wrote is the conjunction **for** (*hoti*), the rest of the clause must be understood as indicated by the brackets in NIV: [**that day will not come**]. The missing clause forms the apodosis of a conditional sentence of which the protasis is **until**, *ean mē*, "if not," "except," **the rebellion occurs** (v. 3) to which the Greek adds "first," i.e., first the rebellion comes and then the day of the Lord. The definite article marks the rebellion as something known to Paul's readers, no doubt from his teaching when he was with them. Without the benefit of that teaching, we can only guess at what the rebellion might be. The word *apostasia*, **rebellion**, is frequently used in a political sense in LXX (e.g., Josh. 22:22; 2 Chron. 29:19; Jer. 2:19; cf. also Josephus, *Life* 43); but in Acts 21:21, the only other occurrence of the word in the NT, it indicates rebellion of a different sort: apostasy from God. In the light of verse 4, this is certainly Paul's meaning here, but the apostasy may have a political expression, so that the other meaning should not be ruled out altogether (since the "governing authorities" are divinely appointed, Rom. 13:1, there is no clear distinction between rebellion and apostasy). At all events, in common with other NT writers and like Jesus himself (Matt. 24:10–13), Paul envisages a final upsurge of evil before the end of the age, heralding the onset of the end. Some have understood the *apostasia* as a falling away within the church, but the word expresses not so much apathy as deliberate opposition, and it is better to see this as a reference to events outside the church which, however, will profoundly affect the church. The rebellion will be the church's "great tribulation" (Rev. 7:14).

Associated with it will be **the man of lawlessness** (*anomia*). The texts vary between this phrase and "the man of sin" (*hamartia*), but the meaning is the same. Sin is essentially lawlessness with regard to God (cf. 1 John 3:4). The phrase **the man of lawlessness**, with the genitive used adjectivally in the semitic manner (see disc. on 1:7), characterizes him in terms of his opposition to God (see further disc. on 2:4). E. Nestle, "2 Thess. 2:3," *ExpT* 16 (1904–5), pp. 472–73, notes that the name translates the OT phrase, "man of Belial." Who or what he is, we cannot say. He might be an individual or a group, a government or an institution. He is called the Beast in Revelation 13, but he is more commonly referred to as the Antichrist. He is not Satan, for he is distinguished from him in verse 9, but he is his instrument imbued with the spirit of Satan. Paul describes him as being **revealed**, *apokalyptō*. This suggests that he exists beforehand (cf. 1:7 for the revelation of Christ) but perhaps only in the sense that he will be the final manifestation of a principle that has always been operative and was active when Paul was writing: namely, that of rebellion against God (see 2:7, cf. 1 John 2:18).

The **man of lawlessness** is further characterized as "the son of destruction" (for the semitic idiom see disc. on 1 Thess. 5:5), NIV **the man doomed to destruction** (the same phrase is used of Judas Iscariot in John 17:12), and "the one opposing (God) and exalting himself." In the Greek, this phrase comprises two participles, each in the present tense expressing what is characteristic to him. The first, *antikeimenos*, is used in LXX 1 Kings 11:23 to render the Hebrew *satan*, "adversary." This may be compared with 1 Timothy 5:14 where *ho antikeimenos* is the ultimate adversary, Satan himself. The description of the man of lawlessness in these terms shows with whose spirit he will be imbued (cf. 2:9). **He will oppose and will exalt himself over everything that is called God**, the sense being "over every so-called god," and over everything that **is worshiped**, where the Greek, *sebasma*, is a comprehensive term denoting any object of worship (Acts 17:23). In short, the man of lawlessness will attempt to usurp the place of every claimant upon us, including the true God and his legitimate claims. This usurpation results (Greek, *hōste*) in the man of lawlessness' self-exaltation. He is described in the language of the OT as setting **himself up in God's temple**, not literally, but in a figure. But this is not a figure of the church, which is sometimes called the temple (cf. 1 Cor. 3:16; Eph. 2:21). He also is **proclaiming himself** (*apodeiknymi* can have this sense) **to be God** (v. 4; cf. Isa. 14:13f.; Ezek. 28:2; Dan. 7:25; 8:9–12; 11:36–39). **Temple** is *naos*, denoting the Holy of Holies, the inner sanctum of the temple in Jerusalem (in contrast with *hieron*, which embraced the whole temple precinct) in which it was believed that God dwelled (cf. 1 Sam. 4:4; Ps. 80:1; 99:1). The man of lawlessness will attempt to put himself in the place of God and to usurp the prerogatives of the true God. Earlier Jesus had drawn on the same OT passages to describe the desecration of the temple that would pre-figure the End (see Mark 13:14 where the masculine participle suggests that a person is meant; cf. also Matt. 24:15). In this connection, the unsuccessful attempt of the emperor Gaius (Caligula) in A.D. 40 to have his statue erected in the temple comes to mind as it must have to Paul's as he wrote. But Jesus' reference was to that "desecration" which would be the temple's destruction and which in fact took place under Titus in A.D. 70. It is noteworthy, however, that for him, as for Paul in describing the End itself, the temple as the symbol of God's presence was thought of also (symbolically) as the locus of the Antichrist's opposition to God.

2:5 / At this point Paul calls up memories of his earlier teaching to flesh out the bare bones of these verses. **Don't you**

remember that when I was with you I used to tell you these things? Notice his use of the first person. As in 1 Thessalonians 5:27, this may suggest a more personal note as he recollects his own role as distinct from that of his companions. The imperfect tense, *elegon*, implies that he had often told the Thessalonians about the matters to which he now refers (reinforcing the view that he was in Thessalonica for much longer than the three Sabbath days of Acts 17; see Introduction on The Founding of the Church).

2:6–7 / Still speaking of the man of lawlessness, Paul adds, **and now you know what is holding him back.** NIV is an improvement on RSV which says, "and you know what is restraining him now," suggesting that the adverb, **now,** qualifies the participle, "restraining." That is highly unlikely given the position of the words. But it remains uncertain how we should understand the **now.** Is it logical, marking the next step in the discussion (as e.g., Acts 3:17)? Or is it strictly temporal, giving the sense, "as concerning the present"? The latter is the more likely.

With the words, **you know what is holding him back,** we are reminded that they did know and that we do not. We can only guess at Paul's meaning. **What is holding him back** translates the neuter participle of the verb *katechō*, meaning (1) "to hold fast" (cf., e.g., 1 Thess. 5:21), (2) "to hold back" (cf. Philem. 13), or (3) "to hold sway" (if intransitive). NIV adopts the second sense, the consensus view. With the participle being neuter, Paul appears to be saying that some *thing* is restraining the man of lawlessness. But we find that in the next verse the participle changes to masculine, so that in verse 7, he appears to be saying that the restraint is embodied in a person: **the one who now holds** (him) **back.** Who this is remains one of the most difficult questions of the entire Pauline corpus.

Some think that God—and more specifically, the Holy Spirit—is in view (see D. Farrow, "Showdown: The Message of Second Thessalonians 2:1–12 and the Riddle of the 'Restrainer,' " *Crux* 25 [1, 1989], pp. 23–6). In Greek, spirit is neuter (*pneuma*), but in Scripture the Holy Spirit is often spoken of as a person, and this might account, they say, for the change in the participle from the neuter to the masculine. But it is difficult to see in what sense the Holy Spirit would be **taken out of the way.** Some advocates of this interpretation say that this would be the case in the

Rapture, but we have already seen that there is nothing to commend the theory of a rapture prior to the coming of the Lord (see disc. on 2:1 and note on 1 Thess. 3:13). Oscar Cullmann saw a reference to Paul's missionary preaching in this passage. According to Cullmann the apostle believed that "before the End the gospel must first be preached to all nations" (Mark 13:10) and that he (Paul) was largely responsible for preaching it. Until he had fulfilled that responsibility, the End would not come. Paul's mission, therefore, was the restraining principle and he himself "the one who now holds back" the man of lawlessness (*Christ and Time* [London: SCM, 1951], p. 164). Not many have accepted his interpretation; nothing in the letter suggests that Paul saw himself and his mission in those terms.

One widely held view is that the principle was the Roman Empire and the person was the emperor. This view fits well with Pauline theology. In Romans 13:3f., Paul states that the emperor ("the one in authority") is "God's servant to do you good." God appointed him to preserve law and order. The antithesis of this is the lawlessness of 2 Thessalonians 2:4 in which the human authority (the man of lawlessness) "sets himself up in God's temple, proclaiming himself to be God" instead of functioning as the servant of God (Paul was writing in the relatively good years of Claudius' reign, A.D. 41–54). But the empire and the emperors have long since gone and, as far as we can tell, still the man of lawlessness has not come. It may be better then to understand **what is holding him back** as the principle of law and order, of which Roman rule was but one instance and of which there have been many others (cf., e.g., Gal. 3:19, 24), and "the one who restrains him" as the human authority that in any particular place and time embodies that principle: when Paul was writing, the Emperor Claudius; in our day, the president or the prime minister and his or her administration.

Whoever or whatever is holding back the man of lawlessness, this restraint is **that he may be revealed at the proper time**. The construction *eis to*, in this instance, is sometimes translated "until." But its usual sense of purpose should be retained as in NIV (see disc. on 1 Thess. 2:12). The purpose is God's, to which both the man of lawlessness and the restraining power are subject. **The proper time** is literally "his own (the man of lawlessness') time," in the sense that it is the time set by God for him to be revealed. Meanwhile (and this is given as an explanation of the statement of v. 7, **for,** *gar*), **the secret power** (*mystērion,* "mystery") **of lawlessness is already at work**. In the NT, "mystery" most often refers to the *revealed* purpose of God—what we could not find out for ourselves, a "mystery" in that sense, but what God has chosen to make known—and to the fulfilment of that purpose in Christ (cf. Mark 4:11; Rom. 11:25; 16:25; 1 Cor. 15:51; Eph. 1:9; 3:3f.; Col. 1:26; 2:2 and such phrases as "the mystery of the faith," 1 Tim. 3:9, and "the mystery of godliness," 1 Tim. 3:16). Thus "the mystery of lawlessness" may be what God has revealed of the matter, with a hint that even lawlessness comes within the ambit of his purpose. At all events, while we await the revelation of the man of lawlessness, the spirit of opposition to God which he will embody is already at work in the world (1 John 2:18), but it is restrained until such time as the restrainer is taken out of the way.

2:8 / **And then the lawless one will be revealed**. This is the third time that Paul has spoken in these terms (cf. vv. 3, 6). The expression **the lawless one** (*ho anomos*) now replaces "the man of lawlessness," but the same person is meant. Paul gives no details beyond what is said (2:4) concerning his activities or concerning how long he will be active. From the revelation of the lawless one, Paul moves at once to speak about his destruction; he does this not in a separate statement, but as a further description of him, as though he is characteristically the one **whom the Lord Jesus will overthrow** (for the title Lord, see note on 1 Thess. 1:1). The sovereignty of God is again to the fore in this verse, while its language is largely dependent on LXX Isaiah 11:4. The verb rendered **overthrow** (*anaireō*) is a particularly strong one, "annihilate," and the qualifying phrase, **with the breath of his mouth**, only here in the NT, underlines the ease of his annihilation—the Lord Jesus will utterly destroy him. As Luther poses it in A Mighty Fortress Is Our God, "A word shall quickly slay him." Parallel with this and forming with it one clause descriptive of the lawless one is the statement that the Lord will destroy him **by the splendor of his coming** (see disc. on 1 Thess. 2:19 for *parousia*). Taken in isolation, **destroy** might be regarded as an over-translation of the verb *katartizō*. "To render inoperative" is more the sense, and the suggestion has been made that Paul was now backing off from the first statement. The lawless one would not be annihilated but made powerless. The difficulty lies in knowing how precisely Paul was using these words, but the parallelism with *anaireō* is probably decisive in accepting **destroy**. So **the splendor of his** (Jesus') **coming** marks the end of the lawless one and of the evil that he represents. It cannot stand in the presence of the Lord. Two words are employed in this phrase, *epiphaneia* and *parousia*. When used alone, each signifies his coming, but in combination they are best expressed as in NIV. *Epiphaneia* often carries with it the idea of splendor (used of Jesus' second coming in 1 Tim. 6:14; 2 Tim. 4:1, 8; Titus 2:13 and of his first in 2 Tim. 1:10).

2:9 / In the Greek, a second relative clause continues the description of the lawless one with a reference again to his revelation, but now in terms of his *parousia*. As Jesus has a *parousia*, so does he. The same word is used and, indeed, the whole description of his coming is something of a parody of Christ's, reminding us of his warning that "false Christs and false prophets will appear and perform signs (*sēmeia*) and miracles (*terata*) to deceive the elect—if that were possible" (Mark 13:22; cf. also 2:5f.). **The coming of the lawless one will be in accordance with the work of Satan** (cf. Rev. 13:2). *Energia*, translated **work**, denotes "operative power" as distinct from *dynamis*, "potential power." In the man of lawlessness, the power of Satan will be seen at work, **displayed in all kinds of counterfeit miracles, signs (*sēmeia*) and wonders** (*terata*). NIV reads *dynamei* as a plural, **miracles**, in line with signs and wonders, but the word is singular with the adjective "all" attached to it. "With all power" would be a better translation. We cannot be certain whether all three nouns (power, signs, and wonders) are qualified by the adjectival genitive, "of falsehood," *pseudous* (see disc. on 1:7). *Pseudous* follows the third noun, but NIV may be correct in applying it to all three. The distinction in number between the first (singular) and the other two (plural), which sets them apart to some extent, might suggest, however, that *pseudous* should be restricted to signs and wonders, i.e., the work of Satan will be seen in the lawless one "with all power and with counterfeit signs and wonders." The same three nouns—miracles, signs, and wonders—are used both of the work of Jesus in Acts 2:22, showing him to be "a man accredited by God," and of the work of his followers (cf. Acts 2:43; Gal. 3:5; Heb. 2:4). Similarly, the signs and wonders of the man of lawlessness mark him as the agent of "the father of lies" (John 8:44; for Satan's activity see disc. on 1 Thess. 2:18).

2:10 / Continuing this thought, Paul adds that Satan's work will also be seen **in every sort of evil that deceives** (lit. "every deceit of evil," another adjectival genitive in which *adikia* is a most comprehensive term indicating evil of every kind; for the construction see disc. on 1:7). Earlier, Jesus had spoken of false Christs and false prophets attempting to deceive the elect, but here it is not the elect who are led astray but **those who are perishing**, whose unbelief already makes them Satan's pawns. The present (passive) participle, *tois apollymenois* (as in 1 Cor. 1:18; 2 Cor. 2:15; 4:3), is particularly vivid. They are in the process of perishing (cf. 1:8f.).

They perish, Paul explains, switching attention from the deceiver to the deceived, **because** (*anth' hōn*, a form used elsewhere in the NT only by Luke [Luke 1:20; 12:3; 19:44; Acts 12:23]) **they refused to love the truth and so be saved**, literally, "did not receive the love of the truth" (a most unusual expression; there is nothing like it elsewhere in the Greek Bible). The truth is the truth of the gospel (cf. 2:12f. and see disc. on 1 Thess. 1:8) with its focus on the person and work of Christ ("I am . . . the truth," John 14:6). Thus **to love the truth** is a way of expressing one's attitude to him. Being saved insofar as we are concerned is a matter of relating to the Savior. These people had the opportunity of doing so. The verb *dechomai* means to receive what is offered (and, indeed, to receive it gladly; see disc. on 1 Thess. 2:13). But they let the opportunity go by and gave him no welcome.

2:11–12 / **For this reason** looks back to the previous verse. Because they refuse to love the truth, those who are perishing consign themselves and are consigned to their fate. Certain spiritual laws of cause and effect come into play (cf. Rom. 6:23), and yet it would be wrong to think of this as something impersonal. Of those whose choice was other than the truth, three times in the opening chapter of Romans Paul declares that "God gave them over" to what they had chosen (Rom. 1:24, 26, 28 and see disc. on 1 Thess. 1:10 and 5:9 for the wrath of God). So here, **God sends them a powerful delusion** (lit. "a working of delusion," *energeion planēs;* see disc. on 2:9). But such a statement presents us with a difficulty. Can it be true of God that he deludes? In discussing a passage like this, we must recognize that the biblical writers were far less concerned with secondary causes than we are. Such was their belief in the sovereignty of God that they attributed to him directly, rather than to their actual source, a range of activities which, being true to his nature, he could not have done. But being God he could turn them to his purpose (e.g., the lying spirits in the mouths of false prophets, 1 Kings 22:23; Ezek. 14:9; cf. esp. 1 Chron. 21:1 with 2 Sam. 24:1 where the same action is attributed to Satan as to God). God does not delude. Much less does he do so, **so that they will believe the lie** (see disc. on 1 Thess. 2:12 for *eis* with the infinitive expressing purpose). Notice the definite article, "the lie"—the denial of *the* truth. Such denial is the work of Satan who blinds "the minds of unbelievers, so that they cannot see the light of the gospel of the glory of Christ" (2 Cor. 4:4). But God is sovereign and even this serves his purpose (*hina*) to condemn all **who have not believed the truth** (cf. 2:10, 13 and see disc. on 2 Thess. 1:8) **but have delighted in wickedness**. The juxtaposition of ideas in this description is significant. Not to believe the truth (the construction with the dative, used nowhere else by Paul except in quotations, means "to give credence to," "to express as true"), to say nothing of loving the one in whom that truth is embodied (see disc. on 2:10), has moral consequences (cf. Rom. 2:8; 1 Cor. 13:6). The verb *eudokeō* means "to give consent to," "to delight in." Those who do not believe, delight in *adikia*, every kind of evil.

Additional Notes §3

2:2 / **Saying that the day of the Lord has already come**: As explained above, common usage supports NIV's rendering of *enestēken*, **has already come** (cf. RV "is now present," RSV "has come," NEB "is already here"), but because of the difficulty that it creates (i.e., in what sense could the Thessalonians have thought that it was present?) a number of versions have shied away from the common usage and have opted instead for the idea of imminence: cf., "the day of Christ is at hand" (AV); "the day of the Lord is just at hand" (ASV). R. D. Aus, for example, in "The Relevance of Isaiah 66:7 to Revelation 12 and 2 Thessalonians 1," *ZNW* 67 (1976), pp. 252–68, accepts this interpretation of the word, suggesting that the severity of the persecution that they were suffering may have led the Thessalonians to think that these days were the eschatological "birth pains" and that the End was near (cf. Mark 13:8; also Eusebius, *Eccl. Hist.* 6.7, for a similar belief for the same reason at a later date). But Paul makes no mention of persecution as a possible cause of their being **unsettled or alarmed**.

Following NIV and other versions in taking *enestēken* to mean **has already come**, some suggest that the Thessalonians, or at least a group within the Thessalonian church, had concluded (under the influence of new teachers) that the kingdom of God in its final form had fully come (realized eschatology). See, e.g., E. von Dobschütz, *Die Thessalonicher— Briefe* (Göttingen: Vandenhoeck & Ruprecht, 1909), pp. 179–82, and more recently, C. L. Mearns, "Early Eschatological Development in Paul: The Evidence of 1 and 2 Thessalonians," *NTS* 27 (1980–81), pp. 147–48. As von Dobschütz formulated his thesis, he rejected the possibility that this group had reinterpreted the events of the Parousia in a gnostic sense similar to the false teachers in the Pastoral Epistles who claimed that the resurrection was past (p. 267, cf. 2 Tim. 2:18). But what he rejected became the basis of the work of W. Lütgert, who claimed that an early Jewish Christian form of Gnosticism was present in a number of Pauline churches including the church at Thessalonica (*Die Vollkommenen im Philipperbrief und die Enthusiasten in Thessalonich* [Gütersloh: C. Bertelsman, 1909], pp. 547–654). Schmithals and Robert Jewett, "Enthusiastic Radicalism and the Thessalonian Correspondence," *SBL Seminar Papers* 1 (1972), pp. 181–232, both are to a greater or lesser degree influenced by Lütgert and accept his, and indeed von Dobschütz's, view that Paul was responding to a group within the church who espoused a realized eschatology (see Introduction on The Writing of 1 Thessalonians). But when we look at what Paul himself says, while there is no disputing that the idea of a realized eschatology was in the air, as far as his readers were concerned that was not the problem. The problem for them was what to make of such an idea in the light of their own firmly held belief in a future eschatology, i.e., that there was something still to come (reflected, e.g., in the presuppositions of the teaching in 1 Thess. 4:13–18). The only firm data that we have to work with are the letters themselves, and Bruce suggests (p. 166) that all we can draw from the letters is that

> Paul and his colleagues, who knew more about their converts' problems than the exegete of today can know, judged that it would help them to be told something about the sequence of events leading up to the Day of the Lord. They had been taught about the actual events, but they needed to have them set in their chronological relationship.

§4 Stand Firm (2 Thess. 2:13–17)

With relief, Paul turns from discussing the delusion of those who are perishing to give thanks again for those who are being saved. The structure of this thanksgiving is almost identical with that of the introductory thanksgiving of this and other letters. So much so, indeed, that some suggest that this could be the remnant of another epistle that has been incorporated into this (see Schmithals, pp. 193f.). Nothing can be proven, of course, and it is better therefore to regard these verses as simply resuming the earlier thanksgiving (1:3f.) in much the same way as 1 Thessalonians 2:13 takes up again the introductory thanksgiving of that letter. In the closing verses of this section (vv. 16–17), thanksgiving turns to petition (another so-called wish-prayer, see disc. on 1 Thess. 3:11–13), with Paul praying that God, Father and Son, would encourage and strengthen the Thessalonians.

2:13 / To begin with, the wording is almost identical with 1:3 (see comment on that verse), expressing the obligation that the missionaries felt **always to thank God** for the Thessalonians. The use of the emphatic pronoun (not in 1:3) and the placing of the verb in a more emphatic position than in 1:3 may be a way of underlining just how strongly this obligation was felt. Again the Thessalonians are affectionately addressed as **brothers** (cf. 1:3 and see disc. on 1:3–12 and on 1 Thess. 1:4) and described as **loved by the Lord**. Since the Father is twice referred to in this verse as **God, the Lord** is probably Jesus (see note on 1 Thess. 1:1), in which case all three persons of the Trinity are mentioned in this verse (as in Matt. 28:19; 1 Cor. 12:4–6; 2 Cor. 13:14; Eph. 4:4–6; 1 Pet. 1:2; Jude 20f. and possibly Acts 20:28). The perfect participle **loved** is the same as in 1 Thessalonians 1:4 and again carries the assurance that the love once shown them in Christ—the love which was the mainspring of their salvation—continues to enfold them, come what may—even the lawless one!

They give thanks **because from the beginning God chose you**. This is the only instance in the NT of the use of the simple verb *haireō* (in the middle voice) of God's choice. It is used, however, in the OT (LXX Deut. 26:18), and, in any case, the idea, whether expressed by compounds of this verb (Gal. 1:4; cf. Deut. 7:6f.; 10:15) or by other means (e.g., 1 Thess. 1:4; Eph. 1:4), is a familiar one linked always with the idea of grace. For his choice is made not on the basis of human merit but according to God's own purposes. A textual problem arises with the phrase, **from the beginning**. NIV accepts the well-attested reading *ap' archēs*, which expresses the idea found elsewhere, for example in Ephesians 1:4, that God "chose us in (Christ) before the creation of the world" (cf. Matt. 19:4; 1 John 2:13). But the alternative reading, *aparchēn*, "first-fruits," is as well if not better attested (see NIV marg. "God chose you as his firstfruits"). On this reading, the most likely meaning would be that Paul saw the Thessalonians as only the beginning—an intimation—of a harvest which was yet to be gathered. Two phrases follow which further qualify this statement. The first expresses his objective: **God chose you** "for salvation" (*eis sōtērian*). This term embraces the whole work of God in Christ on our behalf: past, present, and future (see disc. on 1 Thess. 5:8f.). The second states the means of that salvation (understanding *en* as instrumental, NIV **through**) but only with reference to its application to the believer (see disc. on 2:14 for its publication). No mention is made here of Christ's work (see disc. on 1 Thess. 5:10) but only of the Spirit's work in the hearts of men and women. God chose you—made you his choice—through **the sanctifying work of the Spirit and through belief in the truth** (lit. "by faith in truth," *pistei alētheinas*; see disc. on 1 Thess. 3:2). Some exegetes see in this a reference to the human spirit— "through the sanctification of the whole person, body and spirit." It is far more likely, however, that Paul is speaking of the work of God's Spirit. The thought expressed in *hagiasmos* is primarily of believers being set apart for God, made "saints," *hagioi*, in the NT sense of that word, rather of their being sanctified in the ethical sense, made worthy of their status (see disc. on 1 Thess. 4:3, 4, 7). **Belief in the truth** is in the truth of the gospel (see disc. on 1 Thess. 1:8), as in verses 10 and 12, and in direct contrast with the people described in those verses who do not believe. This verse summarizes the process by which we become Christians. There is the sovereign, gracious choice of God; there is the Spirit's action which makes effective to us the work of Christ; and there is our response of faith in welcoming that work and clearing the way for God's Spirit to act upon us.

2:14 / In verse 13 Paul spoke of God's purpose—"he chose you." In this verse he speaks of the execution of that purpose—**he called you**, where the aorist tense looks back to the time when the missionaries first visited Thessalonica and the call of God was heard in what they said (cf. 1 Thess. 4:7 for another aorist of this verb and 1 Thess. 2:12, 5:24 for the present tense). **To this** refers to the matter of the previous verse, which can be summed up as salvation "by grace . . . through faith" (Eph. 2:8). The means of that salvation (*dia* with the gen.), in terms of making it known to those for whom it was intended, was **through our gospel**, i.e., the gospel given to Paul and his companions to preach. It was, of course, "the gospel of our Lord Jesus" as far as its content was concerned, and in terms of its origin, the gospel of God (see disc. on 1 Thess. 1:5). Earlier, God's objective in making his choice was "for salvation" (2:13). Here that same goal is in terms of "obtaining" **the glory of our Lord Jesus Christ** (*eis peripoiēsin doxēs;* see disc. on 1 Thess. 5:9 and note for "obtaining" and 1 Thess. 2:12 for **glory**; for the titles **Lord** and **Christ** see note on 1 Thess. 1:1). In part, that glory was manifested (John 1:14, cf. also 2 Cor. 4:4, 6), but its complete unveiling awaits Christ's return (2 Thess. 1:10). At his return, our own salvation will be complete; in Christ we are already God's children, "but we know that when he appears, we shall be like him, for we shall see him as he is" (1 John 3:2).

2:15 / **So then, brothers**, repeats Paul's affectionate address (see disc. on 1 Thess. 1:4) and introduces his earnest entreaty: Since God loves you, and since he has chosen you and called you that you might be included in his purpose, and since that purpose cannot fail, **stand firm and hold to the teachings**. Their stand so far greatly encouraged the missionaries (1 Thess. 3:8), and Paul wanted nothing more than that they should continue to stand firm, whatever the present or the future might hold for them. One way of doing so was to hold to the teachings. We should regard the two exhortations of this verse as effectively one, expressing the end and the means to that end and reminding us of what we may have forgotten: the importance of Christian education. With so little teaching evident in our churches, little wonder that our Christian stance is so shaky. **The teachings** are "the traditions" (*paradosis*, pl. *paradoseis*; cf. 3:6 and see note on 1 Thess. 2:13), and the importance of this word is not only that it points to a body of Christian teaching that was passed on by one generation to another (cf. 1 Cor. 11:23; 15:3) but that this teaching is authoritative for the church and stands above the teacher (cf. 1 Thess. 5:19–22). "The prominent idea of *paradosis* . . . is that of an authority external to the teacher" (Lightfoot; see also O. Cullmann, "The Tradition," in *The Early Church*, ed. A. J. B. Higgins [London: SCM Press, 1956], pp. 66-75). In this case authority concerns the divine authority behind Christian *paradosis*. The tradition originated in the teaching of Jesus. This is another way of expressing the truth of 1 Thessalonians 2:13 that the gospel is the word of God. The missionaries **passed** these teachings **on to** the Thessalonians **by word of mouth** and more recently **by letter**. The aorist tense of *edidachthēte* (the traditions that "you were taught") suggests that, insofar as the reference is to a letter, it is 1 Thessalonians. The pronoun, *hēmōn*, "our," not apparent in NIV, qualifies both **word** and **letter**. God's word is spoken with a human voice.

2:16–17 / Thanksgiving turns to petition in these verses, and the pattern of the first epistle is repeated, with Paul bringing the main body of the letter to a close in this fashion (cf. 1 Thess. 3:11ff.). The petition is addressed to God, Father and Son, the Son being named first, **our Lord Jesus Christ himself and God our Father** (cf. 2 Cor. 13:14). For the emphatic pronoun **himself** (*autos*), see the discussion on 1 Thessalonians 3:11, and for the titles of **Jesus** and the description of God as **Father**, see the notes on 1 Thessalonians 1:1. In the prayer of 1 Thessalonians 3:11, the Father is addressed before the Lord Jesus, but either way it is clear that the two were seen as one. The order in which they are named is determined solely by the context. In this instance Paul is speaking of our Lord Jesus Christ (2:14) and therefore Jesus is addressed before the Father. William Neil comments, "The only theological significance to be attached to the variations in order is that there is complete equality in the apostle's mind between the Father and the Son. It is only through his knowledge of Christ that he has come really to know God. For him they are One" (*The Epistles of Paul to the Thessalonians* [London: Hodder & Stoughton, 1950], p. 185). The singular verbs that follow (v. 17) may reinforce this notion that the two are one, but again see the discussion on 1 Thessalonians 3:11.

The subsequent twofold description could apply to both the Father and the Son, although it reads more naturally as concerning only the Father. But, in any case, it speaks of what the Father has done for us in Christ. The description comprises two participles each in the aorist tense, sharing the one definite article. NIV translates as follows: **who loved us and by his grace** (see disc. on 1 Thess. 1:1 and 5:28) **gave us eternal encouragement and good hope**. The tense looks back to the manifestation of God's love and grace in Christ. Especially in the cross of Christ, God's love and grace resulted in **encouragement** or "comfort" (*paraklēsis*; see disc. on 1 Thess. 3:2; cf. Rom. 15:5; 2 Cor. 1:3), i.e., in giving us every reason for confidence before God. The adjective extends that benefit beyond this time into eternity. This leads Paul to add **good hope** (cf. Rom. 15:4), where the thought is of our eternal relationship with God (for **hope**, see disc. on 1 Thess. 1:3).

In that confidence, Paul prays: May God, Son and Father, **encourage your hearts** (*parakaleō*, the verb corresponding to the noun of the previous verse; see disc. on 1 Thess. 3:2 for the verb and 1 Thess. 2:4 for **heart**), **and strengthen you** (*stērizō*, see also disc. on 1 Thess. 3:2) **in every good deed and word**. The repetition of **good** from verse 16 adds a certain emphasis to the word and underscores what Paul is saying in this prayer (for **good work**, *ergon agathon*, cf. Rom. 2:7; 2 Cor. 9:8; Eph. 2:10; Phil. 1:6; Col. 1:10; 1 Tim. 2:10; 5:10; 2 Tim. 2:21; 3:17; Titus 1:16; 3:1; and for the collocation of work and word, cf. Luke 24:19; Acts 7:22). This prayer reminds us that what we are by God's grace is what, increasingly, we should be in word and deed. And the fact that, for Paul, this is a matter of prayer, reminds us of where our help lies to this end.

Additional Notes   §4

2:15 / **The teachings we passed on to you, whether by word of mouth or by letter**: The *eite . . . eite*, **whether . . . or,** of this verse recalls the repeated *mēte* of verse 2. But because there is no reference to the Spirit here as there is in that verse, Schmithals thinks that Paul has Gnosticism in his sights. The Spirit was commonly appealed to as the source of gnostic teaching and, consequently, reference to the Spirit is avoided. Instead, Paul appeals to **the teachings**. Such appeal is never made, says Schmithals, to *didachē* or *paradosis* in Pauline writings "in any context other than the anti-Gnostic battlefront" (p. 209). See Introduction on The Writing of 1 Thessalonians and note on 2 Thessalonians 2:2 for our rejection of the thesis that Gnosticism had infiltrated the church in Thessalonica.

§5 Request for Prayer (2 Thess. 3:1–5)

As in 1 Thessalonians 5:25, Paul closes the letter by asking for prayer for himself and his colleagues (having just prayed for the Thessalonians, 2:16f.). The two passages show a similar structure, with the same verb, the same vocative **brothers**, and the same prepositional phrase **for us** (*peri hēmōn*). In this case, however, unlike 1 Thessalonians 5:25, their particular needs are stated. But the focus of the passage soon shifts from the human weakness expressed in Paul's "standing in the need of prayer" to divine strength, and from their own needs to the needs of others. Surely, this marks true followers of Christ; like their Lord, they are so sure of God and so free from preoccupation with their own wants, that their energies flow naturally towards others and their needs—especially God's people. Verse 5 takes the form of a wish-prayer (see disc. on 1 Thess. 3:6–13).

3:1–2 / **Finally** (*to loipon*, see disc. on 1 Thess. 4:1) signals the nearness of the end of the letter, although this does not prevent Paul from touching on other matters. It means only that he has dealt with what he regards as the most important matter of the letter (see disc. on 1 Thess. 5:25 for both the tense of the verb, *proseuchomai*, "to pray," and the address, **brothers**). He requests prayer first that **the message of the Lord may spread rapidly and be honored**. **The message** is literally "the word" and signifies the gospel of which God is the author—the **Lord** of this reference (see disc. on 1 Thess. 1:5 and 8, and note on 1 Thess. 1:1). Paul characteristically requests prayer for the progress of the gospel (cf. Eph. 6:19f.; Col. 4:3f.), expressed here in terms of its "running" (so the Greek, *trechō*). The idea goes back to Psalm 147:15 where God's word "runs swiftly" (cf. Ps. 19:4f.), but the metaphor would have appealed to Paul as one who often drew on the images of the Greek games to make his point (cf. 1 Cor. 9:24; Gal. 2:2; Phil. 2:16 for reference to himself as running). The notion that the word almost has a life of its own such that it could "run" through the world is reminiscent of Acts 18:5, where Paul is said to have been "seized by the word" (so the Greek). It implies a certain independence of the message; in another sense, however, it is dependent on the messenger to be heard (see disc. on 1 Thess. 1:8 for the gospel "sounding out" like a trumpet call). Perhaps the games are still in mind, with reference now to the spectators and their appreciation of a race well run, when he states as the second objective of this prayer that the message should **be honored** (*doxazō*). In effect, this is a prayer for the people involved with the word, for in large measure, it will be honored only as it is reflected in the lives of those who preach it and hear it (cf. Acts 13:48). It was so honored by the Thessalonians, although it is not clear from the Greek, which lacks a verb (NIV has supplied **was**), whether Paul's reference is to the past—to the time when the missionaries first preached the message in Thessalonica, as NIV implies—or to the present. The absence of the verb may be deliberate to allow for both (but cf. 2:5 and 1 Thess. 1:5ff.; 2:1, 13 where he does look back to the Thessalonians' reception of the gospel when they were there).

Paul's second prayer request is for himself and his colleagues that **we may be delivered from wicked and evil men**. For the verb *rhyomai*, see the discussion on 1 Thessalonians 1:10 and for a similar reference to the dangers that he faced, cf. Romans 15:31. He was writing from Corinth (as we suppose; see Introduction on The Authenticity of 1 Thessalonians) where, clearly, he was facing many difficulties of which Acts tells us little. But what little it does tell may be taken as typical. This would suggest that Paul's greatest danger was from the Jews (cf. Acts 18:12f.). His use of the definite article suggests that he had in mind a particular group of people such as the Jews. He wanted deliverance from *the* **wicked and evil men**. Moreover, the tense of the verb (aorist) may point to a particular need for deliverance, such as the one referred to in Acts. The word translated **wicked** (*atopos*) means literally "out of place," hence "improper," and then the sense that we have here. This passage is the only place in the NT where it is used of people. Elsewhere it describes things (Luke 23:41; Acts 25:5; 28:6). The second adjective, *ponēros*, describes those who not simply acquiesce in evil, but actively pursue it. If the reference is to the Jews, it is not, of course, to the Jews per se, but to them as those who oppose the gospel, hindering it in running its course into all the world. This thought leads to the general observation that **not everyone has faith**—the Jews (if the earlier reference was to them) are not on their own in opposing the gospel. It is not clear in what sense **faith** should be understood, whether subjectively as trust, or objectively as the body of teaching (see disc. on 1 Thess. 3:2). The use of the definite article (in the Greek but not evident in NIV) would suggest the latter, but the idea of trust fits more easily with the next verse— "not everyone trusts the Lord, but the Lord is trustworthy." In any case, it is only a fine line between faith and the faith. The general sense is plain enough: not everyone accepts the Christian position.

3:3 / From commenting on human unbelief, Paul turns to exalt God's faithfulness—we understand **the Lord** of this passage to be God the Father (see note on 1 Thess. 1:1). Like the related noun, *pistis*, the last word of the previous sentence in the Greek text, *pistos*, the first word of this sentence, has more than one meaning. It is **faithful**, either in the active sense of "believing," "trusting," or in the passive sense of "trustworthy," "dependable." Clearly, the latter sense is intended here: God can be relied upon. He will not let his people down. As Paul thinks of God's faithfulness, he also thinks of the needs of the Thessalonians—Paul's heart was ever that of a pastor. God, he says, **will strengthen and protect you from the evil one**. In the Greek, this is not simply a statement as in the English translation, but a relative clause whose antecedent is the Lord. That is to say, it describes God. He is characteristically the one who **will strengthen . . . and protect** (for *stērizō*, "to strengthen," cf. 2:17; 1 Thess. 3:13). The second half of this description is an assurance that God does not leave us to fend for ourselves but is there to protect us. The thought is akin to the petition of the Lord's Prayer, "deliver us from the evil one" (Matt. 6:13). Like that petition, it is unclear whether "the evil" (Gk. *tou ponerou*) is personal (masc.) or impersonal (neut.). **The evil one** is a common name for Satan in the NT (cf. Matt. 13:19, 38; Eph. 6:16; 1 John 2:13f.; 5:18f.), and this reading would give an effective antithesis to the Lord. On that basis we accept the NIV rendering as the most likely, noting the implication that the Evil One stands behind the activities of "the wicked and evil men" of verse 2 and recalling Paul's earlier reference to "the secret power of lawlessness (which) is already at work" (2:7; see disc. and note on 1 Thess. 2:18). The prayer is for deliverance from that satanic power.

3:4 / Paul's confidence in God gives him confidence in the Thessalonians, that they were doing and would continue to do the things that they had been taught (cf. 1 Thess. 4:11; 5:11). A key phrase is **in the Lord**, whether understood as qualifying the verb, **we have confidence**, or the phrase "in you" (*eph' hymas*, not apparent in NIV). Either way it amounts to the same thing: namely, that the maintenance of the good work begun in them (cf. 1:3; 1 Thess. 1:6–8; 2:13f.; 4:9f.) depended on God's faithfulness, specifically as expressed in the previous verse. Again we understand the **Lord** of this verse and the next to be the Father (see note on 1 Thess. 1:1). **The things we command** includes earlier teaching whether by word or by letter (cf. 1 Thess. 4:1 and see disc. on 1 Thess. 4:11 for *parangellō,* "to command"). This teaching remains valid (note the present tense). Some of it as touching community life is found in the verses that follow.

3:5 / The verb *kateuthynō* was used in an earlier prayer (also in the aorist optative) in the sense, "to make straight" (see disc. on 1 Thess. 3:11). Here it carries the sense, "to direct." But in each case the thought is of the removal of obstacles which hinder the desired end. This prayer is that **the Lord** would **direct** their **hearts into God's love and Christ's perseverance**. The **heart** is a comprehensive term for the inner self (see disc. on 1 Thess. 2:4; for Christ see note on 1 Thess. 1:1). Paul is praying, therefore, that their whole being might be concentrated on the love and perseverance of which he speaks. The genitive **God's love** (the love *of God*) could be objective or subjective—either our love of God or God's love for us. Pauline usage would suggest the latter, the context the former. But perhaps the question of what kind of genitive this is, is best left unresolved, for in this case the one love is dependent on the other: "We love because he first loved us" (1 John 4:19). A similar question arises with the second phrase, **Christ's perseverance**. Is this a reference to his perseverance, "who . . . endured the cross . . . who endured . . . opposition from sinful men" (Heb. 12:2f.), or is it a characteristic that he imparts and we should display? AV understands the phrase in the second sense, with reference to the Parousia: "the patient waiting for Christ." This accords well with the major theme of the two letters and with 1 Thessalonians 1:3 in particular which speaks of "your endurance (the same word, *hypomonē*) inspired by hope in our Lord Jesus Christ" (see disc. on that passage). But it is a moot point whether Paul intended such a specific reference here, and again, it may be best to allow the genitive sufficient ambiguity to cover both of the possibilities outlined above.

Paul returns to the theme of idleness touched on in the earlier letter (see disc. on 1 Thess. 4:11f. and 5:14). Obviously, the problem persisted. Judging by the more peremptory tone of the warning, it appears to have worsened. The amount of space allotted to the matter measures how seriously Paul regarded it. But still his pastoral concern is uppermost. The object of the exercise is to help the erring, not to punish them or make the other members feel good. In all matters of church discipline, this distinction is of prime importance. On the form of the exhortation, see the discussion on 1 Thessalonians 4:1–12.

3:6 / The strong-sounding verb, **we command you** (*par-angellō*, see disc. on 1 Thess. 4:11) affords a distinctly military ring to the whole verse. The metaphor contained in the reference to **every brother who is idle** of the soldier who drops out of line (*ataktōs*, see disc. on 1 Thess. 5:14) further enhances this tone. The command is issued, moreover, on the highest authority: **in the name of the Lord Jesus Christ** (cf. 1 Thess. 4:1 and 1 Cor. 5:4f. for the use of this phrase in connection with church discipline; for the titles **Lord** and **Christ** see note on 1 Thess. 1:1). But, for all the authority with which he speaks, Paul's affection for his readers remains. He calls them **brothers** (see disc. on 1 Thess. 1:4), including those who are in error. The church, he says, is **to keep away** (*stellomai*, used of furling sails but here of withdrawing into oneself; cf. 2 Cor. 8:20), from **every brother who is idle**, literally "who walks out of line," i.e., whose conduct is "disorderly"; (see disc. on 1 Thessalonians 2:12 for "walking" as conduct). The present tense of the participle indicates persistence in such conduct, which is not **according to the teaching** (*paradosis*; see disc. on 2:15), **you received from us** (*paralambanō*; see disc. on 1 Thess. 2:13). Some texts read, "they received," with reference to the idlers in particular, but whether one reads **you** or "they" makes little difference. The church had received clear instruction by word (see disc. on 3:10) and then by letter, with regard to conduct no less than to doctrine, and the idle brother was blatantly disregarding that teaching (see further the note on this verse).

3:7 / This appeal to what had been taught is supported by a reminder of the missionaries' own conduct among them. **You yourselves know how you ought to follow our example**. This is not the first time that Paul cites the example of himself and his colleagues (see disc. on 1 Thess. 1:5), but he does it now with special emphasis. The verb *dei*, NIV **ought**, signifies a compelling and often a divine necessity—something that springs from the will of God. We could hardly possess a stronger statement of the importance of Christian conduct or a more striking statement of Paul's own confidence that he was setting an example for others to follow (the verb is *mimeomai*, "to mimic or imitate"; cf. 3:9; Heb. 13:7; 3 John 11). Not that he expected them to be a clone of himself; rather, there were so few Christian examples that it was *necessary* that they should follow the few that they had.

Paul gives three reasons (*hoti*) why the Thessalonians should follow the example set by the missionaries. First, **we were not idle when we were with you**. The verb *atakteō* corresponds to the adverb *ataktōs* of verses 6 and 11 and the adjective *ataktos* of 1 Thessalonians 5:14 (see disc. on that passage).

3:8–9 / Second, **nor did we eat anyone's food without paying for it**. **Food** in this connection represents maintenance of any kind (cf. 2 Sam. 9:7), and the missionaries had received none from the Thessalonians. **On the contrary**—and this is the now the third reason why the Thessalonians should follow their example—**we worked night and day, laboring and toiling so that we would not be a burden to any of you**. The Greek understands "we ate" from the previous clause, adding the qualifying participle, "working," to give the sense, "we ate by working night and day." This statement repeats almost precisely 1 Thessalonians 2:9 (see disc. and note on that passage), although the reason for making it is quite different. Paul is in this instance holding himself and his colleagues up as a model to be imitated; there he was defending their motives and his own in particular against the slanders of their antagonists (see also disc. on 1 Thess. 2:9 for **night and day**, and on that passage again and on 1 Thess. 1:3 for **laboring and toiling**, *kopos* and *mochthos*). The missionaries as apostles of

Christ had every **right** to be a burden to their hosts (cf. 1 Thess. 2:6), but they had foregone that right **in order to make ourselves a model** (*typos*, "example," cf. Phil. 3:17) **for you to follow** ("to mimic," see disc. on 3:7). *Exousia* meant originally the freedom to do as one pleased but came to mean **right** in the legal sense, the right of authority. Paul discusses this right more fully in 1 Corinthians 9:13f., where he shows that it rests on dominical authority (cf. Matt. 10:5–10; see also 2 Cor. 11:12 where in a different situation, he gives another reason for foregoing the right of support).

3:10 / Not only did the missionaries model how the Thessalonians should conduct themselves in this matter of self-support, but they instructed them to the same effect and, judging by the tense of the verb (imperfect), they did so repeatedly. The sense of the Greek is: "we also (a better translation of *kai* than NIV's **even**, meaning in addition to their example) used to command you" (*parangellō*, cf. 3:6 and see disc. on 1 Thess. 4:11). That command is repeated using their original words (the Greek *hoti* is recitative, the equivalent of quotation marks in English): **"If a man** (*tis* could be either a man or a woman, although the reference is undoubtedly to men) **will not work, he shall not eat."** The present imperative, **he shall not eat**, expresses a general rule. Exceptions, of course, can always be made. The words have about them the ring of a proverbial saying which, if proverbial in origin, may go back to Genesis 3:19 (cf. Gen. Rab. 2.2 on Genesis 1:2). But some suppose that it was a Greek proverb. Or it may have been a maxim coined by Paul himself. At all events, the apostle sees this saying now as indicating God's will for his people. Strikingly, however, what is condemned is not worklessness but the unwillingness to work. The verb *thelō* implies a deliberate choice, a conscious decision not to work (see disc. on 1 Thess. 5:14). "It is an impossible exegesis which argues (from this text) that *all* poverty is self-willed, a product of a welfare mentality which should be countered not with food stamps but denial of support. The implication in the letters is that these disruptive persons were perfectly capable of supporting themselves but refused to accept that responsibility, busying themselves instead by meddling in other persons' affairs, compounding the problems they were creating" (Saunders). An implication of the rule laid down in this verse, which lay beyond Paul's interest, is that the ability to earn one's living is an important factor in human well-being. We should understand, then, how demoralizing unemployment is for those unable to work. For the conscious recollection of what was said **when we were with you**, cf. 2:5 and 1 Thessalonians 3:4.

3:11 / The reason for Paul's remarks in verses 6 to 10 surfaces: **We hear that some among you are idle**. Perhaps he learned this from the same report that brought news of their mistaken ideas about the Parousia (see 2:1–12), or perhaps he is referring to the original report brought by Timothy. Nothing in the text indicates that they had just learned about it now or that they had heard of it only once. Again the Greek is literally, "walking in a disorderly manner" (cf. 3:6 and see disc. on 1 Thess. 2:12 and 5:14). What precisely this means is explained: **they are not busy; they are being busybodies**. This play on words in the English reflects a similar play in the Greek, where the two participles are each based on the verb *ergazō*, "to work." The second is a compound found only here in the NT, *periergazomai*, "to waste one's labor about a thing," and so "to be a busybody" (cf. 1 Tim. 5:13 for the corresponding adjective, *periergos*, and 1 Thess. 4:11; 1 Pet. 4:15 for similar warnings against this trait).

3:12 / Paul's response was to **command and urge** the idlers **to settle down and earn the bread they eat**—literally, that "they should eat their own bread," perhaps with some emphasis on "their own," since they were in the habit of eating other people's, "working with quietness" (cf. 1 Thess. 4:11). Such quietness is the antithesis of being a busybody. Paul comes down heavily on the idlers, but even so, his pastoral concern for them is still evident. To spare their feelings, perhaps, he does not address them directly but indirectly as **such people**. Again, he softens the militaristic tone of **we command** (see on 1 Thess. 4:11) by the addition of *parakaloumen*, **we urge**, which has as much to do with encouragement as with admonition (see disc. on 1 Thess. 3:2). Finally, he adds the qualifying phrase, **in the Lord Jesus Christ**. In verse 6 the longer form is used, "in the name of the Lord Jesus Christ," but **in the name of** becomes an assertion of authority. Without it, the phrase is better understood as a reminder of where they stand and of Paul's continuing relationship with them because of it and despite their shortcomings. They were still his brothers in the Lord Jesus Christ (cf. 3:15; see note on 1 Thess. 1:1 for the titles Lord and Christ).

3:13 / The admonition of this verse addresses all of the **brothers** (see disc. on 1 Thess. 1:4). **As for you**—the emphatic **you** marking the change of reference from a particular group to the whole church—**never tire of doing what is right** (cf. Gal. 6:9, and for other exhortations to perseverance, 1 Cor. 15:20, 58; 16:13; Phil. 1:27f.; 2:15f.; 4:1; 1 Thess. 3:5, 13; 5:23). Paul may have had in mind specifically the attitude of the church as a whole to the idlers. The latter's conduct may have been the cause of irritation. But irritation was no less a fault than its cause. The shortcomings of one person or group are no excuse for the failure of another. As Christians we are called to do what is right (Matt. 5:48). If Paul did have in mind a specific situation, his language gives nothing away. The prohibition **never tire**, in the aorist subjunctive, makes no suggestion as the present imperative would, that they had tired. The verb *kalopoieō*, "to do good," is unique to this passage in the NT. The compound with *kalos* rather than with *agathos* might suggest the sense, "to be *seen* to do what is right"—*kalos* is evident goodness. But the distinction between it and *agathos* should not be pressed. The present participle expresses what should be habitual to Christians.

3:14–15 / As in Romans 16:17 and 1 Corinthians 16:22, the letter ends with a warning: **If anyone does not obey our instruction in this letter, take special note of him**. The verb "to obey," *hypakouō*, derives from the verb "to hear" (*akouō*) and means "to act on what is heard," in this instance, **our instruction**, *logos*, "word." The only instruction calling for obedience in this letter (the Greek is literally, "the letter," but at the end of an epistle it was common to refer to the letter in this way) is that they should "stand firm and hold to the teachings" (2:15) and, in particular, as 3:6–16 makes clear, the teaching concerning idleness. The verb *semeioō*, "to take note," has much the same sense as *skopeō* in Romans 16:17, "to keep an eye on" (NIV "watch out for"). It is another word peculiar to this letter in the NT. Anyone marked out as not heeding this particular teaching was to be disciplined by excluding him from the fellowship of the church: **Do not associate with him** (*synanamignymi*, lit. "to mix up [*ana*] together [*syn*]"). In 1 Corinthians 5:9, 11, the only other place in the NT where this verb is used, Paul lays it down that the church should not eat with the offender concerned. Here he may not have intended quite such a rigorous discipline. His purpose was to shame the offender into settling down and becoming a more useful member of the Christian community (v. 12). To that end, he is careful to add: **Do not regard him as an enemy** (see disc. on 1 Thess. 5:13 for *hēgeomai*, "to regard"), **but warn him as a brother** (for *noutheteō*, "to admonish," see disc. on 1 Thess. 5:12). The well-being of the offender was, for Paul, of first importance. Discipline is not to be punitive, but educative, with rehabilitation as its objective.

Additional Notes   §6

3:6 / Keep away from every brother who is idle: In the parenesis of 1 Thessalonians Paul exhorts his readers to a social responsibility (1 Thess. 4:11f.). This theme reappears in 5:14 where the idle are warned not to be idle. Both passages are explained by 2 Thessalonians 3:6–13, where Paul deals at much greater length with the same, worsening problem (G. S. Holland, *The Tradition That You Received From Us: 2 Thessalonians in the Pauline Tradition* [Tübingen: Mohr-Siebeck, 1988], pp. 82f., argues that the problem of the disorderly in 2 Thessalonians is a new one concerning a group setting themselves up as spiritual authorities. There is little to commend this suggestion). Most scholars find the idleness to be rooted in an eschatological excitement stemming from the Thessalonians' belief in the imminence of the Parousia (see, e.g., von Dobschütz, *Die Thessalonicher—Briefe*, pp. 179–82; B. Rigaux, *Saint Paul Les Epîtres aux Thessaloniciens* [Paris: J. Gabalda, 1956], pp. 519–21; Best, pp. 176–78; Bruce, pp. 90f., 204–9; Morris, *Themes*, p. 74; for the suggestion that it was a symptom of Gnosticism, see Introduction on The Writing of 1 Thessalonians). Soon those who had left off working became impoverished and a problem for the church and possibly for non-believers. Von Dobschütz, on the basis of the classical meaning of the terms that Paul uses ("to lead a quiet life, to mind your own business," 1 Thess. 4:11) claims that this group was warning not only believers about Christ's return but non-believers in public places (p. 182). J. Frame adds that the idle demanded that the leaders instruct other members to support them, but this demand was tacitly rejected (1 Thess. 5:12f., 19f.). This led the idle to interfere in the management of church affairs (*The Epistles of St. Paul to the Thessalonians* [Edinburgh: T. & T. Clark, 1912], pp. 159–63). Some also concluded that the idle were responsible for the deception that the day of the Lord had already come (2 Thess. 2:2; cf. C. H. Giblin, *The Threat to Faith* [Rome: Pontifical Biblical Institute, 1967], p. 147; W. G. Kümmel, *Introduction to the New Testament* [Nashville: Abingdon, 1975], p. 268).

The traditional view that belief in the imminence of the Parousia caused this behavior has been modified by some in favor of the view that its cause lay in the belief that the kingdom of God in the final sense had fully come (realized eschatology). We have already considered and rejected this view (see note on 2 Thess. 2:2, and Introduction on The Writing of 1 Thessalonians).

More recently an attempt was made to find a sociological reason for the Thessalonians' idleness. Some scholars suggested that it should be understood against the background of the disdain of the Greeks and Romans for manual labor (cf. W. Bienert, *Die Arbeit nach der Lehre der Bibel: Eine Grundlegung Evangelischer Socialethik* [Stuttgart: Evangelisches Verlagswerk, 1954], pp. 270–72; John Seventer, *Paul and Seneca* [Leiden: E. J. Brill, 1961], p. 213); others that it should be understood in terms of the practice of certain philosophical schools. The Epicureans, for example, were wont to live off others, unmoved by society's disapproval (see Abraham Malherbe, *Social Aspects of Early Christianity* [Philadelphia: Fortress Press, 1983], pp. 24–27; idem, "Gentle as a Nurse: The Cynic Background to 1 Thess. 2," *NovT* 12 [1970], pp. 203–17; idem, "Exhortation in First Thessalonians," *NovT* 25 [1983], pp. 238–56, for the claim that Paul used and modified Stoic language [Dio Chrysostom's criticism of the so-called wandering philosophical preachers] and parenetic *topoi* from philosophic tradition). R. Russell, "The Idle in 2 Thess. 3:6–12: An Eschatological or a Social Problem," *NTS* 34 (1988), pp. 105–19, contributes important insights to this discussion. "Because Paul associated the problem of disorderliness with manual workers, it is more likely," Russell argues, "that the reason and model lies within the situation of the urban poor of the Hellenistic city. In the average Hellenistic city . . . the opportunities for employment were limited, and with the scarcity of work idleness was more widespread and wages even lower—many of the urban poor knew nothing but poverty" (p. 112; cf. A. H. M. Jones, *The Greek City* [Oxford: Clarendon Press, 1940], pp. 268-69; Mikhail Rostovtzeff, *The Social and Economic History of the Hellenistic World* [Oxford: Clarendon Press, 1941], vol. 2, pp. 1126-27; C. Lee, "Social Unrest and Primitive Christianity," *The Catacombs and the Colosseum*, ed. S. Benko, J. O'Rourke [Valley Forge: Judson Press, 1971], p. 129). On occasion, however, the poor developed a relationship with a benefactor from whom they would receive support in exchange for the obligation to reciprocate with an expression of gratitude, and something of this sort may have lain behind the situation that Paul was addressing. Russell continues:

> Paul's converts included the urban poor, and some may have . . . formed a client relationship and obligation to a benefactor. Once brought into the circle of Christian love, they could have appeared to outsiders to be idle beggars who exploited the generosity of the Christian community without any sense of reciprocal response to their new benefactors. If Pauline churches are composed primarily of believers from a lower social position with a minority from higher social levels in positions of leadership, then the idleness is more likely expressed by believers who are manual laborers from a lower social class. Paul urges these idle poor, caught up as beneficiaries of Christian love, to work, being self-sufficient and constructive in their relationship with others (p. 113).

§7 Final Greetings (2 Thess. 3:16–18)

The letter ends with two short wish-prayers (see disc. on 1 Thess. 3:6–13) that the peace of the Lord of peace might be with them and that the Lord himself might be with them also. In effect, Paul signs the letter by drawing attention to his own hand in the final verses (see Introduction on The Sequence of the Letters) and closes with a benediction of grace, as he does in one form or another in all of his letters.

3:16 / For the emphatic pronoun, **himself** (standing first in the Greek sentence), see the discussion on 1 Thessalonians 3:11. For **peace**, signifying well-being in the widest sense, see discussion on 1 Thessalonians 1:1, and for **the Lord of peace**, see discussion on 1 Thessalonians 5:23. While the earlier discussion suggests that the pronoun may reflect a liturgical formula, Morris observes that its effect as the letter draws to a close is to direct the readers' attention away from themselves back to the Lord. Once again we face the difficulty of identifying whether the Father or the Son is intended by **Lord** (see disc. and note on 1:1). The reference is probably to Jesus, whereas before Paul spoke of "the God of peace," a reference to the Father. Again we are reminded that for Paul the two are One (see disc. on 1 Thess. 2:12; 3:11). Paul prays that the Lord might give them an enduring peace—**peace at all times**, *dia pantos*, "through all," the word for **times** being understood, and in every circumstance, *en panti tropō*. The second prayer, **the Lord be with all of you**, may again reflect a liturgical formula, in this case the blessing at the end of a service (cf. Rom. 15:33; Phil. 4:9 where the "God of peace" is the subject; 2 Tim. 4:22; cf. also Matt. 28:20). The answer to this prayer is the answer also to the first, for the Lord (Jesus) is our peace, putting us at peace with each other (to the extent that we allow his influence, his Spirit, to come to bear on our lives) and reconciling us to God through the cross (cf. Eph. 2:14; Col. 1:20; also Mark 9:50).

3:17 / It was unusual for a letter writer in the ancient world to sign his or her name at the end, as is our practice. It was enough that the writer's name should appear in the address (cf. 1:1; 1 Thess. 1:1). On the other hand, it was not unusual for the author to add a few lines at the end if an amanuensis had written the bulk of the letter at his or her dictation. Paul adopts this practice here, claiming in fact that this was **the distinguishing mark in all** (of his) **letters**. Elsewhere he draws attention to it explicitly in 1 Corinthians 16:21; Galatians 6:11; Colossians 4:18 and Philemon 19. In this instance, it may have been prompted by the possibility that a spurious letter was circulating in his name, causing the problem with which he had to deal in 2:1–12 (see disc. on 2:2).

3:18 / **The grace of our Lord Jesus Christ be with you all**. Apart from the addition of **all**, this grace is identical with that of the first letter (5:28), and it is completely identical in Greek with Romans 16:24, which however is not found in the best texts of that letter (for **grace**, see disc. on 1 Thess. 1:1 and 5:28; and for the titles of Jesus, see note on 1 Thess. 1:1). The **all** is perhaps deliberately added to include the idlers. To the end, Paul is practicing what he preached to the others (3:15), demonstrating that he regards these people not as enemies but as his brothers, sharing with him in the grace of God in Christ.

For Further Reading

Commentaries

Bailey, J. W. *The First and Second Epistles to the Thessalonians*. New York: Abingdon Press, 1955.

Best, E. *The First and Second Epistles to the Thessalonians*. HNTC. New York: Harper & Row, 1972.

Bruce, F. F. *1 & 2 Thessalonians*. WBC 45. Waco, Texas: Word, 1982.

Findlay, G. G. *The Epistles to the Thessalonians*. Cambridge: Cambridge University Press, 1925.

Frame, J. E. *The Epistles of St. Paul to the Thessalonians*. ICC. Edinburgh: T. & T. Clark, 1912.

Hendricksen, W. *Thessalonians First and Second*. Grand Rapids: Baker, 1953.

Lightfoot, J. B. *Notes on the Epistles of St. Paul*. London: Macmillan, 1904.

Marshall, I. H. *1 and 2 Thessalonians*. NIC. Grand Rapids: Eerdmans, 1983.

Milligan, G. *St. Paul's Epistles to the Thessalonians*. London: Macmillan, 1908.

Moffatt, J. *The First and Second Epistles to the Thessalonians*. Vol. 4 of *The Expositor's Greek Testament*. 5 vols. London: Hodder & Stoughton, 1897–1910.

Moore, A. L. *1 and 2 Thessalonians*. London: Marshall, Morgan & Scott, 1969.

Morris, L. *The Epistles of Paul to the Thessalonians*. Leicester: Inter-Varsity Press, 1984.

_____. *The First and Second Epistles to the Thessalonians*. Grand Rapids: Eerdmans, 1959.

Neil, W. *The Epistle of Paul to the Thessalonians*. London: Hodder & Stoughton, 1950.

Ockenga, H. J. *The Epistles to the Thessalonians*. Grand Rapids: Baker, 1962.

Saunders, E. W. *1 Thessalonians, 2 Thessalonians Philippians Philemon*. Atlanta: John Knox Press, 1981.

Wanamaker, C. A. *The Epistles to the Thessalonians*. Grand Rapids: Eerdmans, 1990.

Ward, R. A. *A Commentary on 1 & 2 Thessalonians*. Waco, Texas: Word, 1973.

Whiteley, D. E. H. *Thessalonians in the Revised Standard Version*. London: Oxford University Press, 1969.

Related and Background Works

Austin, M. M. *The Hellenistic World from Alexander to the Roman Conquest*. Cambridge: Cambridge University Press, 1981.

Barclay, W. *The Mind of St. Paul*. London: Wm. Collins Sons & Co., 1958.

Bauer, W. *Orthodoxy and Heresy in Earliest Christianity*. London: SCM Press, 1972.

Benko, S. and J. O'Rourke, (eds.) *The Catacombs and the Colosseum*. Valley Forge: Judson Press, 1971.

Bornkamm, G. *Paul*. New York: Harper & Row, 1971.

Bruce, F. F. *The Letters of Paul*. Grand Rapids: Eerdmans, 1965.

_____. *New Testament History*. New York: Doubleday, 1971.

_____. *Paul: Apostle of the Heart Set Free*. Grand Rapids: Eerdmans, 1977.

Bultmann, R. *Primitive Christianity in its Contemporary Setting*. New York: Meridian Books, 1956.

Caird, G. B. *The Apostolic Age*. London: Gerald Duckworth, 1955.

Collins, R. F. *Studies on the First Letter to the Thessalonians*. Leuven: Leuven University, 1984.

Conybeare, W. J., and J. S. Howson. *The Life and Epistles of St. Paul*. London: Longmans, Green & Co., 1889.

Cullmann, O. *Christ and Time*. London: SCM Press, 1951.

_____. *The Christology of the New Testament*. London: SCM Press, 1959.

Deissmann, A. *Light from the Ancient East*. London: Hodder & Stoughton, 1927.

_____. *Paul: A Study in Social and Religious History*. London: Hodder & Stoughton, 1926.

Dibelius, M. and W. G. Kümmel. *Paul*. Philadelphia: Westminster Press, 1953.

Dodd, C. H. *The Apostolic Preaching and its Developments*. London: Hodder & Stoughton, 1936.

Doty, W. G. *Letters in Primitive Christianity.* Philadelphia: Fortress Press, 1979.

Ellis, E. E. *Paul and His Recent Interpreters.* Grand Rapids: Eerdmans, 1961.

_____. *Paul's Use of the Old Testament.* Edinburgh: Oliver & Boyd, 1957.

_____. *Prophecy and Hermeneutic in Earliest Christianity.* Grand Rapids: Eerdmans, 1978.

Exler, F. X. J. *The Form of the Ancient Greek Letter. A Study in Greek Epistolography.* Washington, D.C.: Catholic University of America, 1923.

Farnell, L. R. *The Cults of the Greek States.* Oxford: Clarendon Press, 1909.

Furnish, V. P. *The Moral Teachings of Paul: Selected Issues.* New York: Abingdon Press, 1979.

_____. *Theology and Ethics in Paul.* Nashville: Abingdon Press, 1968.

Giblin, C. H. *The Threat to Faith.* Rome: Pontifical Biblical Institute, 1967.

Glasson, T. F. *The Second Advent—The Origin of the New Testament Doctrine.* London: Epworth Press, 1947.

Grant, R. M. *A Historical Introduction to the New Testament.* Evanston: Harper & Row, 1963.

Guthrie, D. *New Testament Introduction. The Pauline Epistles.* London: Tyndale Press, 1961.

Hamilton, N. Q. *The Holy Spirit and Eschatology in Paul.* Edinburgh: Oliver and Boyd, 1957.

Hock, R. F. *The Social Context of Paul's Ministry. Tent Making and Apostleship.* Philadelphia: Fortress Press, 1980.

Holland, G. S. *The Tradition That You Received From Us: 2 Thessalonians in the Pauline Tradition.* Tübingen: Mohr-Siebeck, 1988.

Hunter, A. M. *The Gospel According to St. Paul.* Philadelphia: Westminster Press, 1979.

Jeremias, J. *New Testament Theology.* New York: Scribners, 1971.

Jewett, R. *Dating Paul's Life.* London: SCM Press, 1979.

_____. *The Thessalonian Correspondence: Pauline Rhetoric and Millenarian Piety.* Philadelphia: Fortress Press, 1986.

Jones, A. H. M. *The Greek City.* Oxford: Clarendon Press, 1940.

Judge, E. A. *The Social Pattern of Christian Groups in the First Century.* London: Tyndale Press, 1960.

Keck, L. E. *Paul and his Letters*. Philadelphia: Fortress Press, 1979.

Kümmel, W. G. *Introduction to the New Testament*. London: SCM Press, 1966.

Ladd, G. E. *A Theology of the New Testament*. Grand Rapids: Eerdmans, 1974.

Lake, K. *The Earlier Epistles of St. Paul*. London: Rivington, 1914.

Lightfoot, J. B. *Biblical Essays*. London: Macmillan, 1893.

Ling, J. *The Significance of Satan—New Testament Demonology and its Contemporary Relevance*. London: S.P.C.K., 1961.

Longenecker, R. N. *Paul, Apostle of Liberty*. New York: Harper & Row, 1964.

Malherbe, A. J. *Paul and the Thessalonians*. Philadelphia: Fortress Press, 1987.

_____. *Social Aspects of Early Christianity*. Philadelphia: Fortress Press, 1983.

Malina, B. J. *The New Testament World*. Atlanta: John Knox Press, 1981.

Meeks, W. A. *The First Urban Christians*. New Haven: Yale University Press, 1983.

_____. *The Moral World of the First Christians*. Philadelphia: Westminster Press, 1986.

Minear, P. S. *Christian Hope and the Second Coming*. Philadelphia: Westminster Press, 1954.

Morris, L. *The Apostolic Preaching of the Cross*. Grand Rapids: Eerdmans, 1955.

_____. *Word Biblical Themes: 1, 2 Thessalonians*. Dallas: Word, 1989.

Moule, C. F. D. *The Origin of Christology*. Cambridge: Cambridge University Press, 1977.

Murphy-O'Connor, J. *St. Paul's Church*. Wilmington, Del.: Michael Glazier, 1983.

O'Sullivan, F. *The Egnatian Way*. Newton Abbott: David & Charles, 1972.

Ramsay, W. M. *The Church in the Roman Empire*. London: Hodder & Stoughton, 1897.

_____. *St. Paul the Traveller and the Roman Citizen*. London: Hodder & Stoughton, 1895.

Reicke, B. *The New Testament Era*. London: Adam & Charles Black, 1968.

Ribberdos, H. N. *Paul: An Outline of his Theology*. Grand Rapids: Eerdmans, 1975.

Robinson, J. A. T. *Jesus and his Coming. The Emergence of a Doctrine.* London: SCM Press, 1957.

_____. *Redating the New Testament.* London: SCM Press, 1976.

Rostovtzeff, M. *The Social and Economic History of the Hellenistic World.* 2 vols. Oxford: Clarendon Press, 1941.

Rowley, H. H. *The Relevance of Apocalyptic: A Study of Jewish and Christian Apocalypses from Daniel to Revelation.* London: Lutterworth, 1963.

Schmithals, W. *Paul and Gnosticism.* New York: Abingdon Press, 1972 (Schmithals).

Schubert, P. *Form and Function of the Pauline Thanksgivings.* Berlin: A. Töpelmann, 1939.

Seventer, J. *Paul and Seneca.* Leiden: E. J. Brill, 1961.

Shires, H. M. *The Eschatology of Paul in the Light of Modern Scholarship.* Philadelphia: Westminster Press, 1966.

Stacey, W. D. *The Pauline View of Man: In Relation to its Judaic and Hellenistic Background.* London: Macmillan, 1956.

Stambaugh, J. E., and D. L. Balch. *The New Testament and its Social Environment.* Philadelphia: Westminster Press, 1986.

Stanley, D. M. *Christ's Resurrection in Pauline Soteriology.* Rome: Pontifical Biblical Institute, 1961.

Stendahl, K. *Paul Among Jews and Gentiles, and Other Essays.* Philadelphia: Fortress Press, 1976.

Theissen, G. *The Social Setting of Pauline Christianity.* Philadelphia: Fortress Press, 1982.

Vos, G. *The Pauline Eschatology.* Grand Rapids: Eerdmans, 1951.

Way, A. S. *The Letters of St. Paul.* London: Macmillan, 1921.

Whiteley, D. E. H. *The Theology of St. Paul.* Philadelphia: Fortress Press, 1964.

Wikenhauser, A. *Pauline Mysticism.* New York: Herder and Herder, 1960.

Wiles, G. P. *Paul's Intercessory Prayers.* Cambridge: Cambridge University Press, 1974.

Williams, D. J. *Acts.* NIBC 5. Peabody, Mass.: Hendrickson Publishers, 1990.

_____. *The Promise of His Coming.* Homebush West, Australia: Anzea Publishers, 1990.

Wright, W. B. *Cities of Paul.* London: Archibald Constable, 1906.

Yarbrough, O. L. *Not like the Gentiles: Marriage Rules in the Letters of Paul.* Atlanta: Scholars Press, 1985.

Works on the Greek Text

Abbott-Smith, G. *A Manual Greek Lexicon of the New Testament.* Edinburgh: T. & T. Clark, 1937.

Bauer, W., W. F. Arndt, and F. W. Gingrich. *A Greek-English Lexicon of the New Testament and Other Early Christian Literature.* Chicago: University of Chicago Press, 1957.

Blass, F., A. Debrunner, and R. W. Funk. *A Greek Grammar of the New Testament and Other Early Christian Literature.* Chicago: University of Chicago Press, 1961.

Hill, D. *Greek Words and Hebrew Meanings: Studies in the Semantics of Soteriological Terms.* Cambridge: Cambridge University Press, 1967.

Liddell, H. G., and R. Scott. *A Greek-English Lexicon.* 9th ed. New York: Oxford, 1940; reprint 1982.

Metzger, B. M. *A Textual Commentary on the Greek New Testament.* New York: United Bible Societies, 1971.

Moule, C. F. D. *An Idiom Book of New Testament Greek.* Cambridge: Cambridge University Press, 1959.

Moulton, J. H., W. F. Howard, and N. Turner. *A Grammar of New Testament Greek.* 3 vols. Edinburgh: T. & T. Clark, 1908, 1929, 1963.

Moulton, J. H., and G. Milligan. *The Vocabulary of the Greek Testament.* London: Hodder & Stoughton, 1930.

Moulton, W. F., and A. S. Geden. *A Concordance of the Greek Testament.* Edinburgh: T. & T. Clark, 1957.

Subject Index

Abbott-Smith, G., 39
Achaia, 6, 9, 10, 31, 32
Adikia, 130, 131
Agapē, 67, 76
Alexander the Great, 1
Amanuensis, 105, 152
Amphipolis, 1
Andronicus, 49
Angels, 67, 84, 114
Annihilation, 87, 116, 128
Anomia, 124
Antichrist, 121, 125
Antioch in Syria, 63
Apokalyptō, 124
Apostasia, 124
Apostasy, 124
Apostle, 40, 49, 51
Apostolic decree, 71
Apostolic parousia, 53
Appolonia, 1
Aquila, 32
Archangel, 83, 84
Armor, 89
Atakteō, 96, 145
Ataktos, 96, 144, 145
Ataktōs, 145
Athens, 63
Aus, R. D., 110, 131
Avenger, 74

Bailey, J. W., 70
Barnabas, 49, 57
Beast, the, 124
Beelzebub, 60
Belial, man of, 124
Believers, 67, 88, 117
Benefactor, 150
Berea, 1, 56
Best, E., 23, 149
Bienert, W., 150
Bruce, F. F., 14, 16, 17, 30, 35, 38, 52, 65, 69, 77, 86, 92, 111, 121, 123, 132, 149
Busybody, 147

Caesar, 5
Caligula, 125
Cassander, 1
Catechesis, 51
Chara, 99
Charis, 21, 99
Church: founding of at Thessalonica, 2; in Jerusalem, 46, 120; in Judea, 46, 51, 120; leaders, 7, 13, 94–96, 111, 149; members, 94, 96
Civil order, 97
Claudius, 5, 10, 127
Collection, the, 49
Collins, R. F., 78
Comfort, 43, 86, 137
Coming, the, 83, 85, 118
Corinth, 6, 9, 10, 14, 32, 56, 62, 63, 120, 140
Credal statement, 90
Cullmann, O., 127, 136
Cyrus, 24

Day of the Lord, 11, 50–51, 87, 117, 131, 149
Dead, the, 83, 85, 86
Dead, the Christian, 6, 9, 80–81; resurrection of, 7, 81, 82, 85
Death, 81, 84, 91; as sleep, 81, 92
Deception, 38, 130
Dechomai, 31, 45, 130
Deissmann, A., 55
Delphi, 10
Dibelius, M., 17
Dodd, C. H., 34
Doxa, 56, 116
Doxazō, 140
Dynamai, 40

Edersheim, A., 24
Elect, the, 28, 130
Election, 28–29
Ellis, E. E., 17
Encouragement, 43, 58, 61–62, 86, 92, 135, 137, 147

End, the, 125, 127
Endurance, 26–27
Epicurians, 150
Epimenides, 23
Ēpioi, 40
Epiphaneia, 129
Ergon, 26, 137
Eternal life, 116
Euangelion, 34
Euangelizomai, 34
Evil, 131

Faith, 26, 43, 58, 90, 111; of the Thessa-
    lonians, 6, 12, 32, 61–63, 65, 111–13
False Christs, 129, 130
False prophets, 129, 130
Farrow, D., 126
Findlay, G. G., 64
Fowl, S., 41
Frame, J. E., 17, 149
Funk, R. W., 53

Galilee, 46
Gallio, 9, 10
Gaius (Caligula), 125
Gentiles, 3, 11, 47, 115
Giblin, C. H., 149
God-fearers, 2, 3, 4, 35
God: approval of, 38; calling by, 44,
    118, 134–35; faithfulness of, 141–42;
    forgiveness of, 50; glory of, 44, 85,
    117, 119; love of, 26, 34, 90, 100, 114,
    133, 135, 137, 142; separation from,
    87, 116; serving, 33, 54; slave of, 33;
    sovereignty of, 50, 128, 130–31;
    waiting for, 33; will of, 15, 39, 73–
    74, 78, 100, 106, 146; work of, 57, 90;
    wrath of, 34, 36, 49, 90
God the Father, 22–24, 28, 66, 141
Glory: of the Parousia, 114; our, 118
Gnosticism, 7, 8, 81, 132, 137–38
Grace: of God, 16, 22, 26, 35, 93, 98, 99,
    109, 113, 119; prayer for, 22, 152
Great tribulation, 124
Greed, 39
Greek games, 37, 55, 139
Greeks, 77

Hagiasmos, 67, 71, 73–75, 134
Hagiazō, 71
Hagioi, 67, 117, 134

Hagiosynē, 67, 71, 73
Hahn, H. C., 34
Hardship, 42
Harpazō, 84
Hengel, M., 16
Higgins, B., 136
Hock, R. F., 50
Holiness, 16, 34, 67, 71, 88, 103, 118
Holland, G. S., 17, 149
Holy of Holies, 125
Holy Spirit, 29, 100, 126, 134, 137, 151
Hope, 27, 33, 90, 111, 137, 143

Idleness, 14, 96–97, 144, 148, 149, 152
Idlers, 7, 8, 11, 13, 14, 121, 147, 149, 152
Idolatry, 32
Idols, 11, 32, 33, 35, 39
Ignorance of God, 73
Imitators, 30, 31, 46, 96, 145
Immorality, 38, 71
Insult, 37, 49

James, 49
Jason, 4, 5
Jeremias, J., 23, 106
Jerusalem: fall of, 36, 48; church in,
    46, 120
Jesus Christ: 5, 23–24; as judge, 33, 74;
    as Lord, 5, 22–24, 47, 83, 101, 114,
    122, 143, 151; as Savior, 26, 33–34;
    as Son, 22, 66; miracles of, 51; resur-
    rection of, 33, 51, 65, 82; return of,
    6, 9, 33, 44, 51, 56, 67, 86, 90; work
    of, 26, 135
Jewett, R., 7, 17, 52, 132
Jews, 2, 3, 21, 46–49, 77, 115, 140; in
    Thessalonica, 37, 38, 46
Jones, A. H. M., 150
Joy, 31, 56, 64–65, 99, 112
Judas Iscariot, 124
Judea, 46, 52
Judgment, 33–34, 50, 74, 113, 115; of
    Christians, 74, 118; of non-believ-
    ers, 50
Junia(s), 49
Justice, 114
Justification, 74, 118

Kardia, 39
Katheudō, 89, 91
Kauchēsis, 55, 56

Kilner, J. F., 67
Kingdom of God, 44, 50, 88, 113, 132, 149
Kiss, 104
Koimaō, 81, 91
Kopos, 26, 42, 60, 145
Kümmel, W. G., 149

Lake, K., 17
Lautenschlage, M., 91
Lawlessness, 124, 127–28, 141
Letters: authenticity of, 8, 11; date of, 9; forged, 123; relevance of, 15; sequence of, 13–15; writing of, 6, 10–11
Lifestyle, 30
Light, 88–89
Lightfoot, J. B., 16, 70, 83, 93, 136
Liturgical formula, 22, 151
Love, 66, 67, 76, 96
Lundstrom, G., 50
Lütgert, W., 7, 8, 17, 132
Lydia, 57

Macedonia, 6, 31, 32, 47
Malherbe, A. J., 4, 16, 94, 150
Man of lawlessness, 124–29, 134; parousia of, 129; signs and wonders of, 129
Manual labor, 77, 97
Marcion, 8
Marcionite canon, 13
Marriage, 72, 79
McGehee, M., 78, 79
Mearns, C. L., 132
Meeks, W. A., 41
Messiah, 24, 50
Metaphor, 32, 41, 53, 55, 72, 86, 88–90, 106, 118, 144
Michael, archangel, 84
Milligan, G., 17, 41, 70, 119
Miracles, 29
Mission (today), 33, 43
Morris, L., 12, 17, 22, 30, 32, 34, 41, 54, 64, 70, 73, 85, 103, 105, 113, 114, 119, 149, 151
Moule, C. F. D., 63, 70
Moulton-Milligan, 73, 85, 123
Muratorian Fragment, 8, 13
Murphy-O'Connor, J., 16

Neil, W., 12, 17, 136
Nēpioi, 40, 41
Nestle, E., 124

Obedience, 26, 148
Opposition from Jews, 4, 6, 31, 38

Pagans, 32, 35
Paradidomi, 45, 51
Paradosis, 51, 97, 136, 138, 144
Parakaleō, 38, 43, 58, 70, 76, 86, 137
Paraklēsis, 37, 58, 137
Paralambanō, 45, 51, 70, 144
Parangelia, 71
Parangellō, 77, 142, 144, 146
Parousia, 55, 56, 85, 103, 114, 122, 129
Parousia, 15, 68, 82; anticipation of, 11, 67, 117–18; and hope, 111; and judgment, 74; events before, 11, 83–86, 117; of the man of lawlessness, 129; timing of, 7, 80, 86–89
Patience, 98
Paul: as father, 15, 43; as mother, 15, 41, 43; conduct of, 42; longing of, 14, 55, 64; love of, 25, 41; maintenance of, 40, 145–46; motives of, 37–40, 49, 145; persecution by, 51; prayer of, 26, 64, 65, 67, 99, 102–3, 136–37, 139, 142; preaching of, 30, 32, 35, 37, 39, 55, 127, 152; self-support of, 50, 146; signature of, 13, 14, 151–52; slanders against, 36, 39, 145
Peace, 21, 22, 102, 109, 151
Pentecost, 51
Perfection, 44, 67, 76
Peripateō, 44
Persecution, 46, 58
Perseverance, 112, 142
Persistent Widow, parable of, 99
Persistence, 44
Phoebe, 95
Pistis, 58, 59, 141
Politarch, 1, 4, 5
Power, 29, 30, 100, 116, 129
Praise, 40
Prayer, 99; wish-prayer, 61, 133, 151
Preacher, wandering, 6, 17
Preaching, 29, 41, 61, 106
Priscilla, 32
Prophecy, 7, 101, 106, 122
Prophet, 47, 82, 122

Proselyte, 2, 3
Punishment, 116, 117

Rabbi, 24, 50
Rackham, R. B., 16
Ramsay, W. M., 16
Rapere, 68
Rapture, the, 68, 127
Rebellion, the, 11, 124
Redemption, 27
Restraining power, 126–28
Resurrection, of the dead, 7, 81, 82, 85
Revelation, the, 68
Reward, 34
Rhyomai, 33, 140
Rigaux, B., 78, 149
Righteousness, 34, 90
Rostovtzeff, M., 150
Russell, R., 150

Sacrifice, 42
Saints, 85, 117, 122, 134
Salvation, 33, 34, 43, 45, 90, 91, 93, 114, 134, 135
Samaria, 46
Sanctification, 71, 78, 102–3, 134
Satan, 5, 50, 54, 55, 60, 65, 125, 129, 131, 141
Saunders, E. W., 65, 104, 146
Schmithals, W., 7, 8, 49, 132, 133, 137, 138
Schubert, P., 25
Semitism, 88, 114, 124
Seventer, J., 150
Sexual behavior, 8, 74
Signs and wonders, 29; counterfeit, 129
Silas: co-author, 8, 11, 21, 25; in Berea, 56; in Thessalonica, 31; member of the team, 1, 6, 10, 31, 40, 42, 46, 82
Sin, 34, 75, 82, 100, 124
Skeuos, 72, 73
Sleep, 82, 89
Son of Man, 83, 85, 88
Spiritual growth, 70
Suffering, 31, 46
Synagogue, 2, 3, 35; liturgy of, 65

Tasker, R. V. G., 34
Temple, 125, 127; massacre in, 49
Thanksgiving, 25–28, 45, 63–64, 99, 100, 110, 133
Theodidaktos, 76
Therma, 1
Thessalonians: love of, 61, 65, 66, 76, 112, 150; persecution against, 5, 10, 13–15, 22, 31, 112, 131; prayer of, 103–4; preaching of, 31
Thessalonica, riot in, 4, 46
Thlibō, 59, 114
Thlipsis, 31, 58, 62, 112, 114
Threat, 33
Times and dates, 14, 86, 87
Timothy: as apostle, 50; as co-author, 8, 11, 21, 25; as member of the team, 1, 6, 31, 40, 42, 46; report to Paul, 6, 10, 69; return to Thessalonica, 53, 56–57
Tradition, the, 51, 136
Trumpet, 84, 140
Truth, 130–31, 134, 136
Trust, 112, 141

Via Egnatia, 1
Ventidius Cumanus, 52
von Dobschütz, E., 132, 149
von Harnack, A., 17

Wandering preacher, 6, 17
Watson, D. F., 17
Way, A. S., 110
Whitton, J., 78
Wife, 72, 79
Wiles, G. P., 61
Williams, D. J., 49, 51, 68, 75, 84, 91, 118
Women, prominent, 4
Work, as occupation, 11, 42, 77–78; work ethic, 78; work(s), our, 26, 57, 95

Yarbrough, O. L., 78

Zealot, 52
Zeus, 84

Scripture Index

OLD TESTAMENT

Genesis **3:19**, 146

Exodus **3:2**, 114; **4:22**, 23; **19:16**, 84, 85; **19:18**, 114; **24:15–18**, 85; **34:6**, 98; **40:34**, 85

Leviticus **4:3**, 24; **6:22**, 24; **19:18**, 76

Numbers **11:12**, 41; **22:22**, 60

Deuteronomy **4:37**, 28; **6:4**, 66; **7:6f.**, 134; **10:15**, 134; **26:18**, 134; **32:2**, 67; **32:6**, 23; **33:12**, 28

Joshua **22:22**, 124

1 Samuel **4:4**, 125; **10:1**, 104; **21:5**, 72; **24:1**, 131; **24:10**, 24

2 Samuel **4:10**, 34; **9:7**, 145; **19:21**, 24; **23:1**, 24

1 Kings **2:10**, 81; **3:8**, 28; **8:10f.**, 85; **11:23**, 125; **19:16**, 24; **19:18**, 104; **22:23**, 131

2 Kings **6:16**, 116

1 Chronicles **21:1**, 60, 131; **28:9**, 39; **29:7**, 131; **29:17**, 39

2 Chronicles **29:19**, 124

Nehemiah **9:7**, 28; **13:26**, 28

Job **1:7–2:9**, 60; **31:27**, 104

Psalms **2:2**, 24; **7:9**, 39; **9:17**, 115; **18:8**, 114; **19:4f.**, 139; **22:19**, 65; **32:8**, 65; **34:14**, 95; **37:23**, 65; **40:2**, 65; **79:6**, 115; **80:1**, 125; **87:6**, 91; **89:5**, 67; **97:2**, 85; **99:1**, 125; **103:8**, 98; **103:20**, 114; **105:15**, 24; **109:6**, 60; **139:23**, 39; **147:15**, 139

Proverbs **3:6**, 65; **4:26**, 65; **16:9**, 65; **25:21**, 98

Isaiah **1:16f.**, 102; **2:10**, 116; **2:11**, 117; **2:17**, 117; **2:19**, 116; **2:21**, 116; **11:4**, 128; **13:6–8**, 88; **14:13f.**, 125; **21:3**, 88; **27:13**, 84; **37:3**, 88; **40–66**, 34; **40:9**, 34; **41:8f.**, 28; **43:10**, 28; **44:1f.**, 28; **45:1**, 24; **45:4**, 28; **49:7**, 28; **52:7**, 34; **54:13**, 76; **59:17**, 89; **60:6**, 34; **61:1**, 34; **66:15f.**, 115

Jeremiah **2:19**, 124; **4:31**, 88; **6:14**, 88; **6:24**, 88; **11:20**, 39; **12:3**, 39; **17:10**, 39; **20:9**, 101; **31:33f.**, 76; **31:34**, 50

Lamentations **4:20**, 24

Ezekiel **1:13**, 114; **1:27**, 114; **13:10**, 88; **14:9**, 131; **28:2**, 125

Daniel **7:9f.**, 115; **7:10**, 67; **7:13**, 85; **7:25**, 125; **8:9–12**, 125; **11:36–39**, 125; **12:2**, 91

Hosea **1:10**, 23; **11:1**, 23; **13:2**, 104

Joel **2:1**, 84; **2:15**, 84; **2:28**, 50; **2:31**, 50, 87

Amos **2:12**, 101; **5:18**, 87; **5:18–20**, 50

Micah **2:6**, 101

Habakkuk **3:13**, 24

Zechariah **3:1f.**, 60; **9:14**, 84; **14:5**, 67

Malachi **4:5**, 50, 87

NEW TESTAMENT

Matthew **3:11**, 100; **3:11f.**, 115; **4:1–11**, 60; **4:3**, 59; **5:10**, 113; **5:11f.**, 58; **5:32**, 72; **5:34**, 105; **5:44–48**, 98; **5:48**, 44, 67; **6:13**, 141; **6:24**, 97; **10:5–10**, 146; **10:5–15**, 40; **10:25**, 60; **11:27**, 116; **11:28**, 44; **12:24**, 60; **12:27**, 60; **13:19**, 141; **13:38**, 141; **13:21**, 112; **13:41**, 67; **16:23**, 60; **16:27**, 44; **19:4**, 134; **19:9**, 72; **19:28**, 44; **20:3**, 97; **20:6**, 97; **23:8**, 28; **23:29–36**, 36; **23:32**, 48; **23:37**, 47; **24:3**, 56; **24:10–13**, 124; **24:15**, 125; **24:27**, 56; **24:30**, 44; **24:31**, 80, 84; **24:37**, 56; **24:39**, 56; **24:43**, 82, 86, 89; **25:6**, 85; **25:31**, 44, 67; **28:19**, 133; **28:20**, 151

Mark **1:15**, 51; **1:22**, 50; **1:27**, 50; **3:34**, 28; **4:11**, 128; **4:17**, 112; **5:39**, 91; **6:3**, 59; **7:22**, 39; **8:34ff.**, 58; **8:38**, 67; **9:7**, 85; **9:50**, 96, 151; **10:30**, 112; **10:45**, 42; **12:29–31**, 26; **12:31**, 76; **13**, 48; **13:7**, 122; **13:8**, 88, 131; **13:10**, 127; **13:14**, 125; **13:22**, 129; **13:26**, 83, 85; **13:26f.**, 67; **13:27**, 68; **13:32**, 87; **13:36**, 89; **14:36**, 66; **14:62**, 85; **15:34**, 34

Luke **1:19**, 61; **1:20**, 130; **1:26**, 84; **3:16**, 100; **4:18**, 34; **6:27–36**, 98; **6:29**, 37; **6:32–36**, 66; **9:26**, 67; **10:1–12**, 40; **11:47–51**, 47; **12:3**, 130; **12:15**, 39; **12:39**, 82, 86, 89; **12:39f.**, 87; **12:49**, 100; **13:33f.**, 47; **15:3–10**, 90; **16:8**, 88; **16:13**, 97; **17:21**, 51; **17:24**, 83; **17:24–32**, 87; **18:1**, 99; **19:27**, 114; **19:44**, 130; **20:35**, 113; **21:34**, 87; **21:34–36**, 80, 87, 89; **21:36**, 88; **22:3**, 60; **23:2**, 5; **23:41**, 140; **24:19**, 137

John **1:1**, 59; **1:14**, 135; **3:16**, 66, 99; **3:18**, 74; **3:30**, 40; **5:24–27**, 84; **5:28**, 83; **8:12**, 89; **8:44**, 60, 129; **10:28–30**, 22; **10:29**, 22; **11:9f.**, 89; **12:21**, 23; **12:31**, 58; **12:36**, 88; **12:46**, 89; **13:1**, 76; **13:16**, 42, 50; **13:27**, 60; **13:34**, 44, 76; **14:6**, 130; **14:30**, 58, 60; **15:18–21**, 58; **16:11**, 58; **16:21**, 88; **16:22**, 99; **16:33**, 58; **17:3**, 115; **17:10**, 119; **17:12**, 124; **17:21–23**, 119; **19:12**, 5; **19:15**, 5; **20:30**, 82

Acts **1:2**, 49; **1:6**, 49; **1:6–8**, 33; **1:7**, 86; **1:9–11**, 85; **1:12**, 49; **1:21**, 50; **1:24**, 39; **2:3**, 100; **2:10**, 2; **2:22**, 129; **2:32–36**, 47; **2:36**, 23, 101, 114; **2:37**, 28; **2:43**, 49, 129; **2:47**, 57; **3:15**, 81; **3:16**, 103; **3:17**, 126; **4:35**, 49; **4:37**, 49; **5:2**, 49; **5:3**, 60; **5:12**, 49; **5:18**, 49; **5:28**, 71; **5:41**, 31, 113; **6:1**, 46; **6:5**, 2; **7:2**, 28; **7:22**, 137; **7:52**, 47; **8:1**, 46, 49, 112; **8:1–3**, 52; **8:4**, 46; **8:39**, 85; **9:1f.**, 52; **9:2**, 44; **9:11**, 99; **9:15**, 72; **9:27**, 37; **9:29**, 37; **9:31**, 46, 120; **10:2**, 2; **10:22**, 2; **10:42**, 74; **11:19**, 46; **11:22**, 46; **11:27**, 106; **11:28**, 100; **12:1**, 46, 52; **12:23**, 130; **13:1**, 46, 82, 106; **13:1ff.**, 63; **13:2f.**, 99; **13:10**, 60; **13:15**, 28; **13:16**, 2; **13:26**, 2; **13:43**, 2; **13:46**, 37; **13:48**, 140; **13:50**, 47, 112; **13:52**, 99; **14:3**, 37; **14:4**, 49; **14:4f.**, 4; **14:5**, 47; **14:14**, 49; **14:15**, 32, 32, 35; **14:19**, 4, 47; **14:22**, 58; **14:23**, 99; **14:27**, 32, 45, 56; **15:4**, 57; **15:8**, 39; **15:20**, 71; **15:29**, 71; **15:32**, 106; **16:14**, 2, 28, 57; **16:16–40**, 37; **16:22–24**, 49; **16:22–25**, 504; **16:24**, 71; **16:25**, 99; **17**, 25, 126; **17:1–14**, 47; **17:2**, 2; **17:2f.**, 3; **17:2–3**, 91; **17:3**, 92; **17:4**, 2, 35; **17:5**, 4, 55; **17:5–10**, 31, 53; **17:5–19**, 37; **17:7**, 4, 5; **17:9**, 5, 55; **17:10–14**, 6; **17:13**, 4, 47; **17:14f.**, 56; **17:15**, 6; **17:17**, 2; **17:22–31**, 32, 33; **17:23**, 125; **17:28**, 23; **17:31**, 33, 74; **18:1–17**, 9; **18:2**, 32, 49; **18:5**, 45, 56, 140; **18:6**, 47, 62; **18:7**, 2 ; **18:9f.**, 62; **18:12f.**, 140; **18:12ff.**, 62; **18:22**, 49; **18:26**, 37; **19**, 49; **19:8**, 37; **19:9**, 44, 47; **19:23**, 44; **20:2f.**, 53; **20:20**, 15; **20:27**, 15, 39, 106; **20:28**, 133; **20:31**, 42; **20:34**, 50, 77; **20:35**, 82; **20:36**, 99; **21:5**, 99; **21:10**, 106; **21:11**, 100; **21:21**, 124; **21:25**, 71; **22:17–21**, 99; **23:3**, 37; **23:10**, 85; **24:14**, 44; **24:17**, 49; **24:22**, 44; **25:5**, 140; **26:26**, 37; **27:35**, 99; **28:6**, 140; **28:8**, 99; **28:15**, 85; **28:17**, 28

Romans **1:1**, 29, 33; **1:1–3**, 29; **1:1–7**, 21; **1:4**, 24, 67; **1:7**, 22, 109; **1:8**, 28,

32; **1:9**, 26, 29; **1:13**, 81; **1:16**, 29; **1:18**, 34, 48; **1:21**, 100; **1:24**, 73, 74, 130; **1:26**, 74, 130; **1:28**, 73, 74, 115, 130; **1:29**, 39; **2:7**, 116, 137; **2:8**, 131; **2:16**, 29, 34; **2:17**, 23; **3:25**, 35; **3:25f.**, 112; **3:27**, 55; **5:1–5**, 26; **5:2**, 27; **5:3**, 31; **5:3–5**, 31; **5:5**, 29, 31, 76; **5:6**, 91; **5:6ff.**, 102; **5:8**, 28, 47; **5:9**, 34; **5:11**, 23; **5:20**, 64; **5:21**, 116; **6:17**, 51; **6:22f.**, 116; **6:23**, 82, 116, 117, 130; **8:8**, 47; **8:9**, 113; **8:11**, 81; **8:19**, 67; **8:22f.**, 119; **8:23**, 27; **8:24**, 27; **8:28**, 100, 113; **8:30**, 44; **8:32**, 91; **8:35**, 112; **8:38**, 123; **8:39**, 84; **9–11**, 47; **9:1**, 29; **9:3**, 47; **9:11**, 28; **9:22f.**, 72; **9:26**, 32; **10:15**, 34; **10:16**, 115; **10:17**, 51; **11:5**, 28; **11:7**, 28; **11:25**, 81, 128; **11:28**, 28; **12:1**, 69; **12:8**, 95; **12:11**, 33; **12:12**, 99; **12:17**, 98; **12:18**, 96; **13:1–7**, 97; **13:1**, 124; **13:3f.**, 127; **13:4**, 74; **13:8–10**, 26, 76; **13:12**, 51, 89; **13:13**, 97; **14:1**, 97; **14:8f.**, 91; **14:15**, 91; **14:17**, 99, 102; **14:18**, 33; **14:19**, 96; **15:1**, 97; **15:4**, 137; **15:5**, 137; **15:13**, 29; **15:16**, 29; **15:19**, 29; **15:20**, 92; **15:22**, 54; **15:25–31**, 49; **15:30**, 104; **15:31**, 140; **15:33**, 102, 151; **16:2**, 95; **16:3**, 57; **16:4**, 120; **16:7**, 50; **16:9**, 57; **16:16**, 104; **16:17**, 148; **16:18**, 33; **16:20**, 102; **16:21**, 57; **16:24**, 152; **16:25**, 29, 128

1 Corinthians **1:1**, 21; **1:2**, 120; **1:3**, 22, 109; **1:7**, 68; **1:8**, 51; **1:9**, 44, 103; **1:16**, 70; **1:18**, 27, 29, 130; **1:24**, 29; **1:30**, 67; **2:2**, 35; **2:3**, 57, 62; **2:8**, 47; **3:11**, 118; **3:11–15**, 55; **3:13**, 51; **3:16**, 75, 125; **3:22**, 123; **4:2**, 70; **4:3–5**, 55; **4:5**, 74; **4:12**, 50; **4:17**, 44; **5:1**, 72; **5:3–5**, 53; **5:5**, 51; **5:9**, 148; **5:10f.**, 39; **5:11**, 148; **5:14**, 144; **6:2**, 67; **6:4**, 83; **6:10**, 39; **6:14**, 83; **6:18f.**, 75; **6:20**, 73; **7:1**, 76; **7:5**, 59; **7:10–12**, 82; **7:26**, 123; **8:1**, 92; **8:5**, 113; **8:6**, 24; **9:1**, 50; **9:3–18**, 40; **9:3–19**, 50; **9:6**, 50; **9:12**, 29, 57; **9:13f.**, 146; **9:22**, 39; **9:24**, 139; **9:25**, 55; **10:1**, 81; **10:13**, 103; **10:23**, 92; **10:32**, 120; **11:4f.**, 105; **11:7**, 56; **11:22**, 120; **11:23**, 45, 136; **11:23–26**, 35; **12:1**, 76, 81; **12:3**, 29, 101; **12:4–6**, 133; **12:8**, 123; **12:10**, 101; **12:10f.**, 100; **12:28**, 100; **12:28f.**, 106; **13:4**, 97;

13:6, 131; **13:7**, 57; **13:12**, 51; **13:13**, 26; **14:1**, 100; **14:2f.**, 106; **14:4**, 160; **14:8**, 32; **14:16**, 78; **14:17**, 160; **14:23f.**, 78; **14:24f.**, 106; **14:26ff.**, 106; **14:29**, 101, 106; **14:33**, 97; **14:37f.**, 101; **14:39**, 100; **14:39f.**, 97; **5:2**, 27; **15:3**, 45, 91, 136; **15:3f.**, 81, 92; **15:3–8**, 35; **15:7**, 49; **15:9**, 120; **15:14**, 118; **15:18**, 84; **15:23**, 56, 81; **15:24f.**, 51; **15:37f.**, 91; **15:50**, 148; **15:50–53**, 85; **15:51**, 128; **15:52**, 83, 84; **15:54**, 82; **15:58**, 148; **16:1**, 76; **16:1–4**, 49; **16:7**, 56; **16:9**, 32; **16:12**, 76; **16:13**, 148; **16:20**, 104; **16:21**, 152; **16:22**, 148; **16:24**, 104

2 Corinthians **1:1**, 21, 120; **1:2**, 22, 109; **1:3**, 137; **1:8**, 81; **1:9**, 81; **1:11**, 104; **1:14**, 51; **1:18**, 103; **2:11**, 60; **2:12**, 29, 32; **2:13**, 114; **2:14**, 32; **2:15**, 27, 130; **3:3**, 32; **3:7–11**, 40; **4:2**, 39, 44; **4:3**, 29, 130; **4:4**, 60, 131, 135; **4:6**, 135; **4:7**, 40, 72; **4:8–11**, 100; **4:14**, 82, 83; **5:15**, 91; **5:20**, 38; **5:21**, 91; **6:2**, 44; **6:6**, 29; **6:7**, 89; **6:10**, 31; **6:11**, 66; **6:13**, 66; **6:16**, 32; **7:4**, 64; **7:5**, 114; **7:6**, 56; **8–9**, 49; **8:1–5**, 32; **8:13**, 114; **8:20**, 144; **8:23**, 50, 56; **8:24**, 112; **9:5**, 39; **9:8**, 137; **9:13**, 29; **10:2**, 44; **10:4**, 89; **10:14**, 29; **11:7–11**, 40; **11:7ff.**, 50; **11:10**, 55; **11:12**, 146; **11:14**, 60; **11:17**, 55; **11:23–29**, 114; **12:7**, 55; **12:10**, 112; **12:12**, 29; **12:15**, 41; **12:17f.**, 39; **13:4**, 85; **13:11**, 96, 102; **13:12**, 104; **13:14**, 105, 133, 136

Galatians **1:1f.**, 21; **1:3**, 22, 109; **1:4**, 87, 91, 112, 123, 134; **1:7**, 29; **1:10**, 33; **1:11f.**, 45; **1:19**, 49; **1:22f.**, 52; **2:2**, 55, 139; **2:20**, 91; **3:1**, 35; **3:2**, 51; **3:5**, 51, 129; **3:15**, 75; **3:19**, 127; **3:24**, 127; **4:19**, 41; **4:20**, 53; **5:5**, 26; **5:6**, 61, 90; **5:7**, 54; **5:11**, 39; **5:22**, 76, 97, 99; **6:2**, 77; **6:5**, 77; **6:8**, 116; **6:9**, 148; **6:10**, 66; **6:11**, 105, 152; **6:14**, 35

Ephesians **1:2**, 22, 109; **1:3–14**, 28; **1:4**, 134; **1:9**, 128; **1:14**, 93, 120; **1:16**, 26; **1:20**, 81; **1:22**, 120; **2:2**, 60, 85; **2:5**, 27; **2:8**, 27, 135; **2:8–10**, 26; **2:10**, 117, 137; **2:12**, 89, 116; **2:13ff.**, 102; **2:14**,

151; **2:20**, 100, 106; **2:21**, 125; **3:3f.**, 128; **3:5**, 100, 106; **3:9**, 23; **3:10**, 120; **3:18**, 90; **3:19**, 102; **3:21**, 120; **4:1**, 69, 118; **4:2**, 97; **4:3**, 96; **4:4–6**, 133; **4:6**, 28; **4:11**, 100, 106; **4:13**, 92, 118; **4:14**, 122; **4:19**, 39; **4:27**, 60; **4:28**, 77, 78; **5:1f.**, 96; **5:3**, 97; **5:4** , 100; **5:5**, 39; **5:8**, 88; **5:14**, 89, 92; **5:20**, 100; **5:21–23**, 72; **5:23ff.**, 120; **5:29**, 41; **6:7**, 33; **6:11**, 60; **6:11–17**, 89; **6:12**, 55; **6:16**, 141; **6:19**, 104; **6:19f.**, 139; **6:20**, 37

Philippians **1:1**, 9, 21, 33; **1:2**, 109; **1:6**, 51, 55, 90, 106, 237; **1:10**, 51; **1:12**, 22; **1:19**, 104; **1:23**, 85; **1:27**, 29; **1:27f.**, 148; **1:28**, 112, 113; **1:29**, 58; **2:13**, 119; **2:15f.**, 148; **2:16**, 51, 55, 139; **2:22**, 33; **2:25**, 50, 57; **3:1**, 70; **3:6**, 120; **3:12**, 71, 76; **3:17**, 146; **3:21**, 71; **4:1**, 148; **4:4**, 99; **4:6**, 100; **4:8**, 70; **4:9**, 51, 102, 151; **4:15f.**, 39, 50; **4:16**, 4, 54

Colossians **1:1**, 21; **1:2**, 22, 109; **1:4f.**, 26; **1:6**, 32; **1:10**, 137; **1:11**, 97; **1:20**, 151; **1:24**, 31; **1:26**, 128; **1:27**, 27; **1:28**, 43; **2:1**, 81; **2:2**, 128; **2:6f.**, 51; **2:7**, 100; **2:12**, 81; **2:15**, 47; **3:3**, 23; **3:5**, 39, 69, 96; **3:5–4:6**, 51; **3:12**, 97; **3:15**, 100; **3:17**, 100; **3:18–4:1**, 97; **3:24**, 33; **4:2**, 100; **4:3**, 32; **4:3f.**, 104, 139; **4:5**, 77; **4:16**, 105; **4:18**, 105, 152

1 Thessalonians **1:1**, 8, 24, 28, 29, 65, 105, 120, 152; **1:2**, 12, 44, 99, 100; **1:2f.**, 105; **1:2–10**, 44; **1:2–2:2**, 7; **1:3**, 23, 24, 58, 61, 63, 64, 65, 76, 95, 111, 142; **1:3f.**, 9; **1:4**, 12, 27, 134; **1:5**, 37, 40, 45; **1:5ff.**, 140; **1:6**, 29, 45, 46, 58, 99; **1:6–10**, 6; **1:7**, 3, 65; **1:7f.**, 76; **1:8**, 24, 58; **1:9**, 11, 112; **1:10**, 24, 49, 83, 114; **2:1**, 29; **2:1–12**, 6; **2:2**, 1, 29; **2:3**, 7, 38, 58, 75; **2:4**, 15, 29, 40, 59; **2:6**, 15, 24, 146; **2:7**, 15, 53; **2:8**, 29; **2:9**, 4, 26, 29, 30, 77, 145; **2:11**, 15, 41, 53, 111; **2:11f.**, 15; **2:12**, 58, 103, 118, 122, 135; **2:13**, 25, 99, 133, 136, 140; **2:13–16**, 25; **2:14**, 5, 14, 24, 30, 58, 63, 112, 113, 119; **2:14–16**, 4, 31, 37; **2:15**, 5, 23, 38; **2:17**, 39, 41, 59, 61, 62; **2:17f.**, 6, 64; **2:17–3:5**, 14; **2:18**, 4, 5, 58, 59; **2:19**, 4, 23, 27, 56, 64, 118;

2:19f., 105; **2:20**, 112; **3:1**, 8, 21; **3:1f.**, 6; **3:1ff.**, 54; **3:1–5**, 5; **3:2**, 24, 29, 44, 61, 70; **3:3**, 15, 31, 59; **3:3f.**, 113; **3:4**, 31, 147; **3:5**, 26, 54, 55, 57, 58, 60, 148; **3:5f.**, 64; **3:6**, 10, 58, 65, 76; **3:7**, 31, 58, 59, 76; **3:7–9**, 105; **3:8**, 24, 135; **3:9**, 55, 62, 100; **3:9–10**, 25; **3:10**, 8, 42, 44, 58; **3:11**, 22, 23, 136; **3:11ff.**, 136; **3:11–13**, 23, 25, 69, 103; **3:12**, 24, 76, 111; **3:13**, 23, 27, 39, 44, 55, 56, 64, 68, 71, 102, 141, 148; **4:1**, 23, 38, 44, 47, 58, 63, 66, 96, 118, 121, 122, 142, 144; **4:1–8**, 6; **4:2**, 23, 75; **4:3**, 87, 102; **4:3ff.**, 67; **4:3–8**, 102; **4:6**, 24; **4:7**, 38, 103, 135; **4:9**, 13, 44, 86; **4:10**, 58, 66, 70, 96; **4:11**, 7, 12, 96, 142, 147, 149; **4:11f.**, 97, 149; **4:12**, 44; **4:13**, 13, 27; **4:13ff.**, 89, 91; **4:13–18**, 8, 132; **4:13–5:11**, 7, 97; **4:14**, 67, 68, 92; **4:15**, 48, 56, 122; **4:15–17**, 24; **4:16**, 24, 33, 92, 114; **4:16f.**, 68, 80, 123; **4:17**, 15, 68, 122; **4:18**, 58, 91; **5:1**, 13, 13, 76; **5:1f.**, 83; **5:1–11**, 123; **5:2**, 24, 51, 82, 89; **5:4**, 51, 89; **5:5**, 114; **5:6**, 91; **5:7**, 89; **5:8**, 26, 27, 58, 89; **5:8–11**, 80; **5:9**, 23, 24, 27, 34; **5:10**, 3, 81, 89; **5:11**, 58, 86, 142; **5:12**, 3, 8, 9, 24, 26, 69, 70, 96, 121; **5:12f.**, 7, 149; **5:13**, 64, 77; **5:14**, 7, 13, 43, 58, 69, 95, 145, 149; **5:15**, 8, 66; **5:17**, 25, 44; **5:18**, 24; **5:19f.**, 122, 149; **5:19–22**, 7, 136; **5:21**, 38, 126; **5:21f.**, 122; **5:22f.**, 69; **5:22–24**, 6; **5:23**, 21, 23, 24, 56, 61, 65, 71, 148; **5:24**, 8, 135; **5:25**, 139; **5:27**, 24, 126; **5:28**, 22, 23, 24, 152

2 Thessalonians **1:1**, 21, 23, 152; **1:2**, 12, 21, 22, 23, 24, 105; **1:3**, 12, 43, 58, 66, 133, 142; **1:3f.**, 133; **1:3–12**, 11, 12; **1:4**, 13, 22, 27, 31, 32, 58; **1:5**, 44; **1:5–10**, 11, 121; **1:6**, 5, 31, 64; **1:6f.**, 59; **1:7**, 23, 67, 83, 124; **1:8**, 23, 29, 73, 74; **1:8f.**, 130; **1:9**, 24, 87; **1:10**, 51, 67, 122, 135; **1:11**, 28, 58, 122; **1:11f.**, 16; **1:12**, 22, 23, 24, 105; **2:1**, 12, 15, 23, 24, 56, 68, 70; **2:1–12**, 8, 11, 13, 14; **2:2**, 9, 13, 14, 24, 44, 51, 117, 137, 138; **2:3**, 86; **2:4**, 127, 128; **2:5**, 4, 105, 140, 147; **2:5f.**, 129; **2:6**, 101; **2:7**, 124, 142; **2:8**, 23, 56; **2:9**, 54, 55, 125, 130; **2:9f.**, 114; **2:10**, 45, 131; **2:12f.**, 130; **2:13**,

12, 24, 28, 58, 71, 90, 131, 135; **2:13f.**, 67; **2:14**, 23, 24, 29, 44, 93, 118, 136; **2:15**, 4, 12, 123, 148; **2:16**, 22, 23, 24, 27, 58, 105; **2:16f.**, 23, 61, 65, 66, 139; **2:17**, 12, 39, 58, 141; **3:1**, 12, 24, 31; **3:1f.**, 104; **3:1–5**, 95; **3:2**, 33, 58; **3:3**, 24, 54, 60; **3:4**, 12, 24, 77; **3:5**, 12, 23, 24, 27, 39, 66; **3:6**, 4, 8, 12, 23, 24, 44, 45, 69, 71, 77, 96, 97, 136, 146, 147; **3:6–10**, 51; **3:6–12**, 77, 96; **3:6–13**, 149; **3:6–15**, 11; **3:7**, 30, 96, 146; **3:7–9**, 40; **3:7–10**, 77; **3:8**, 4, 26, 42, 50; **3:9**, 145; **3:10**, 8, 12, 77, 97; **3:11**, 13, 14, 44, 96; **3:11f.**, 112; **3:12**, 12, 23, 24, 58, 69, 77; **3:13**, 12; **3:15**, 12, 16, 95, 152; **3:16**, 21, 24, 61, 65, 102; **3:17**, 9, 14, 105; **3:18**, 22, 23, 24, 105

1 Timothy **1:2**, 22, 50, 109; **1:5**, 71; **1:12–14**, 52; **1:18**, 71; **2:7**, 42; **2:10**, 137; **3:4**, 95; **3:5**, 95; **3:7**, 60; **3:9**, 128; **3:12**, 95; **3:15**, 32; **3:16**, 128; **4:10**, 32; **5:3–8**, 78; **5:10**, 137; **5:13**, 97, 147; **5:14**, 125; **5:17**, 95; **6:9**, 87; **6:14**, 129; **6:21**, 105

2 Timothy **1:2**, 22, 109; **1:9**, 27; **1:10**, 129; **1:11**, 42; **2:8**, 29; **2:13**, 103; **2:18**, 132; **2:21**, 72, 137; **2:22**, 96; **2:26**, 60; **3:11**, 112; **3:13**, 38; **3:17**, 137; **4:1**, 129; **4:2**, 45; **4:8**, 129; **4:22**, 105, 151

Titus **1:1**, 33; **1:4**, 22, 109; **1:9**, 97; **1:12**, 97; **1:16**, 137; **2:13**, 68, 88, 129; **3:1**, 137; **3:5**, 27; **3:8**, 95; **3:14**, 95; **3:15**, 105

Philemon **1**, 21, 57; **3**, 22, 109; **4**, 26; **13**, 126; **19**, 152; **24**, 57

Hebrews **2:4**, 29, 129; **2:14**, 60; **2:14f.**, 81; **3:12**, 32; **4:2**, 51; **9:9**, 123; **9:14**, 32; **10:22–24**, 26; **10:23**, 103; **10:25**, 51; **10:31**, 32; **10:39**, 93; **11:11**, 103; **12:1f.**, 87; **12:2**, 31; **12:2f.**, 142; **12:14**, 96; **12:22**, 32; **13:7**, 145; **13:18**, 104; **13:20**, 102

James **1:4**, 103; **1:12**, 31; **1:13**, 113; **4:7**, 60; **5:7f.**, 56

1 Peter **1:2**, 133; **1:6f.**, 31; **1:21f.**, 26; **1:23**, 32; **2:9**, 93; **3:7**, 72; **4:15**, 147; **5:2f.**, 95; **5:8**, 60, 89; **5:14**, 104

2 Peter **1:16**, 56; **3:4**, 56; **3:10**, 51; **3:11f.**, 118; **3:12**, 56

1 John **1:5f.**, 89; **2:13f.**, 141; **2:13**, 134; **2:18**, 124, 128; **2:28**, 56; **3:2**, 117, 119, 135; **3:4**, 124; **3:8**, 60; **4:8**, 28; **4:10**, 28; **4:16**, 28, 44; **4:19–21**, 26; **4:19**, 142; **5:18f.**, 141

3 John **11**, 145

Jude **9**, 84; **14f.**, 67; **20f.**, 133

Revelation **1:7**, 85; **1:10**, 84; **1:13–16**, 114; **2:2**, 26; **2:23**, 39; **3:3**, 86; **3:20**, 45; **4:1**, 84; **7:14**, 124; **11:11f.**, 68; **11:12**, 85; **11:15**, 84; **13**, 124; **13:2**, 129; **14:13**, 84; **14:14–16**, 85; **16:15**, 82, 86, 89; **19:14**, 67; **20:5**, 84

APOCRYPHA

Sirach **45:1**, 28

Baruch **3:36**, 28

4 Maccabees **10:15**, 116

PSEUDEPIGRAPHA

2 Baruch **78:2**, 22

2 Enoch **3:1ff.**, 85

RABBINIC LITERATURE

'Abot **6.1**, 28

Genesis Rabbah **2.2**, 146

Mart. Isaiah **5:1–14**, 47

Pirqe 'Abot **2.2**, 50

QUMRAN

1QH **9:35f.**, 23

JOSEPHUS

Antiquities **3.80**, 56; **3:203**, 56; **9.55**, 56; **20.105–112**, 49; **20.105–135**, 52

Against Apion **2.121**, 47

Life **43**, 124

War **2.224–227**, 49

CHURCH FATHERS

Augustine, *The City of God* **20.19**, 121

Eusebius, *Eccl. Hist.* **6.7**, 131

Hippolytus, *Apostolic Constitutions* **2.57.17**, 104

Iranaeus, *Adv. Haer.* **5**, 91

Jerome, *Adversus Jovinianum* **2.37**, 47

Justin Martyr, *First Apol.* **65.2**, 104

Tertullian, *Scorpiace* **8**, 47

OTHER EARLY WRITINGS

Aeschylus, *Eumenides* **651**, 81, 84

Catallus, **5.4–6**, 81

Cicero, *Ad Att.* **8.16.2**, 85; **16.11.6**, 85

Homer, *Iliad* **11.241**, 81

Plutarch, *Vit. Crassi* **29**, 92

Suetonuis, *Claudius* **25.4**, 49

Tacitus, *Annals* **15.44.5**, 47

Tacitus, *History* **5.5.2**, 47